CAMBRIDGE LIBRARY COLLECTION

Books of enduring scholarly value

Travel and Exploration

The history of travel writing dates back to the Bible, Caesar, the Vikings and the Crusaders, and its many themes include war, trade, science and recreation. Explorers from Columbus to Cook charted lands not previously visited by Western travellers, and were followed by merchants, missionaries, and colonists, who wrote accounts of their experiences. The development of steam power in the nineteenth century provided opportunities for increasing numbers of 'ordinary' people to travel further, more economically, and more safely, and resulted in great enthusiasm for travel writing among the reading public. Works included in this series range from first-hand descriptions of previously unrecorded places, to literary accounts of the strange habits of foreigners, to examples of the burgeoning numbers of guidebooks produced to satisfy the needs of a new kind of traveller - the tourist.

Description of the Coasts of East Africa and Malabar

The publications of the Hakluyt Society (founded in 1846) made available edited (and sometimes translated) early accounts of exploration. The first series, which ran from 1847 to 1899, consists of 100 books containing published or previously unpublished works by authors from Christopher Columbus to Sir Francis Drake, and covering voyages to the New World, to China and Japan, to Russia and to Africa and India. This 1866 volume contains an English translation of a Spanish manuscript version of a document originally written in Portuguese about 1514. The supposed author, Duarte Barbosa, who may have been a relative of Magellan, is said to have spent sixteen years exploring the Indian Ocean. The complex history of this manuscript narrative is given in detail in the translator's preface, and the book has explanatory notes and an index.

Cambridge University Press has long been a pioneer in the reissuing of out-of-print titles from its own backlist, producing digital reprints of books that are still sought after by scholars and students but could not be reprinted economically using traditional technology. The Cambridge Library Collection extends this activity to a wider range of books which are still of importance to researchers and professionals, either for the source material they contain, or as landmarks in the history of their academic discipline.

Drawing from the world-renowned collections in the Cambridge University Library, and guided by the advice of experts in each subject area, Cambridge University Press is using state-of-the-art scanning machines in its own Printing House to capture the content of each book selected for inclusion. The files are processed to give a consistently clear, crisp image, and the books finished to the high quality standard for which the Press is recognised around the world. The latest print-on-demand technology ensures that the books will remain available indefinitely, and that orders for single or multiple copies can quickly be supplied.

The Cambridge Library Collection will bring back to life books of enduring scholarly value (including out-of-copyright works originally issued by other publishers) across a wide range of disciplines in the humanities and social sciences and in science and technology.

Description of the Coasts of East Africa and Malabar

In the Beginning of the Sixteenth Century

Duarte Barbosa

CAMBRIDGE UNIVERSITY PRESS

Cambridge, New York, Melbourne, Madrid, Cape Town, Singapore, São Paolo, Delhi, Dubai, Tokyo

Published in the United States of America by Cambridge University Press, New York

www.cambridge.org
Information on this title: www.cambridge.org/9781108010412

This edition first published 1866
This digitally printed version 2010

ISBN 978-1-108-01041-2 Paperback

WORKS ISSUED BY

The Hakluyt Society.

DESCRIPTION OF THE COASTS OF EAST AFRICA AND MALABAR.

M.DCCC.LXVI.

A DESCRIPTION

OF THE COASTS OF

EAST AFRICA AND MALABAR

IN THE BEGINNING OF

THE SIXTEENTH CENTURY,

BY

DUARTE BARBOSA,

A PORTUGUESE.

TRANSLATED FROM

AN EARLY SPANISH MANUSCRIPT IN THE BARCELONA LIBRARY

WITH NOTES AND A PREFACE,

BY

THE HON. HENRY E. J. STANLEY.

LONDON:

PRINTED FOR THE HAKLUYT SOCIETY.

M.DCCC.LXVI.

LONDON: T. RICHARDS, 37, GREAT QUEEN STREET, W.C.

COUNCIL

OF

THE HAKLUYT SOCIETY.

TRANSLATOR'S PREFACE.

The Spanish manuscript from which this volume has been translated is in the handwriting of the beginning of 1500, full of abbreviations, and without punctuation or capital letters at the beginnings of sentences or for the proper names, which adds much to the difficulty of reading it. It contains eighty-seven leaves. The handwriting more resembles an example of the year 1510 than those dated 1529 and 1531, given at p. 319 of the "Escuela de Leer Letras Cursivas Antiguas y Modernas desde la entrada de los Godos en España, por el P. Andres Merino de Jesu Christo, Madrid, 1780." This work was translated into Spanish from the original Portuguese in 1524, at Vittoria, by Martin Centurion, ambassador of the community of Genoa, with the assistance of Diego Ribero, a Portuguese, cosmographer and hydrographer to his Majesty Charles V. There are reasons (as will be shewn in the notes) for supposing that the Spanish translation, probably this copy and not the Portuguese original, assisted the compilers of the early atlases, especially that of Abraham Ortelius, of Antwerp, 1570, other editions of which were published in succeeding years.[1] The

[1] I have been informed by Mr. Winter Jones that Diego Ribero drew up a map of the world in 1529, of which Sprengel

similarity of the orthography of this manuscript and of that of the names in maps as late as that of Homann, Nuremberg, 1753, shews how much geography up to a recent period was indebted to the Portuguese and Spaniards. It may also be observed that from their familiarity at that time with the sounds of Arabic, the proper names are in general more correctly rendered in European letters, than used to be the case in later times.

This MS. is in the Barcelona Library and is there catalogued "Viage por Malabar y costas de Africa, 1512 : letra del siglo xvi." It was supposed to be an original Spanish work, for the statement of its having been translated is in the body of the MS., no part of which can be read without more or less difficulty. This work is not a book of travels as the title given in the catalogue, though not on the MS., indicates ; it is rather an itinerary, or description of countries. It gives ample details of the trade, supplies, and water of the various sea-ports mentioned in it. It contains many interesting historical details, some of which, such as the account of Diu, the taking of Ormuz, the founding of the Portuguese fort in Calicut, their interruption of the Indian trade to Suez by capturing the Indian ships, the rise of Shah Ismail, etc., fix pretty nearly the exact date at which this narrative was composed as the year 1514.

wrote an account in 1795, called, Über J. Ribero's alteste Welt-charte. He gives the western hemisphere only, the eastern hemisphere has been published by the Vte. Santarem. This might be the means by which the orthography and errors of this work passed into the maps of Ortelius.

Two other MS. copies of this work are preserved in the Royal Library at Munich: the first of these, Nó. 570 of the catalogue of that library, is in a handwriting very similar to that of the Barcelona MS., and apparently of the same period. It consists of one hundred and three leaves, and is stated to have proceeded from the episcopal library of Passau. This MS. does not contain the appendix respecting the prices of the precious stones. The other MS. No. 571, is of fifty-three leaves, and is written in two handwritings, both of which are much rounder and dearer than that of No. 570; the catalogue states that this MS. came from the library of the Jesuits of Augsburg. There are several verbal differences between the two MSS., and perhaps No. 571 agrees more exactly with the Barcelona MS. The two Munich MSS. frequently write words such as rey with a double r, as *rrey*, which does not occur in the Barcelona MS., where, however, words begin with a large r, which is also used for a double r in the middle of a word.

The piracies of the Portuguese are told without any reticence, apparently without consciousness of their criminality, for no attempt is made to justify them, and the pretext that such and such an independent state or city did not choose to submit itself on being summoned to do so by the Portuguese, seems to have been thought all sufficient for laying waste and destroying it. This narrative shows that most of the towns on the coasts of Africa, Arabia, and Persia were in a much more flourishing condition at that time than they have been since the Portuguese ravaged some of them, and interfered with the trade of all. The description of the early introduction of the cultivation and weaving of cotton into South Africa by the Arab traders will be read with interest; and the progress then beginning in those regions three hundred and fifty years ago, and the subsequent stand still to which it has been brought by the Portuguese and by the slave-trade to America, may be taken as supporting the views lately put forward by Captain R. Burton and others at the Anthropological Society.

The greater part of this volume was printed in Italian by Ramusio in 1554 in his collection of travels (Venetia, nella Stamperia de' Giunti), as the narration of Duarte Barbosa, and a large part of this work must have been written by Barbosa; and a Portuguese manuscript of his was printed at Lisbon in 1812 in the "Collecçaō de noticias para a historia e geografia das naçoes ultramarinas." This manuscript of Barbosa's, however, is much less full than this Spanish MS. of Barcelona, or than the Italian version of Ramusio, and the Lisbon editors have added from Ramusio translations of the passages which were wanting in their MS. These publications do not contain the number of leagues between one place and another which are given in the Spanish translation.

That the Portuguese manuscript printed at Lisbon in 1812 belongs to Barbosa, stands only on the authority of Ramusio, who gives an introduction by Odoardo Barbosa of the city of Lisbon, which is not to be found either in the Barcelona MS. or in the Portuguese MS., and which has been translated from the

Italian of Ramusio and published in the Lisbon edition. The introduction to the Lisbon edition states that the Portuguese MS. is not an autograph MS., and that the account of Barbosa is bound up along with other papers. This introduction refers to the passages in the Portuguese MS. which are not to be found in Ramusio, and says it may be doubted whether these were additions posterior to the work of Duarte Barbosa.

It had occurred to me that this work might be attributed to the famous navigator Magellan, and that it must have been through him that it found its way to Charles the Fifth's court : there are several reasons for this supposition, and some difficulties in the way of it ; I will, however, follow Sr. Larrañaga's advice, and state both sides of the question.

Duarte Barbosa, cousin of Magellan, Alvaro de Mezquita, Estevan Gomez, Juan Rodrigues de Carvalho were Portuguese employed by Spain along with Magellan[1] in the fleet which sailed on the 21st September 1519, from San Lucar de Barrameda to Brazil and the straits which bear the name of that Admiral.

Now the *Panorama* or Spanish version of the *Univers Pittoresque* states (page 140) : "It was at that time, although it has not been possible to ascertain exactly the year, when the illustrious Viceroy of the Indics sent Francisco Serrano to the Moluccas, a

[1] The Portuguese are scarcely justified in their censure of Magellan for serving Spain, after the neglect he had met with at the hands of the King of Portugal, since disnaturalisation was a custom of the country frequently practised at that period : and it is the necessary complement of naturalisation.

friend, and also, as it is believed, a relation of Magellan, the same person who by reason of the exact and precise data which he furnished to the celebrated navigator deserved later to see his name inscribed amongst those of other notable persons, whose fame will last as long as history endures."

* * * * *

"At the beginning of the same century Duarte Barbosa also proceeded to the Moluccas, and cruised among those countries for the space of sixteen years, collecting interesting notes, which although they were not published till three centuries after the event, are not on that account the less admirable and precious; these reports were published in Lisbon in a work which bears the following title: *Collecçao de Noticias para a historia e Geografia das naçoes ultramarinas*; those reports which relate to Barbosa are contained in the second volume."

Now this Barcelona MS. contains in an appendix the voyage of three Portuguese, a Spaniard, and five Malays, whose captain was Francisco Serrano, to the Moluccas in the year 1512: this supplies the date of his voyage which the above quoted paragraph says could not be ascertained, and this account is not in Ramusio's collection, and there is every reason to suppose that it was as yet unpublished.

In addition to what has been said by the writers of the *Panorama* and *Univers Pittoresque*, in which statement they follow the 3rd Decade of the "Asia" of Barros, lib. v. cap. 8 :—

"We wrote before how Francisco Serrão wrote some

letters from the Maluco Islands where he was, to Fernão de Magalhaēs, on account of being his friend from the time when both were in India, principally at the taking of Malaca :" it was to be expected that Barbosa and Serrano would furnish their information to Magellan, whether as the head of their family, or as the Portuguese who had been longest at the Spanish Court, and through whom they might hope for advancement and further employment, such as Duarte Barbosa obtained with the fleet which discovered the Straits of Magellan.

Magellan returned to Europe in 1512. Duarte Barbosa probably did not return till 1517, since he is said to have remained sixteen years in the Indian Ocean, and in that case he could not have returned before 1515—however, it is said in the introduction to the Lisbon edition that he is the son of Diego Barbosa, named in the Decades as having sailed in 1501 with the first fleet with João de Nova : the same introduction also says that the time of his departure to and return to India are unknown.

Ramusio's edition of Barbosa's narrative says the writing of it was finished in 1516 ; it does not, however, mention any facts which occurred later than the year 1514. There is reason to suspect that Ramusio obtained his copy from the same source as the Barcelona manuscript, because the name of the precious stone zircon is spelled differently, giagonza, jagonza, and gegonza, and this difference of orthography coincides in the same places in the Spanish manuscript and in Ramusio. Ramusio gives an appendix containing the prices of precious stones and of spices, but has not got the voyage to the Moluccas of Francisco Serrano. The only reason I can conjecture for this not having reached Ramusio is, that it was a confidential paper, on account of the rivalry of Spain and Portugal with regard to those islands; and it is stated in history that Serrano increased the distances so as to enable Magellan to persuade the Spaniards that the Moluccas were more to the eastward, and that they fell within the demarcation of territories assigned by the Pope to Castille. This account of Francisco Serrano's voyage, and of his remaining behind married at Maluco, was either written by the Spaniard who accompanied him, or was translated by some other person than Diego Ribero and the Genoese ambassador Centurione, since all the points of the compass which in the body of the work are indicated by the names of winds, are here described by their names, as este, sudoeste, etc. Tramontana, greco, maestro, siloque, are all Spanish terms, but are less literate than the names of the points of the compass, and seem to be owing to the Genoese translator, to whom they would be familiar. It must be observed that the handwriting and paper of the narrative and two appendices of the Barcelona MS. are identical, and the leaves are numbered consecutively, so that there is no reason for supposing that the whole papers were not originally, as they now are, placed together.

Ramusio in various parts of the narrative leaves a blank with the words, *Here several lines are wanting*; this may be owing to passages having been struck out for political reasons. The Portuguese edition has a short passage not in the Spanish MS., the only apparent motive for its omission being that it was to the glorification of the Portuguese.

Since so large a portion of the present volume is contained in the Portuguese manuscript of Barbosa printed at Lisbon, it would be natural to follow Ramusio in attributing the work to him: at the same time it is not easy to understand how Barbosa, who was in the Indian Ocean at the time, should have confounded the two naval actions at Diu in 1508 and 1509, which he relates as one only, although the Portuguese were beaten in the first and victorious in the second. It is also difficult to imagine that one person visited all the places described in this volume, even in the space of sixteen years, at a period when travelling was slower than at present: and the observations on the manners and customs show a more intimate knowledge than what could be acquired by touching at a port for a few days only.

This work is that of no ordinary capacity; it shews great power of observation, and also the possession by the writer of great opportunities for inquiry into the manners and habits of the different countries described. It could hardly have been drawn up by an ecclesiastic, there is too great an absence of condemnation of idolatrous practices, and the deficiencies of St. Thomas's Christians are too lightly spoken of. An ecclesiastic would not have been so indifferent to their mode of communion and to the sale of the sacraments, which caused many to remain unbaptized. The scanty mention of

Albuquerque and of Goa, and its being the sort of political memorandum which a person in Magellan's position, seeking service from Spain, and desirous of pushing the Spanish government to eastern as well as western enterprise, would be likely to write; the commercial details, which are not those of a merchant, but rather of a soldier, for the prices given chiefly relate to provisions, horses and elephants, things useful in war, whilst the prices of jewels and spices, drawn up in a business-like manner, are in an appendix and not referred to in the narrative,—all these circumstances seem almost to justify the conclusion that this volume was drawn up by Magellan, or under Magellan's guidance, for the purpose of being laid before Charles V, at the time that Magellan was seeking the command which he received a short time later.

This volume derives additional value from the numerous passages in which it runs parallel to the *Lusiad*, so that the two confirm one another, and this prose description serves as a commentary to Camoens. Several passages descriptive of the customs of the nairs of Malabar in this work present very forcibly the connection between Plato and the Hindus.

The travels of Varthema, a former publication of the Hakluyt Society, gave evidence of the good administration of India especially in regard to justice in olden times; similar testimony will be found in this volume. The expedient of the King of Narsinga for correcting his high officials, without either removing them or lowering them in the eyes of those they had to rule, has not, I believe, been before narrated. Though Suttee has been so often described, the account of it in these pages possesses much interest and novelty, probably from having been written by an eye-witness, before that institution was disturbed by European influence. An allusion to the English longbow as to a weapon in actual use, gives an appearance of antiquity to this narrative even greater than that which belongs to its date. The orthography of the manuscript is not always uniform, therefore where a name is spelt in two different ways, I have left them as they are given. I have altered the original spelling of the names of only a few familiar places, and have retained the Portuguese expressions of Moor and Gentile, which mean Mussulman and heathen, one of which has survived up to the present time in Southern India as Moorman.

Any further observations I may have to make on this manuscript will be found in the notes.

I wish to express my thanks to Sr. D. Gregorio Romero Larrañaga, the head of the Barcelona Library, and to the other gentlemen of his department, for the cordial manner in which they have supplied me with the contents of their Library, and for their assistance in discussing doubtful points.

London, October 21, 1865.

viaje que hizo Juan Estevano quando huyo de ma
laca con tres portogueses e xpo valdemorales
sevillano en una cara dela que huyo de malaca en
la qual metio ciertos marineros malayos natu
rales de malaca cerca de los años de nro señor Jhu
xpo de mill e quinientos e doze años /

En el nonbre de dios salimos dela cibdad de malaca en una
caravela con quatro marineros e pilotos malayos el capitan era
franco Estevano con los tres xpianos que por todos eran nue
ve los marineros naturales de malaca los xpianos tres por
togueses e un castellano e en el año de mill e quis e doze
de calle navegamos hasta la cibdad de pegu y esta cibdad es
ta en tierra firme y no muy lexos dela mar mas cerca de malaca
leste oeste con ella y esta cerca faya norte sur con la canal
de malaca e ys la guardan /

Finis

Acabose de trasladar este libro de su original
en lengua portoguesa traduzida en lengua cas
tellana en vitoria estando en ella el enperador y rey
de españa a primero dia de marzo año de mill e quinien
tos e veynte e quatro años por mj ynterpretacion enba
xador dela comunidad de genova con ynterpetracion
de diego rribero portugues cosmografo de su mag^t
y maestro de cartas de navegar /.

PREFACE.

(TRANSLATED FROM THE PORTUGUESE EDITION, LISBON, 1812.)

I, Duarte Barbosa, a native of the very noble city of Lisbon, having navigated for a great part of my youth in the Indies discovered in the name of the king our lord, and having travelled through many and various countries neighbouring to the coast, and having seen and heard various things, which I judged to be marvellous and stupendous, and which had never been seen nor heard of by our ancestors, resolved to write them for the benefit of all, as I saw and heard of them from day to day, striving to declare in this my book the towns and limits of all those kingdoms to which I went in person, or of which I had trustworthy information; and also which were kingdoms and countries of the Moors and which of the Gentiles, and their customs. Neither have I left in silence their traffic, the merchandise which is met with in them, the places where they are produced, nor whither they are transported. And besides what I saw personally, I always delighted in inquiring of the Moors, Christians, and Gentiles, as to the usages and customs which they practised, and the points of information thus gained I endeavoured to combine together so as to have a more exact knowledge of them, this being always my special object, as it should be of all those who write on such matters; and I am convinced that it will be recognized that I have not spared any diligence in order to obtain this object, as far as the feeble extent of the power of my understanding allows of. It was in the present year of 1516 that I finished writing this my book.

DESCRIPTION OF THE EAST INDIES AND COUNTRIES ON THE SEABORD OF THE INDIAN OCEAN IN 1514.

[1] THE CAPE OF ST. SEBASTIAN AFTER PASSING THE CAPE OF GOOD HOPE.

HAVING passed the Cape of Good Hope in a north-easterly direction, at Cape San Sebastian, there are very fair mountain lands, and fields, and valleys, in which there are many cows and sheep, and other wild animals; it is a country inhabited by people who are black and naked. They only wear skins with the fur of deer, or other wild animals, like some cloaks in the French fashion, of which people the Portuguese, up to the present time, have not been able to obtain information, nor to become acquainted with what there is in the interior of the country. They have no navigation, neither do they make use of the sea, neither have the Moors of Arabia and Persia, or the Indies, ever navigated as far as this, nor discovered them, on account of the strong currents of the sea, which is very stormy.

ISLANDS OF THE GREAT UCIQUES.[2]

Having passed Cape San Sebastian towards the north-east for India, there are some islands close to the mainland to the east, which are called the Great Uciques; in which,

[1] Here the Barcelona manuscript begins.

[2] Insula Bocicas, 23 deg. S. lat., just N. of C. S. Sebastian, Homann's Atlas, Nuremberg, 1753.

on the side towards the mainland there are a few small towns of Moors, who deal with the people of the continent, and they provision themselves from them. In these Uciques much amber is found of good quality, which the Moors collect and sell in other places, and likewise many pearls and small seed pearls are found in the sea in beds (crusts), which they cannot gather or fish up, and whenever they do get them out they boil them, and extract the said pearls and seed pearls dingy and burnt, and there is no doubt that there are many and good ones, if they knew how to extract them, as is done in Sael, Cochoromandel, and in Barahe,[1] which will be mentioned hereafter.

THE LITTLE VCIQUES ISLANDS IN RIVERS.

Having passed the Vciques grandes towards Sofala, a fortress which the King of Portugal made there, and where there is much gold, at xvii or xviii leagues from it there are some rivers, which make between their branches, islands, called the Little Vciques, in which there are some villages of the Moors, who also deal with the Gentiles of the mainland in their provisions, which are rice, millet, and meat, and which they bring in small barks to Sufala.[2]

SOFALA.

Having passed the Little Vciques, for the Indies, at xviii leagues from them there is a river which is not very large, whereon is a town of the Moors called Sofala,[3] close to which town the King of Portugal has a fort. These Moors established themselves there a long time ago on account of the great trade in gold which they carry on with the Gentiles of the mainland: these speak somewhat of bad Arabic (garabia), and have got a king over them,

[1] Probably Bahrein.

[2] Cujus rex Quitove, Atlas, 1753. Reg. Munica cujus rex Chicanga.

[3] Cefala, Ortelius.

who is at present subject to the King of Portugal.[1] And the mode of their trade is that they come by sea in small barks which they call zanbucs (sambuk), from the kingdoms of Quiloa, and Mombaza, and Melindi; and they bring much cotton cloth of many colours, and white and blue, and some of silk; and grey, and red, and yellow beads, which come to the said kingdoms in other larger ships from the great kingdom of Cambay, which merchandise these Moors buy and collect from other Moors who bring them there, and they pay for them in gold by weight, and for a price which satisfies them; and the said Moors keep them and sell these cloths to the Gentiles of the kingdom of Benamatapa who come there laden with gold, which gold they give in exchange for the before mentioned cloths without weighing, and so much in quantity that these Moors usually gain one hundred for one. They also collect a large quantity of ivory, which is found all round Sofala, which they likewise sell in the great kingdom of Cambay at five or six ducats the hundred weight, and so also some amber, which these Moors of Sofala bring them from the Vciques. They are black men, and men of colour—some speak Arabic, and the rest make use of the language of the Gentiles of the country. They wrap themselves from the waist downwards with cloths of cotton and silk, and they wear other silk cloths above named, such as cloaks and wraps for the head, and some of them wear hoods of scarlet, and of other coloured woollen stuffs and camelets, and of other silks. And their

[1] Lusiadas, Canto v, stanza 76.

Ethiopes são todos, mas parece,
Que com gente melhor communicavam:
Palabra alguma Arabia se conhece
Entre a linguagem sua, que fallavam:
E com panno delgado, que se tece
De algodão, as cabeças apertavam,
Com outro, que de tint azul se tinge,
Cada hum as vergonhosas partes cinge.

victuals are millet, and rice, and meat, and fish. In this river near to the sea there are many sea horses, which go in the sea, and come out on land at times to feed. These have teeth like small elephants, and it is better ivory than that of the elephant, and whiter and harder, and of greater durability of colour. In the country all round Sofala there are many elephants, which are very large and wild, and the people of the country do not know how to tame them: there are also many lions, ounces, mountain panthers, wild asses, and many other animals. It is a country of plains and mountains, and well watered. The Moors have now recently begun to produce much fine cotton in this country, and they weave it into white stuff because they do not know how to dye it, or because they have not got any colours; and they take the blue or coloured stuffs of Cambay and unravel them, and again weave the threads with their white thread, and in this manner they make coloured stuffs, by means of which they get much gold.

KINGDOM OF BENAMATAPA.

On entering within this country of Sofala, there is the kingdom of Benamatapa, which is very large and peopled by Gentiles, whom the Moors call Cafers. These are brown men, who go bare, but covered from the waist downwards with coloured stuffs, or skins of wild animals; and the persons most in honour among them wear some of the tails of the skin behind them, which go trailing on the ground for state and show, and they make bounds and movements of their bodies, by which they make these tails wag on either side of them. They carry swords in scabbards of wood bound with gold or other metals, and they wear them on the left hand side as we do, in sashes of coloured stuffs, which they make for this purpose with four or five knots, and their tassels hanging down, like gentlemen; and in their hands azagayes, and others carry bows and arrows: it must be mentioned that the bows are of middle size, and the iron points of the arrows are very large and well wrought. They are men of war, and some of them are merchants: their women go naked as long as they are girls, only covering their middles with cotton cloths, and when they are married and have children, they wear other cloths over their breasts.

ZINBAOCH.[1]

Leaving Sofala for the interior of the country, at xv days journey from it, there is a large town of Gentiles, which is called Zinbaoch; and it has houses of wood and straw, in which town the King of Benamatapa frequently dwells, and from there to the city of Benamatapa there are six days journey, and the road goes from Sofala, inland, towards the Cape of Good Hope. And in the said Benamatapa, which is a very large town, the king is used to make his longest residence; and it is thence that the merchants bring to Sofala the gold which they sell to the Moors without weighing it, for coloured stuffs and beads of Cambay, which are much used and valued amongst them; and the people of this city of Benamatapa say that this gold comes from still further off towards the Cape of Good Hope, from another kingdom subject to this king of Benamatapa, who is a great lord, and holds many other kings as his subjects, and many other lands, which extend far inland, both towards the Cape of Good Hope and towards Mozambich. And in this town he is each day served with large presents, which the kings and lords, his subjects, send to him; and when they bring them, they carry them bareheaded through all the city, until they arrive at the palace, from whence the king sees them come from a window, and he orders them to be taken up from there, and the bearers do not see him, but only hear his words; and afterwards, he bids them call the persons who

[1] Zimbro, Ortelius, Zimbaon, Atlas, 1753. Sedes Regia.

have brought these presents, and he dismisses them. This king constantly takes with him into the field a captain, whom they call Sono, with a great quantity of men-at-arms, and amongst them they bring six thousand women, who also bear arms and fight. With these forces he goes about subduing and pacifying whatever kings rise up or desire to revolt. The said king of Benamatapa sends, each year, many honourable persons throughout his kingdoms to all the towns and lordships, to give them new regulations, so that all may do them obeisance, which is in this manner: each one of the envoys comes to a town, and bids the people extinguish all the fires that there are in it; and after they have been put out, all the inhabitants go to this man who has been sent as commissary, to get fresh fire from him in sign of subjection and obedience; and, whoever should not do this is held as a rebel, and the king immediately sends the number of people that are necessary to destroy him, and these pass through all the towns at their expense: their rations are meat, rice, and oil of sesame.[1]

RIVER ZUAMA.

Leaving Sofala for Mozambich, at forty leagues from it, there is a very large river, which is called the Zuama;[2] and it is said that it goes towards Benamatapa,[3] and it extends more than 160 leagues. In the mouth of this river there is a town of the Moors, which has a king, and it is called

[1] Ajonjo (Agiongoli) plant with a viscous substance. Ajonjoli Sesame plant. Ajonjera, carlina aqualis bruised in water makes birdlime.

[2] Zuama, Ortelius.

[3] Vê do Benomotapa o grande imperio,
De selvatica gente, negra e nua,
Onde Gonçalo morte e vituperio
Padecerá pela Fé sancta sua:
Nasce por este incognito hemispherio
O metal, porque mais a gente sua
Vê que do lago, donde se derrama
O Nilo, tambem vindo está Cuama,
Camoens, Canto x, stanza 93.

Mongalo.[1] Much gold comes from Benamatapa to this town of the Moors, by this river, which makes another branch which falls at Angos, where the Moors make use of boats (almadias), which are boats hollowed out from a single trunk, to bring the cloths and other merchandise from Angos, and to transport much gold and ivory.

ANGOY.

After passing this river of Zuama, at xl leagues from it, there is a town of the Moors on the sea coast, which is called Angoy,[2] and has a king, and the Moors who live there are all merchants, and deal in gold, ivory, silk, and cotton stuffs, and beads of Cambay, the same as do those of Sofala. And the Moors bring these goods from Quiloa, and Monbaza, and Melynde, in small vessels hidden from the Portuguese ships ; and they carry from there a great quantity of ivory, and much gold. And in this town of Angos there are plenty of provisions of millet, rice, and some kinds of meat. These men are very brown and copper coloured ; they go naked from the waist upwards, and from thence downwards, they wrap themselves with cloths of cotton and silk, and wear other cloths folded after the fashion of cloaks, and some wear caps and others hoods, worked with stuffs and silks ; and they speak the language belonging to the country, which is that of the Pagans, and some of them speak Arabic. These people are sometimes in obedience to the king of Portugal, and at times they throw it off, for they are a long way off from the Portuguese forts.

MOZAMBIQUE ISLAND.

Having passed this town of Anguox, on the way to India, there are very near to the land three islands, one of which

[1] The old maps have a kingdom of Mongale stretching N. from the R. Zuama.

[2] Angoches, 16 deg. S. lat., Homann.

is inhabited by Moors, and is called Mozambique.[1] It has a very good port, and all the Moors touch there who are sailing to Sofala, Zuama, or Anguox. Amongst these Moors there is a sheriff, who governs them, and does justice. These are of the language and customs of the Moors of Anguox, in which island the King of Portugal now holds a fort, and keeps the said Moors under his orders and government. At this island the Portuguese ships provide themselves with water and wood, fish and other kinds of provisions; and at this place they refit those ships which stand in need of repair. And from this island likewise the Portuguese fort in Sofala draws its supplies, both of Portuguese goods and of the produce of India, on account of the road being longer by the mainland.

Opposite this island there are many very large elephants and wild animals. The country is inhabited by Gentiles, brutish people who go naked and smeared all over with coloured clay, and their natural parts wrapped in a strip of blue cotton stuff, without any other covering; and they have their lips pierced with three holes in each lip, and in these holes they wear bones stuck in, and claws, and small stones, and other little things dangling from them.

ISLAND OF QUILOA.

After passing this place and going towards India, there is another island close to the mainland, called Quiloa,[2] in which there is a town of the Moors, built of handsome houses of stone and lime, and very lofty, with their windows like those of the Christians; in the same way it has streets, and these houses have got their terraces, and the wood worked in with the masonry, with plenty of gardens, in which there are many fruit trees and much water. This island has got a king over it, and from hence there is trade with Sofala with ships, which carry much gold, which is dispersed thence

[1] Mozambique, Ortelius.

[2] Quiloa, Ortelius.

through all Arabia Felix, for henceforward all this country is thus named on account of the shore of the sea being peopled with many towns and cities of the Moors; and when the King of Portugal discovered this land, the Moors of Sofala, and Zuama, and Anguox, and Mozambique, were all under obedience to the King of Quiloa, who was a great king amongst them. And there is much gold in this town, because all the ships which go to Sofala touch at this island, both in going and coming back. These people are Moors, of a dusky colour, and some of them are black and some white; they are very well dressed with rich cloths of gold, and silk, and cotton, and the women also go very well dressed out with much gold and silver in chains and bracelets on their arms, and legs, and ears. The speech of these people is Arabic, and they have got books of the Alcoran, and honour greatly their prophet Muhamad. This King, for his great pride, and for not being willing to obey the King of Portugal, had this town taken from him by force, and in it they killed and captured many people, and the King fled from the island, in which the King of Portugal ordered a fortress to be built, and thus he holds under his command and government those who continued to dwell there.

ISLAND OF MOMBAZA.

Passing Quiloa, and going along the coast of the said Arabia Felix towards India, close to the mainland there is another island, in which there is a city of the Moors, called Bombaza,[1] very large and beautiful, and built of high and handsome houses of stone and whitewash, and with very good streets, in the manner of those of Quiloa. And it also had a king over it. The people are of dusky white, and brown complexions, and likewise the women, who are much adorned with silk and gold stuffs. It is a town of great trade in goods, and has a good port, where there are always

[1] Mombaza, Ortelius.

many ships, both of those that sail for Sofala and those that come from Cambay and Melinde, and others which sail to the islands of Zanzibar, Manfia, and Penda, which will be spoken of further on. This Monbaza is a country well supplied with plenty of provisions, very fine sheep, which have round tails, and many cows, chickens, and very large goats, much rice and millet, and plenty of oranges, sweet and bitter, and lemons, cedrats, pomegranates, Indian figs, and all sorts of vegetables, and very good water. The inhabitants at times are at war with the people of the continent, and at other times at peace, and trade with them, and obtain much honey and wax, and ivory. This King, for his pride and unwillingness to obey the King of Portugal, lost his city, and the Portuguese took it from him by force, and the King fled, and they killed and made captives many of his people, and the country was ravaged,[1] and much plunder was carried off from it of gold and silver, copper, ivory, rich stuffs of gold and silk, and much other valuable merchandize.

MELINDE.

After passing the city of Mombaza, at no great distance further on along the coast, there is a very handsome town on the mainland on the beach, called Melinde,[2] and it is a town of the Moors, which has a king. And this town has fine houses of stone and whitewash, of several stories, with their windows and terraces, and good streets. The inhabitants are dusky and black, and go naked from the waist

[1] Camoens confirms the author's statement of the flourishing condition of Mombaza, and of its devastation by the Portuguese. Canto x, stanzas 26, 27—

> Ambos darâo com braço forte armado
> A Quiloa fertil aspero castigo,
> Fazendo nella Rei leal e humano,
> Deitado forá o perfido Tyranno.
>
> Tambem farâo Mombaça, que se arrea
> De casas sumptuosas e edificios,
> Co'o ferro e fogo seu queimada e fea
> Em pago dos passados maleficios.

[2] Melinde, Ortelius.

upwards, and from that downwards they cover themselves with cloths of cotton and silk, and others wear wraps like cloaks, and handsome caps on their heads. The trade is great which they carry on in cloth, gold, ivory, copper, quicksilver, and much other merchandise, with both Moors and Gentiles of the kingdom of Cambay, who come to their port with ships laden with cloth, which they buy in exchange for gold, ivory, and wax. Both parties find great profit in this. There are plenty of provisions in this town, of rice, millet, and some wheat, which is brought to them from Cambay, and plenty of fruit, for there are many gardens and orchards. There are here many of the large-tailed sheep, and of all other meats as above; there are also oranges, sweet and sour. This King and people have always been very friendly and obedient to the King of Portugal, and the Portuguese have always met with much friendship and good reception amongst them.[1]

ISLAND OF SAN LORENZO.[2]

Opposite these places, in the sea above the Cape of the Currents,[3] at a distance of eighty leagues, there is a very large island, which is called San Lorenzo, and which is peopled by Gentiles, and has in it some towns of Moors. This island has many kings, both Moors and Gentiles. There is in it much meat, rice, and millet, and plenty of oranges and lemons, and there is much ginger in this country, which they do not make use of, except to eat it almost green. The inhabitants go naked, covering only their middles with cotton cloths. They do not navigate, nor does any one do so for them; they have got canoes for fishing on their coast. They

[1] Melinde hospicio gazalhoso e charo.
Camoens, Canto x, stanza 96.

[2] Lusiade, Canto x, stanza 137—
De São-Lourenço vê a ilha affamada,
Que Madagascar he d'alguns chamada.

[3] Cabo dos Corrientes, Ortelius.

are people of a dark complexion, and have a language of their own. They frequently are at war with one another, and their arms are azagayes, very sharp, with their points very well worked; they throw these in order to wound, and carry several of them in their hands. They are very well built and active men, and have a good method of wrestling. There is amongst them silver of inferior quality. Their principal food is roots, which they sow, and it is called yname,[1] and in the Indies of Spain it is called maize. The country is very beautiful and luxuriant in vegetation, and it has very large rivers. This island is in length from the part of Sofala and Melinde three hundred leagues, and to the mainland there are sixty leagues.

PENDA, MANFIA, AND ZANZIBAR.

Between this island of San Lorenzo and the continent, not very far from it, are three islands, which are called one Manfia, another Zanzibar, and the other Penda;[2] these are inhabited by Moors; they are very fertile islands, with plenty of provisions, rice, millet, and flesh, and abundant oranges, lemons, and cedrats. All the mountains are full of them; they produce many sugar canes, but do not know how to make sugar. These islands have their kings. The inhabitants trade with the mainland with their provisions and fruits; they have small vessels, very loosely and badly made, without decks, and with a single mast; all their planks are sewn

[1] Yname, in Portuguese, Inhame. Root in the form of a gourd, composed of two bulbs, which grow one above the other, the larger one below the smaller one. It is cut into slices and eaten instead of bread. It throws out very large leaves, without fruit. The ancients erroneously called it Fava Ægyptia, others have called it Arum Egyptium, which Bahuino, in his Historia Universal das Plantas, does not approve of. Bluteau, Dict., Coimbra, 1713. ñame—Genus of monocotyledonous plants of the family of the dioscoreas. Dico. Encyclopedico, Madrid, 1855. The "maize" mentioned in the text must be a mistake of the author or of the translators: it should be yams.

[2] Penda and Zenzibar, Ortelius.

together with cords of reed or matting, and the sails are of palm mats. They are very feeble people, with very few and despicable weapons. In these islands they live in great luxury, and abundance; they dress in very good cloths of silk and cotton, which they buy in Mombaza of the merchants from Cambay, who reside there. Their wives adorn themselves with many jewels of gold from Sofala, and silver, in chains, ear-rings, bracelets, and ankle rings, and are dressed in silk stuffs: and they have many mosques, and hold the Alcoran of Mahomed.

PATE.

After passing Melinde, and going towards India, they cross the Gulf (because the coast trends inwards) towards the Red Sea, and on the coast there is a town called Pate,[1] and further on there is another town of the Moors, called Lamon;[2] all these trade with the Gentiles of the country, and they are strongly-walled towns of stone and whitewash, because at times they have to fight with the Gentiles, who live in the interior of the country.

BRAVA.

Leaving these places, further on along the coast is a town of the Moors, well walled, and built of good houses of stone and whitewash, which is called Brava. It has not got a king; it is governed by its elders,[3] they being honoured and respectable persons. It is a place of trade, which has already been destroyed by the Portuguese, with great slaughter of the inhabitants, of whom many were made captives, and great riches in gold, silver, and other merchandise were taken here, and those who escaped fled into the country, and after the place was destroyed they returned to people it.

[1] Pato, Ortelius, Homann. [2] Lamon, Ortelius.

[3] Brava, Ortelius. The German Atlas of 1753 adds Respubl. to the name of Brava.

MAGADOXO.[1]

Leaving the before-mentioned town of Brava, on the coast further on towards the Red Sea, there is another very large and beautiful town, called Magadoxo, belonging to the Moors, and it has a king over it, and is a place of great trade in merchandise. Ships come there from the kingdom of Cambay and from Aden with stuffs of all sorts, and with other merchandise of all kinds, and with spices. And they carry away from there much gold, ivory, beeswax, and other things upon which they make a profit. In this town there is plenty of meat, wheat, barley, and horses, and much fruit; it is a very rich place. All the people speak Arabic; they are dusky, and black, and some of them white. They are but bad warriors, and use herbs with their arrows to defend themselves from their enemies.

AFUNI.[2]

Having passed the district and town of Magadoxo, further on along the coast is another small town of the Moors, called Afuni, in which there is abundance of meat and provisions. It is a place of little trade, and has got no port.

CAPE GUARDAFUN.

After passing this place the next after it is Cape Guardafun,[3] where the coast ends, and trends so as to double towards the Red Sea. This cape is in the mouth of the Strait of Mecca, and all the ships which come from India, that is to say, from the kingdom of Cambay, of Chaul, Dabul, Baticala, and Malabar, Ceylon, Choromandel, Bengal, Sumatra, Poggru, Tanaseri, Malacca, and China, all

[1] The river of this place is called Mecadesso in the German Atlas, which shows the Arabic origin of the name; in Ortelius Magadazo.

[2] Orfuni, in Atlas of 1753.

[3] Guardafun, Ortelius.

come to meet at this cape, and from it they enter into the before-mentioned Red Sea with their merchandise for Aden, Berbera, and Zeyla, and Guida, the port of Mecca, for which ships the ships of the King of Portugal sometimes go and lie in wait and take them with all their riches.

MET.

In doubling this Cape of Guardafun, towards the inner part of the Red Sea, there is, just near the said cape, a town of the Moors called Met,[1] not very large, where there is plenty of meat; it is of little trade.

BARBARA.

Further on, on the same coast, is a town of the Moors called Barbara;[2] it has a port, at which many ships of Adeni and Cambay touch with their merchandise, and from there those of Cambay carry away much gold, and ivory, and other things, and those of Aden take many provisions, meat, honey, and wax, because, as they say, it is a very abundant country.

ZEYLA.

Having passed this town of Berbara, and going on, entering the Red Sea, there is another town of the Moors, which is named Zeyla,[3] which is a good place of trade, whither many ships navigate and sell their cloths and merchandise. It is very populous, with good houses of stone and whitewash, and good streets; the houses are covered with terraces, the dwellers in them are black. They have many horses, and breed much cattle of all sorts, which they make use of for milk, and butter, and meat. There is in this country abundance of wheat, millet, barley, and fruits, which they carry thence to Aden.

[1] Met, Ortelius, and the Atlas of 1753.

[2] Barbara, Ortelius.

[3] Zeila, Ortelius.

DALAQUA.

After continuing along the coast from the town of Zeyla, there is another place of the Moors, called Dalaqua,[1] the seaport which is most made use of by the Abaxins[2] of the country of Prester John. And all round this place there are much provisions, and much gold comes there from the country of Prester John.

MASAVA SAVAQUIN[3] AND OTHER PLACES.

Leaving Dalaqua for the interior of the Red Sea, there are Massowa, Suakin, and other towns of the Moors; and this coast is still called Arabia Felix, and the Moors call it Barra Ajan,[4] in all which there is much gold which comes from the interior of the country of Prester John, whom they call Abexi. All these places on this coast trade with the country with their cloths and other merchandise, and they bring from it gold, ivory, honey, wax and slaves; and sometimes they are at war with them, for they are Christians, and they capture many of them; and such captives are much valued by the Moors, and amongst them are worth much more money than other slaves because they find them sharp and faithful, and well-built men in body, and when they turn Moors, they become greater emperors than the original Moors. These Moors of Arabia Felix are all black[5] and good fighting men; they go bare from the waist upwards, and from thence downwards they cover themselves with cloths of cotton; and the more honourable men amongst

[1] Dalacca, Ortelius.

[2] Abyssinians, Habeshin in Arabic.

[3] Saachem, Ortelius.

[4] Berr Ajem. The spelling of this name is a proof that the Spanish j still had the value of the English j and the Arabic jim.

[5] This refers to the Sawahily of Abyssinia, not to the people of Arabia, and applies to them.

them wear their cloths over them like Almalafas,[1] and the women are covered in the same way:[2] . . . .

KINGDOM OF PRESTER JOHN.

Leaving these towns of the Moors and entering into the interior of the country, the great kingdom of Prester John is to be found, whom the Moors of Arabia call Abexi;[3] this kingdom is very large, and peopled with many cities, towns, and villages, with many inhabitants: and it has many kings subject to it and tributary kings. And in their country there are many who live in the fields and mountains, like Beduins: they are black men, very well made: they have many horses, and make use of them, and are good riders, and there are great sportsmen and hunters amongst them. Their provisions are flesh of all kinds, milk, butter, and wheaten bread, and of these things there is a great abundance. Their clothes are of hides because the country is wanting in cloths; and there is a law amongst them by which certain families and ranks of persons may wear cloths, and the rest of the people may wear only hides well dressed and tanned. Amongst them there are men and women who have never drunk water, but only milk, which greatly supports them, and quenches the thirst, on account of its being more healthy and substantial, and there is great abundance of it in the country. These people are Christians of the doctrine of the blessed Saint Bartholomew, as they say; and their baptism is in three kinds, of blood, fire, and water: that is to say,

[1] Almalafa, a cloak, plaid, old Spanish, not in dictionaries, from Arabic.

[2] "Estas cosen a sus hijas sus naturas quando son chiquitas dexandoles solamente un meadero y asi las traen cosidas fasta que son en hedad de casar y las entregan a sus maridos y estonces les cortan la carne questa soldada como sy nacieron asy." The Portuguese edition states that Barbosa knew this by experience.

[3] Habeshy, Abyssinian.

that they circumcise themselves, and mark themselves on the temples and forehead with fire, and also in water, like the Catholic Christians. Many of them are deficient in our true faith, because the country is very large, and whilst in the principal city of Babel Malech, where Prester John resides, they may be Christians, in many other distant parts they live in error and without being taught; so that they are only Christians in name.

BABEL MELECH.

In the interior of this country is the great city of Babel Melech,[1] where Prester John holds his residence. The Moors call him the great King of the Habeshys: he is Christian, and lord of many extensive countries and numerous people, with whom he makes subject many great kings. He is very rich, and possesses more gold than any other prince. This Prester John holds a very large court, and he keeps many men at arms continually in his pay, whom he takes about with him. He goes out very rarely from his dwelling; many kings and great lords come to visit him. In this city a great feast takes place in the month of August, for which so many kings and nobles come together, and so many people that they are innumerable: and on this day of the feast in August they take an image out of a church, which is believed to be that of Our Lady, or that of St. Bartholomew, which image is of gold and of the size of a man; its eyes are of very large and beautiful rubies of great value, and the whole of it is adorned with many precious stones of much value, and placing it in a great chariot of gold, they carry it in procession with very great veneration and ceremony, and Prester John goes in front of this car in another gold car, very richly dressed in cloth of gold with much jewellery. And they begin to go out thus in the morning,

[1] Babel Mandel, Ortelius.

and go in procession through all the city with much music of all sorts of instruments, until the evening, when they go home. And so many people throng to this procession, that in order to arrive at the car of the image many die of being squeezed and suffocated; and those who die in this wise are held as saints and martyrs; and many old men and old women go with a good will to die in this manner.

SUEZ.

Leaving this country of Prester John and the coast of the sea of Arabia Felix. and turning to the other part of the Red Sea, which is also called Arabia, and the Moors call it Barra Arab, there is a village, a sea-port called Suez,[1] and thither the Moors of Guida, the port of Mecca, bring all the spices, drugs, precious stones, seed pearl, amber, musk, and other merchandise of great value from the parts about India; and from there they load them on camels to carry them by land to Cairo, and from Cairo other merchants carry them to Alexandria; and from there the Venetians and other Christians usually export them. And this trade now, in a great measure, ceases on account of the Portuguese, whose fleets prohibit the navigation of the Moors from India to the Red Sea.[2] And the Great Sultan, lord of Cairo, who loses

[1] Zues, Ortelius.

[2] Camoens thus describes the interruption by the Portuguese of the Indian voyages to the Red Sea. Canto ix, stanzas 3 and 4:—

Gidá se chama o porto, aonde o trato
De todo o Roxo mar mais florecia,
De que tinha proveito grande, e grato
O Soldão, que esse reino possuïa.
Daqui os Malabares, por contrato
Dos infieis, formosa companhia
De grandes naos pelo Indico Oceano
Especiaria vem buscar cada anno.

Por estas nãos os Mouros esperavam,
Que, como fossem grandes e possantes,
Aquellas, que o commercia lhe tomavam,
Com flammas abrazassem crepitantes:

most by this, ordered a fleet to be built in the port of Suez, for which he had the wood and artillery, and other equipments transported by land, in which much money was expended; and this fleet was of ships and galleys, in order to pass with it to India and there forbid the Portuguese from cruising. And when this fleet was built many people of different nations went with it to the first India, which is the Kingdom of Cambay; and the Captain of it was Amir Uçen,[1] and with this fleet they met that of Portugal in front of a city named Dyu, and there they fought vigorously, and many people were killed, and at last the Moors, Turks, and Mamelukes were conquered and all their fleet was taken and part of it burned, and on this account and several other victories which the Portuguese gained over the before-mentioned Moors, they lost their navigation in the Red Sea, and the said port of Suez remains without the trade in spices.

MOUNT SINAI.

Near the said city of Suez there is in the country of Arabia on the Red Sea, the mountain of Sinai, where lies the blessed Saint Catharine in a church, in which there are Christian friars, under the lordship of the Sultan, to which building the devout of all Christian countries come in pilgrimage, and the chief part of those that throng thither are from the country of Prester John and Armenia, Babilonia, Constantinople, and Jerusalem.

Neste socorro tanto confiavam,
Que já não querem mais dos navegantes,
Senão que tanto tempo alli tardassem,
Que da famosa Meca as naos chegassem.

And Canto x, stanza 50:—

Barbará se teme
Do mal, de que o emporio Zeila geme.

[1] Hussein.

ELIOBON AND MEDINA.

Having passed Mount Sinai, which the Moors call Tur, along the coast of the Red Sea going out of it, there is a village of the Moors, a sea-port called Eliobon,[1] and it is a port where they disembark for Medina, which is another town of the Moors, up the country at three days' journey from the port, and the body of Mahomed is buried in it.

GUIDA PORT OF MECA.

Leaving the port of Eliobon to go out of the Red Sea, there is a town of the Moors, called Guida, and it is the port of Mecca, whither the ships used to come every year from India with spices and drugs, and they returned thence to Calicut with much copper, quicksilver, vermillion, saffron, rose-water, scarlet silks, camelots, tafetans and other goods, of stuffs used in India, and also with much gold and silver; and the trade was very great and profitable. And from this port of Guida these spices and drugs were transported in small vessels to Suez, as has been already said.

MECA.

At one day's journey up the country from the port of Guida is the great city of Meca, in which there is a very large mosque, to which all the Moors from all parts go in pilgrimage, and they hold for certain that they are saved by washing with the water of a well which is in this mosque: and they carry it away from there in bottles to their countries as a great relic. In the aforesaid Guida port of Mecca a fortress has been lately built by Emir Hussein, the Moorish captain of the ships of the Sultan, which the Portuguese destroyed in India: this captain when he saw himself defeated, did not dare return to his country without performing some service to his king, and he decided on begging of the

[1] Eliobon, Atlas of Ortelius and Iambut or Yembo.

King of Cambay (who is called Sultan Mahamud) assistance in money, and so also from the nobles and merchants of his kingdom and from other Moorish kings, in order to construct this fortress, saying: that since the Portuguese, (whom they call Franks) were so powerful, it would not be wonderful if they were to come into this port and were to go and destroy the house of Mahomet. And these Moorish kings and people hearing his petition, and seeing the power of the King of Portugal, it seemed to them that this might come to pass, and thus all gave him great gifts, by means of which he loaded three ships with spices and other merchandise, and went with them to the Red Sea, and arrived at Guida, where he sold them, and with the money he made the said fortress, and during the time that he was building it, the Portuguese were making another inside the town of Calicut,[1] and the King of Calicut begged the Captain Major of the King of Portugal to give him permission to send then a ship laden with spices to Mecca. And this permission was given him, and the ship was sent. And there went in it as captain an honourable person of the Moors named Califa, and he arrived at Guida the port of Mecca, where he came on shore very well dressed out, along with his people, and he found Emir Hussein building his fortress, and was asked by him news of the Portuguese. And this Califa answered him, telling him how they were in great peace at Calicut, and making a handsome fortress. And Emir Hussein asked him, how dare you come to Mecca being a friend of the Portuguese? Califa

[1] Voyages and Travels by R. Kerr, vol. ii, p. 512. Letter from merchants of Spain to their correspondents respecting a treaty of peace and league between the Kings of Portugal and Calicut.

We have been informed by those who were on board the fleet which sailed from Lisbon to India in May, 1502, and returned on the 15th December, 1503, that the King of Calicut has concluded a peace with our Sovereign on the following conditions. . . . That our king, if so inclined, may build a fort at Calicut, and shall be supplied with a sufficient quantity of stones, lime, and timber for that purpose.

answered him, I am a merchant and am unable to do anything, but you who are a captain of the great Sultan if you go to India to turn them out of it, how came you to leave them there, and to make a fortress here? At which Emir Hussein was much put out, and ordered Califa immediately, and well dressed as he was, to take stones and mortar, he and his people, and help to build the fortress: and he made him work for the space of an hour.[1] And Califa related this in Calicut later when he returned there.[2]

JAZAN, HALI, ALHOR.

Leaving Jiddah the port of Mekkah, to go out of the Red Sea there are three towns of the Moors, which have got kings over them, one is called Jazan,[3] another Hali, and the other Alhor; in these there are many horses and plenty of provisions. This king does not obey the Sultan nor any other

[1] Probably Admiral Hussein had heard of Monçaide, the spy of Vasco de Gama, of whom Camoens says:—

Estava para dar ao Gama aviso
E merecer por isso o Paraiso.
Este, de quem se os Mouros naô guardavam,
Por ser Mouro, como ellos, antes era
Participante em quanto machinavam.
Canto ix, stanzas 5 and 6.

[2] The above anecdote of the fortitude and perseverance of Mir Hussein after his defeat, is new; and seems conclusive as to this MS. having remained unpublished, and almost unread; since, the *Panorama* (or Spanish version of the *Univers Pittoresque) Historia de Portugal*, por M. Fernando Denis, Conservador de la Biblioteca de Santa Jenoveva: traducida por Una Sociedad Literaria, Barcelona, Imprenta del Fomento, 1845; says at p. 123:—"This battle, as Simon Goulard relates it, brought the power of the Mussulmans of Egypt to an end, and so convinced of this was Melek-Jaz that he hastened to conclude a peace with the Portuguese. Mir-Hosein, who had manifested such distinguished valour and such profound knowledge in this struggle, fearing the inconstancy of Melek-Jaz, who might have given him up to Almeida, went off hurriedly to the kingdom of Cambay, and later removed himself to Upper Hindustan: but the historians lost his trace here and never again make any mention of the chief of the confederation of the Rumys."

[3] Jizan.

king whatever; he holds many countries under him in which he has many towns with many sea ports, from which the Moorish merchants used to export a few horses to India in their merchant ships, because there they are worth a good deal.

HODEYDA, MAHA, BABEL MENDE.

Having passed these places and kingdom, there are three places further on the coast which belong to the kingdom of Aden; the one they call Hodeyda, the other Maha,[1] the other Babelmende, which is in the mouth of the strait of the Red Sea where the ships enter it, and at this place the ships take pilots as far as Jiddah, who live by it.

ISLAND OF CAMARON.

In the sea of these other places, there is a small island called Camaron,[2] inhabited by Moors, in which the ships were accustomed to take refreshments when they passed by it to Jiddah. This island was ravaged by Alonso de Alboquerque, captain of the King of Portugal; and he staid there for some days repairing his fleet in order to leave the Red Sea, for the season did not allow him to go as far as Jiddah, to which he wished to arrive.

ADEM.

Coming out of the Red Sea by Babelmendel, which is in the straits, as has been said, towards the open sea, further on the coast there are several towns of Moors, which all belong to the kingdom of Aden, and having passed these villages you arrive at the town of Aden, which belongs to the Moors, and has a king over it. It is a very handsome city, with very large and fine houses, and a place of much trade, with good streets, and surrounded with a strong wall in their fashion. This city is on a point between a mountain and the sea; and this mountain ridge on the side of the main land is a pre-

[1] Mocha.

[2] Camaran, Ortelius.

cipitous rock, in such manner that on that side it has no more than one entrance, and on the top of this ridge, where the town is, there are many small towers, which look very pretty from the sea. Inside the city there is no water at all, and outside of the gate towards the main land there is a building to which they make water come in pipes from another mountain at some little distance from there, and between one ridge and the other ridge there was a great plain. In this city there are great Moorish merchants, and many Jews.[1] They are white men, a few of them black, they dress in cloth of cotton, silk, scarlet wool, and camelots. Their clothes are long robes, and they wear caps on their heads, and with low shoes on their feet. Their victuals are plenty of meat, wheaten bread, and rice which comes from India: there is plenty of fruit as in our parts, and there are in this place many horses and camels. The king is always in the interior of the country, and he maintains his governor in this city. Many ships, great and small, come there from many parts; that is to say, from Jiddah, whence they bring them much copper and quicksilver, and vermillion, coral, cloths of wool and silk. And they take from here in return spices, drugs, cotton cloths, and other things from Cambay, with provisions and other goods. Many ships also touch there from Zeyla and Berbera with provisions and other goods, and carry away from there stuffs from Cambay, alaquequas,[2] and large and small beads perforated for stringing, with which they trade in Arabia Felix, and in the country of Prester John. Some ships from Ormuz likewise touch there to trade, and also from Cambay, whence they bring much cotton stuff, spices, drugs, jewels and pearls, alaquequas, spun cotton, and unspun; and they take from these madder, opium, raisins, copper, quicksilver, vermillion, rose-water which they make there, woollen and silk stuffs, coloured

[1] Or Indians.

[2] Alaquequa is an Indian stone which stops the flow of blood; alaquequas are glass beads. Dictionary of V. Salva, Paris, 1856.

stuffs from Mecca, and gold in ingots or coined, and thread and camelots. And these ships of Cambay are so many and so large, and with so much merchandise, that it is a terrible thing to think of so great an expenditure of cotton stuffs as they bring. There come likewise to this port of Aden many ships from Chaul and Dabul, and from Bengal and the country of Calicut; they used to come there with the beforementioned goods and with a large quantity of rice and sugar, and cocoanuts which grow on the palm trees, and which are like nuts in flavour, and with the kernels[1] they make drinking cups. There also arrive there ships from Bengal, Samatra, and Malaca, which bring much spices and drugs, silks, benzoin, alacar,[2] sandal-wood, aloes-wood, rhubarb, musk, and much cotton stuffs from Bengal and Mangala,[3] so that it is a place of as much trade as there can be in the world, and of the richest merchandise. The fleet and armament of the King of Portugal came to this city, and took and burned in its harbour several ships laden with much merchandise, and several empty ships, and it made an assault to enter the town, and mounted the walls with scaling ladders, which broke with the weight of the many people on them; so that the Portuguese went out again, and abandoned the town: and at this entry the Moors defended themselves very vigorously, and many of them died, and some of the Christians.

KINGDOM OF FARTACH.

Having passed the said kingdom of Aden, going out of the strait towards the East, there is another kingdom of the Moors about twenty-five leagues off, near the sea, it has three or four towns on the coast, and they are called Xebech,

[1] The cocoa-nut shell is within a very thick husk, and so may be called a kernel.

[2] Lac.

[3] Mangala, fortress of Sumatra, in the country of Lampong, on the shore of the Tulang-Buvang, nine leagues and two-thirds from the mouth of that river. *Geographical Dictionary*, Barcelona, 1832.

Diufar,[1] and Fartach.[2] These Moors have got a king over them and are very good fighting men: they have got horses which they make use of in war, and good arms with short blades; the said king is subject to the King of Aden and is his servant.

CAPE FARTACH AND THE ISLAND OF SACOTORA.

In this country and kingdom there is a cape which is called Cape Fartach, where the coast turns and makes a bend towards the said sea between north-east and east,[3] and between this cape and that of Guardafun, is the mouth of the strait of Mecca, which runs north-west and south-east,[4] and it is xl leagues in width, where all the ships pass for those voyages and to the Red Sea. Above Cape Guardafun, to the north-east by east, twenty-seven leagues off, is an island called Sacotora, with very high mountains, it is inhabited by dusky people, who are said to be Christians; but they are deficient in the teaching of the Christian law and baptism, and have got only the name of Christians: they have in their chapels crosses, +.[5] It was in former times a country of Christians, and the Christian doctrine was lost there on account of Christian navigation having ceased there; and the Moors say that this was an island of Amazons, who later in the course of time mixed with men, and something of this appears to be the case, since there the women administer property and manage it, without the husbands having a voice in the matter. These people have a language of their own; they go without clothes, and only cover their nakedness with cotton cloths and skins: they have many cows and sheep, and date palms. Their victuals are meat, milk,

[1] Dhafar. [2] Fartach, Ortelius, Fartaque, Atlas of 1753.

[3] Greco y levante, N.E.E., Gregal, Grech, N.E. wind, still used in Catalan.

[4] Mastro y Soroco, Mistral & Sirocco.

[5] Marked with a cross thus in the MS.

and dates. In this island there is much dragon's blood[1] and aloes of Socotra. And the Moors of Fartach built in it a fortress, to subjugate them, and turn them Moors; and some of those that lived around the fortress were Moors, and served the Moors of the fort like their slaves, both in their persons and property. A fleet of the King of Portugal arrived at this island, and took this fortress by force of arms from the Moors of Fartach, fighting with them: and they defended themselves much more vigorously than any men of these parts; so that they never would give themselves up, and all died in the fight, for none of them escaped; so that they are very good and daring fighting men. The Captain of this fleet left troops and artillery in this fortress in order to keep it in the name of the King of Portugal. And quite near to this island of Sacotora there are two other islands inhabited by coloured people and blacks, like the people of the Canary Islands, without law or knowledge, and they have no dealings with any other people. In these two islands much amber and of good quality is found, and many shells of the valuable and precious kind in the mine, and much dragon's blood and aloes of Socotra; and there are large flocks of sheep and oxen.

DIUFAR.

Leaving Cape Fartach towards the coast of the open sea to the north-east by east, going along the coast L leagues off is a town of the Moors and sea-port called Diufar,[2] a city of the kingdom of Fartach, in which the Moors of Cambay trade in cotton stuffs, rice, and other goods.

XEHER.[3]

Further on from this place, in the direction of the same wind, at XX leagues off, along the same coast, is another

[1] Sangre de dragon.

[2] Dolfar, Ortelius.

[3] Shehir, one of the chief sea-ports of Hadramant. Zeher, Ortelius.

town of the Moors, called Xeher; it also belongs to the kingdom of Fartach, and is very large; it has a large trade in the stuffs, which the Moors of Cambay, Chaul, Dabul, and Baticala, and the country of Malabar, bring in their ships to this port and town of Xeher; these are coarse and fine cotton stuffs, with which they clothe themselves; granates on strings and several other jewels of small value, much rice, sugar, and spice of all kinds, cocoa-nuts, and other goods, which they sell there to the merchants of the country, who carry them from there to Aden and all this part of Arabia. And the importers afterwards employ the money in horses for India: these are very large and very good, and each one of them in India is worth five or six hundred ducats. And they also take from there much wormwood,[1] which grows in that country. And in the interior of the country all the people are Beduins: in this country there is much wheat and plenty of meat and dates, grapes, and all other fruits which are in our parts. And all the ships which sail from India for the Red Sea, and having been delayed cannot arrive in good time[2] with their merchandise at the place of their destination, remain to sell them in this port of Xeher, and from there they go to India along the coast to Cambay. And so this port is large and of much trade at all times. This King of Fartach is, with the whole of his kingdom, in obedience to the King of Aden, because he holds a brother of his a prisoner. The wormwood which grows in this country of Xeher is carried from here to all the world, and the ships of this place load[3] the said wormwood, which is there worth a hundred and fifty maravedis the hundred weight.

[1] Enciencio, antient for ajenjo, Absinthe; perhaps the Kat or Katta, a very expensive leaf of a shrub.

[2] This refers to the monsoon; if it is unfavourable the ships cannot get up the Red Sea.

[3] This word is illegible, it reads *se enpegen*.

FASALHAD.

Having passed this town of Xeher, along the coast there are other small towns, and Beduins in the interior of the country. This coast lasts as far as Cape Fasalhat, which is xxv leagues from Xeher, between north-east and east, where the kingdom and rule of the King of Ormuz begins. At this cape there is a fortress which the King of Ormuz holds there which is called Cor: and from there the coast begins to bend inwards towards Ormuz.

KINGDOM OF ORMUZ.

After passing this Cape of Fasalhat along the coast to the north-east, there are many towns and castles of the kingdom of Ormuz in Arabia, fifty leagues to the north-east, and then twenty-five leagues to the east, and as much again to the north-east and north, and then it makes a bay to the north-west for twelve leagues, and turns to the north-east twenty-five leagues as far as Cape Refalcate,[1] and then it turns to the north-west, making bays until Madea, which are eighty-six leagues off, and from there it trends to the north-east by north thirty leagues until Cape Mocondon,[2] which is at the mouth of the sea of Persia, which is twelve leagues in width, and on this sea also further on, this rule and lordship continue to extend, and there are in it many towns and forts; and islands which are in the midst of the said sea of Persia, inhabited by Moors.. These places belonging to this kingdom are the following. In the beginning of this kingdom on the coast outside of this sea of Persia, is:—

First Calhat,[3] a very large town of handsome houses, and

[1] Probably an error of the pen for Ras al Gat.

[2] Cape Mussendom, in Ortelius and the German Atlas of 1753 also Mocandon, here it is evident that the cedilla of the c has been forgotten, and the error has been perpetuated. Ç is often used for s in old manúscripts.

[3] In the German Atlas there is a place called Kellat, and another close by called Calajute; Calata, Ortelius.

well situated; the inhabitants are rich nobles and merchants: it is forty-four leagues from Cape Fasalhat. Thirty-two leagues further on there is another small place called Tybi, which has good water with which the ships navigating all this coast provide themselves.

Twenty-five leagues further on is another small place called Daxnia, also a sea-port.

Thirty leagues further on is another large place which is a very good town of much trade in merchandise, which is called Curiat,[1] in which, as well as in the others in the neighbourhood, there is plenty of meat, wheat, dates, and other fruit in abundance: there are plenty of horses, which are bred in the country, and they are very good, and the Moors of Ormuz come to buy them for exportation to India.

Leaving this town of Curiat, at twelve leagues along the coast is another place with a fortress which is called Sar,[2] which the King of Ormuz keeps there.

Having doubled the Cape of Resalcate, the coast turns to the sea of Persia. Forty leagues further on from this cape is another town upon the coast itself called Mazquate. It is a large town, and of very honourable people, and of much trade in merchandise, and a place of great fisheries: they catch large fish there, which they export dried and salted to other parts.

Going along the coast further on to the sea of Persia there is at a distance of ten leagues another place called Sohar.[3]

Leaving this town of Sohar, further inland from the coast, at fourteen leagues off is another fortress of the King of Ormuz called Rosach; and with these fortresses this king is better able to keep all this country in subjection.

Having passed the fortress of Rosach, there is another fortress called Nahel twelve leagues off.

1 Curiate in Ortelius and the German Atlas.

2 This may be read Sar, or Sari.

3 Soar Ortelius, Sohar in the German Atlas (map of Persia).

Twelve leagues further on is another place they call Madeha; it is a small place, of few inhabitants, inside the mouth of the Sea of Persia, thirty leagues to the south-west.[1]

Further on, there is a large place of many inhabitants called Corfasan,[2] around which and the other neighbouring places are many very agreeable country houses belonging to the chief men and most honoured of the Moors of Ormuz, who come during certain months of the year there to repose, and to collect their provisions, and enjoy their fruit.

Fifteen leagues further on there is another place on the coast, called Dadena.

As much again further on to the south-west, another place called Daba. Further on, on the coast to the south-west by west, at a distance of lxxxv leagues, is another very large town called Julfar,[3] where there are many very respectable people, and many merchants and sailors. And there they fish up many large pearls and seed pearls, which the merchants of the city of Ormuz come there to buy, to carry them to India and other parts. This place is one of much trade, and produces a great deal to the king of Ormuz.

Further along the coast of the Persian Sea, in the before-mentioned inner part, are three other places belonging to the king of Ormuz: Raçolhiman,[4] which is a good town, at a distance of twenty-four leagues, and another beyond this, called Melquehoan,[5] and six leagues further on there is a fortress called Calba,[6] which the king maintains to defend his country from the Bedouins, who live in the interior of

[1] Lebeche or leveche, S.W. wind.

[2] In the German Atlas Corscan, there is also another place there inland a long way off called Orfacan, both these seem to be corruptions of the name in the text Khor Fakan.

[3] Julphar or Giotoffar in the German Atlas.

[4] Roccalima in the Atlas of Abraham Ortelius, Antwerp, 1570: the Ras el Khyma of Captain Felix Jones's Chart.

[5] Probably Amulgowein of Captain F. Jones.

[6] Calba, Ortelius.

the country, and who are governed by sheikhs ; and at times they go against these towns of the kingdom of Ormuz, and make war upon them, and sometimes they make them rebel against the king.

This king of Ormuz possesses, besides these places already mentioned, on the coast of Arabia, many other towns in the country of Persia, on the sea-coast, and in the midst of the Persian Sea many islands inhabited by Moors, in which he has many large towns, very rich and handsome, all of which are named separately further on, and afterwards the island and city of Ormuz and its customs are mentioned.

On this coast the king of Ormuz has a town called Baha,[1] in which he maintains his governors.

Having passed this place, further along the coast is another place called Dexar.

Further on another place called Xahen.

Further on another place called Ygun.[2]

Further on another place called El-guadun.

Further on another place called Nabani,[3] from which place they carry much water to drink to Ormuz, because there is no drinkable water there ; and from this and all those other places they carry to Ormuz all its supplies.

Further on is another place called Guan-meda, and from there further on there are also some other places belonging to the king of Ormuz, which are the following—Lefete, Quesebi,[4] and from here further on the coast turns to the north-west by north as far as the mouth of the river Eufrates, and it begins here to be a wide estuary. Berohu,[5] Caljar, Xuza, Mohimasim,[6] Lima,[7] Gorbaz, Alguefa, Carmon.[8] Which

1 Baha, Ortelius.

2 Iguir in Ortelius, 1570.

3 Naban, Ortelius, 1570.

4 Quesibi, Ortelius.

5 Berou, ibidem.

6 Moy Macina, Ortelius, 1570.

7 Lima, Ortelius.

8 Carmon, Ortelius.

This list of towns is thus introduced without anything to connect it with the narrative; they would apparently be places on the Shat el

lasts two hundred and forty leagues, and then Bazera, a castle of Sophi. At the entrance of the river Eufrates the land turns to the sea in a southerly direction eighty leagues, and then returns as much again to the north, and after that turns again to the south, when there begin these towns—Cohomo, Barque Guex,[1] Ganguan, Basido,[2] Goxtaque, Conch, Conga, Ebrahemi,[3] and as far as this there are one hundred and sixty-five leagues, and after that Xenase,[4] Menahao Xamile, Leytam, Bamtani, Doani,[5] and from this point the coast trends to the east for a distance of thirty leagues as far as Lorom.[6] Between these places there are many large towns with much trade, and very respectable inhabitants, and great merchants; and many castles, which the King of Ormuz maintains for the defence of his country, and they are all on the coast of the Persian Sea. They are

Arab, between the sea and Basrah, but from the Atlas of Ortelius it is clear that they are intended to follow after Quesebi, from which word to "estuary" should be read in a parenthesis: from the entire absence of punctuation and capital letters in the MS. there is great difficulty in ascertaining always the correct meaning. This passage seems to show that those who made the early maps had had a copy of this MS. under their eyes. "Quesebi: y dende aqui adelante da vuelta la costa a maestro y tramontana hasta la boca del Rio eufrates y comiença en esa vuelta una tabla berohu caljar," et cetera. The word *tabla* can hardly as here placed mean a list, and one of its meanings, dead water, or water without a current, in speaking of a river, seems here most applicable. Ortelius, however, followed by the German Atlas of 1753, has got *Tabla* as a town between Quesibi and Berou, in which case the sense of comienza and una would be imperfect. As the word *tabla* is Spanish, and in Portuguese is *tabula*, it would appear that this Spanish translation and not the Portuguese original has been made use of for the ancient atlases. This view is confirmed by there being no such place as Tabla in Captain F. Jones's Chart. Ramusio's edition has Tabla between Quesibi and Berohu.

[1] Gues, Ortelius, on the Persian shore.

[2] Gues, before named, re-appears as Cuez, Basida, Costaque, Conga, which are placed on the Arabian shore: Gonga also appears on the Persian shore in Ortelius's Atlas, 1570.

[3] Braimu, Ortelius.

[4] Denaze, ibid.

[5] Doan, ibid., on Persian shore.

[6] Laron, ibid.

places abundantly supplied with meat and wheaten bread, barley, vines, and all other things which are found in our parts, and many dates; and the inhabitants of these towns are white, and very polite people; they dress in long clothes of silk and cotton stuffs and camelots; and this is a very rich country.

THE ISLANDS OF THE KINGDOM OF ORMUZ.

In the mouth of this sea of Persia there are the following islands belonging to the king of Ormuz. Cuyx, Andrany,[1] Baxeal, *Quiro*,[2] *Lar*,[3] Cojar,[4] Tomon,[5] *Firror* Guolar, Melugan,[6] Gory, Queximi,[7] Baharem.[8]

These two islands of Queximi and Baharem are large; and Queximi has eight inhabited towns and has plenty of provisions. Baharem has a large town of many Moors, important and honourable personages. And it is distant from Lorom to the north-east xxxiv leagues, and to the island of Queximi fifty leagues of channel; and between it and the mainland from two to four leagues; and after that the coast turns between north-east and east, until the island of Ormuz for xxxv leagues, of which island mention is made lower down.[9]

Merchants from many parts reside in this island, and it is situated in the middle of this sea, and many ships with great merchandise sail to it; and here and in the neighbourhood much seed pearl and many pearls are produced, and they fish them on the island itself, from which there is a great profit to the inhabitants; and the king draws from this

[1] Andrani, Ortelius. [2] Quaro, ibid.
[3] Lar, ibid. [4] Coiar, ibid. [5] Tome, ibid.
[6] Mulugan, ibid. [7] Quezimi, ibid.
[8] Baharem, ibid. Besides these islands, Ortelius has got Gicolar and Ficor, which names might have been made out of the above list from this very MS. by reading differently the names which are written in italics.
[9] Here there appears to be a gap in the MS. of three quarters of a line.

island and from all the others large revenues. The merchants of Ormuz go to this island of Baharem to buy the pearls and seed pearl for India and other parts where they find it profitable, and for the kingdom of Narsinga; and also those of Persia and Arabia go there to buy them, and in all this sea of Persia these pearls are found, but not in such quantity as in this island of Baharem.

COUNTRY OF SHEIKH ISMAIL.

After passing these countries along the coast of Persia, there are many towns, places, and villages of the Moors, very handsome and rich enough. From here further on it is no longer the country of the king of Ormuz, but belongs to other lords, of whom we do not possess so much information, except that Xeque Yzmael[1] subjugates and governs them. He is a Moor, and a young man, who in a short time has subjugated these parts, and a great part of Persia and Arabia, and many kingdoms and lordships of the Moors, not being a king nor the son of a king, except that he was only a sheikh of the house and lineage of Aly, the brother-in-law[2] of Mahomed; and, being poor, he united with other young Moors, and they took up the habit of going without clothes, which is a custom amongst them; they abandoned their property, honours, and clothes, and only covered themselves with skins of goats, and leopards, and deer with the fur, which many are in the habit of carrying, and they mark their arms and breasts with many scars of burns; and they carry heavy iron chains, and in their hands some weapons, different from those of other people, such as small battle-axes of much workmanship, and iron maces; they go as pilgrims, and do not sustain themselves except by alms; and to such

[1] Shah Ismail, King of Persia, contemporary of the writer of this MS. and founder of the Shiah rite as at present existing.

[2] Son-in-law. This account is like that of Ramusio and differs somewhat from the Portuguese.

people, wherever they go, much honour and entertainment is shown by the other Moors; and they always go shouting and crying out in the villages the name of Mahomet. So this Sheikh Ismail took this habit, and determined to shout and cry out for Aly, whilst he took no heed of Mahomed. Many people began to collect round him, so that he began soon to take towns and to grant property to the persons who flocked to him, and were with him at a conquest; and, in case they took nothing, he decided on making some hoods of scarlet wool, of ample dimensions, and ordering them to be worn by the persons who followed him;[1] thus he collected many people, and with them he went on taking many towns, and making war in many parts; and he did not choose to be called king, but the leveller of property, who took from those who had much, and gave to those who had little; neither did he choose to rest in any place.

But all that he conquered he gave away and distributed to those who followed and obeyed him; whenever he found any very rich people whose riches did not profit any one, he took them away and distributed them amongst honourable people and the poor; and to the owners of the property he left a share equal to that which he gave to each one of the others; this he did many times, on which account they called him the Equaller. This king sent ambassadors to all the Moorish kings to persuade them to wear those coloured hoods, and if they did not choose to accept them, he sent to challenge them, and to say that he would come against them, to take their country, and make them believe in Aly. He sent this embassy to the great Sultan of Cairo and to the Grand Turk, who gave him a hostile answer and made a league against him. As soon as Sheikh Ismail saw their answers he determined to go against the Grand Turk, and he went against him with large forces, horse and foot, and the Turk came out to receive him, and they had a

[1] The origin of the Kizilbashes.

great battle,[1] in which the Grand Turk was the conqueror, on account of the quantity of artillery which he brought with him, which Sheikh Ismail did not bring, and he only fought with his men with the strength of their arms. They killed there many of his people, and he took to flight, and the Turk followed him, killing many of his troops, until he left him within Persia, when he returned thence to Turkey. This was the first time that this Sheikh Ismail was routed, for which he said that he wished to return to Turkey with greater power and provided with artillery. This king ruled over a part of Babilonia, and Armenia, and Persia, and a large part of Arabia, and of India, near to the kingdom of Cambay. His design was to get into his hands the house of Mekkah. This sheikh sent an embassy with many presents to the captain of the king of Portugal, who was exercising his functions in India, and asked him to agree to peace and friendship. And the Portuguese captain-major received this embassy and presents, and in return sent another embassy.[2]

At the extremity of this Sea of Persia there is, as has been said, a fortress called Basera, inhabited by Moors, in subjection to Sheikh Ismail, at which there comes out from the mainland to the sea a very large and beautiful river of good fresh water, which is called Frataha.[3] This is said to be one of the four rivers which flow out of the terrestrial Paradise, which river is the Eufrates, and these Moors say it has sixty thousand branches, and that one of the principal ones comes out at the kingdom of Dahulcino, in which is the first

[1] Chalderan, 3rd Rejeb 920, or August 1514. Vicente Rocca, in his history of the Turks, printed at Valencia 1556, says that the corpses of many Persian women who had accompanied their husbands in disguise, were found after the battle, and that Sultan Selim ordered them to receive an honourable burial.

[2] This embassy came to Albuquerque when he was at Ormuz the last time, the envoy sent by Albuquerque was Fernan Gomez. San Roman Hist. de la India, pp. 239, and 246-249. Valladolid, 1603.

[3] Frat, with a Persian termination.

India, which we call the river Indus; and the river Ganges is the other branch, which comes out in the second India to the sea; and the Nile, which is another branch, which comes through the country of Prester John, and waters Cairo.[1]

ISLAND AND CITY OF ORMUZ.

On coming out of the Sea and Strait of Persia, in its mouth there is a small island, in which is the city of Ormuz, which is small and very handsome, and with very pretty houses, lofty, of stone, whitewash, and mortar, covered with terraces, and because the country is very hot, they have fans made in such a manner that they make the air come from their summits to the lower part of the houses and rooms. It is a very well situated town, which has very good streets and squares. Outside of this city, in the island itself, there is a small mountain, which is entirely of rock salt and sulphur; this salt is in great lumps, and very white and good: they call it Indian salt, because nature produces it there; and the ships which come there from all parts take this salt as ballast, because in all other parts it is worth much money.

The inhabitants of this island and city are Persians and Arabs, and they speak Arabic and another language which they call Persian. They are very white, and good-looking people, of handsome bodies, both men and women; and there are amongst them black and coloured people also, who are from the country of Arabia. And the Persians, who are very white, are fat and luxurious people, who live very well. They are very voluptuous, and have musicians with various instruments. There are among them very rich merchants, and many ships, because they have a good port, and they trade in many kinds of goods, which are imported there from

[1] With respect to this geography of the four rivers of Paradise, see M. Renan's remarks on the Persian traditions, in his Hist. des Langues Semitiques, pp. 481-483. Paris, 1863.

many parts, and exported thence to other parts of India. They bring there all sorts of spices, drugs, precious stones, and other goods, such as pepper, ginger, cinnamon, cloves, mace, nutmeg, long pepper, aloes-wood, sandal-wood, brasil-wood, balsam, tamarinds, Indian saffron, beeswax, iron, sugar, rice, cocoa-nuts, rubies, sapphires, giagonzas,[1] amethysts, topazes, chrysolites, hyacinths, porcelain, benzoin; and upon all these goods much money is made, and many stuffs from the kingdom of Cambay, Chaul, Dabul, and Bengala, which are called Sinabasos, Chautars, Mamonas, Dugasas, Soranatis, which are kinds of stuffs of cotton very much valued amongst them for caps and shirts, which are much made use of by the Arabs and Persians, and people of Cairo, Aden, and Alexandria. They also bring to this city of Ormuz, quicksilver, vermillion, rose-water, brocade and silk stuffs, scarlet woollens, coarse camelots, and silk. And from China and Catuy they bring to this city by land much fine silk in skeins, and very rare musk and rhubarb;[2] and they bring from Babilonia very fine torquoises, and some emeralds, and very fine lapis lazuli from Acar. And from Baharem and Julfar they bring much seed pearl and large pearls, and many horses from Arabia and Persia, of which they carry away to India every year as many as five or six hundred, and at times a thousand; and the ships which export these horses load much salt, dates, and raisins, and sulphur, and of the other goods which the Indians are pleased with.

These Moors of Ormuz are very well dressed, with very white, long, and fine cotton shirts, and their fine drawers[3] of cotton, and above that, very rich silk clothes and camelots, scarlet cloth, and very rich gauzes, with which they wrap their waists, and they wear in their girdles daggers and knives, ornamented with gold and silver, and some heavy

[1] Zircon or jargon, a stone of which false diamonds are made.

[2] Reubarbaro.

[3] Sarahueles, Serwal or Shalwar.

[4] Almaizar.

short swords, all adorned with gold and silver, according to the rank of the wearers: and large round shields, richly garnished with silk, and in their hands they carry Turkish bows, painted with gold and very pretty colours, and their cords are of silk. These bows are of stiff wood and of buffaloe's horn; they carry very far, and these people are very good archers; their arrows are slender and well worked. Others carry in their hands iron maces, well wrought and elegant; others again, battle-axes of various patterns and of very good temper, and inlaid or enamelled.[1] They are very agreeable and polite people, and very civil in their mutual relations. Their food is of very good meats, very well cooked, wheaten bread, and very good rice, and many other dishes very well prepared, and many kinds of conserves, and preserved fruits, and others fresh: that is to say, apples, pomegranates, peaches, apricots, figs, almonds, melons, radishes, salads, and all the other things which there are in Spain; dates of many kinds, and other eatables and fruits not used in our parts. They drink wine of grapes in secret, because their law forbids it them; and the water which they drink is flavoured with pistachio nuts, and set to cool, for which purpose they employ and seek many methods for cooling and preserving it cool. And all the noblemen and honourable merchants always take, wherever they go, both in the streets and public places, and on the road, a page with a bottle of water, which is covered underneath with silver, or with a silver cup, as much for state and show as for use and comfort. All these people possess gardens and farms, to which they go to enjoy themselves for some months of the year.[2]

This city of Ormuz is, as has been said, very rich and well supplied with everything in the way of provisions, but everything is very dear, because it is brought by sea from the towns of Arabia and Persia, for in the island there is no-

[1] Atuxsia, Moorish workmanship of inlaying metals.

[2] This description of Persian customs is very exact.

thing that can be made use of except salt; neither have they water to drink, for they bring it each day in boats from the mainland or other neighbouring islands. But for all that, the squares are full of all sorts of things, and everything is sold by weight, and with great order and regulation. And they give a very proper punishment to whoever falsifies the weights or sells above the regulation price; and they also sell cooked and roasted meat by weight, and so with all other cooked victuals; and all these so well arranged and so clean that many people do not have cooking done in their houses, but eat in the squares.

The king is always in this city of Ormuz, in which he has some beautiful palaces, and a fortress, where he has his residence, and where he keeps his treasury; and there he holds all his court, and out of it provides governors or judges for all his states and lordships. But it is his council that does everything; and he does not meddle with any affair, but only amuses himself, neither would it have been in his power to do otherwise; for if he wished to govern in person, and wished to be free and exempt like other kings, immediately they would put his eyes out, and would put him in a house with his wife, and maintain him there miserably; and they would raise up another son of his as king, or some one else more fitting for it, of his lineage, in order that his council may govern all his kingdoms and territories peacefully in his name. And with respect to all the other heirs of the kingdom, as they grow up and become persons able to command and govern, if it should appear to the council that they desire to meddle with the government, they take them and put their eyes out also, and put them also in a house; so that there are always ten or twelve of these blind men, and those who reign live with this fear before them.[1] They give

[1] The Jewish traveller Pedro Teixeira (or Teireira, according to Rodriquez de Castro, Biblica, Rabinica Esp.) at the end of the sixteenth or beginning of the seventeenth century, wrote a history of Persia,

food there to them and to their wives and children. This king has many men-at-arms, and many gentlemen who guard and serve him, and they receive very good pay and rations, and are always at the court with their arms; and they send some to the frontiers on the mainland whenever they are required.

They make gold and silver money in this city; the gold coins are called Sarafin, and are worth three hundred maravedis, and most of them are halves, which are worth a hundred and fifty, a round coin like ours,[1] and with Moorish letters on both sides, and about the size of a fanon of Calicut, with Moorish letters, and it is worth fifty-five maravedis; they call these tanga, and they are of very fine silver, and of the standard of twelve dinars.[2] There is a large quantity

translated from Mirkhond, and a "Journey from the East Indies to Italy Overland," Antwerp, Jerome Verdassen. Teixeira wrote the first part of this work in Portuguese, and afterwards translated it into Spanish, adding the second part. Both were translated into French by C. Cotolendi in 1681, and printed at Paris under the title of "Voyages de Teixeira, ou l'Histoire des Rois de Perse." He died at Verona. Teixeira says: "It was a custom much in use, both formerly and in later times among the kings of Persia and Harmuz, in order to assure themselves of those whom they might have reason to fear, and who commonly were their relations. And even this day may be seen at Harmuz, on a hill near the hermitage of Santa Lucia, at a little more than a mile from the city, the ruins of some towers, in which the kings placed their relations who had been blinded for this reason. The method which they used for depriving them of sight was this: they took a brass basin, and heating it in the fire as much as possible, passed it two or three or more times before the eyes of the person they intended to blind; and without other lesion of the eyes they lost their sight, the optic nerves being injured by the fire, but the eyes remaining as limpid and clear as before." Amador de Los Rios, Estudios sobre los Judios de España, p. 557. Madrid, 1848.

Ramusio has translated to blind "cavar gli occhi," which in this case would not apply.

[1] This observation is owing to the Moorish coins of the Almohade dynasty having been square, which gave rise to the Spanish saying of spendthrifts: "My money rolls, as it is not Moorish."

[2] The standard of modern Spanish silver coin is eleven dinars, or dineros.

of this money, both gold and silver, and much of it goes out to India, where it has much currency.

There came a Portuguese fleet to this kingdom of Ormuz, and its captain-major was Alfonso de Alborquerque, who attempted to come to an understanding with this kingdom of Ormuz, but the Moors would not agree, and on that account this captain began to make war upon the whole kingdom at all the sea-ports, and he did them much injury, and at last he came and touched at the port of Ormuz with his fleet, and there was a great battle there, with many and great ships full of many and smart well-armed men. And the said captain routed the fleet of the Moors, and killed many of them, and sunk many of their ships, and took and burned many which were moored in the harbour, drawn up by the wall of the city. And when the king and the governors of the country saw such great destruction of their people and ships, without being able to assist them, they offered peace to the before-mentioned captain, who accepted it under the condition that they should let him make a fortress at one extremity of the city; and they agreed, and this began to be done; and the work having commenced, the Moors repented again, and did not choose that more should be built; and then the Portuguese began again to make war upon them, and they did them so great damage, and slaughtered so many people, that they made them tributary to the King of Portugal to the amount of fifteen thousand serafins of gold each year.

Some years from that time the king and governors of Ormuz sent an ambassador with offers of services and letters to the King of Portugal, and the before-named captain returned with his answer and a good fleet to the city of Ormuz,[1] and there they received him very peacefully in this

[1] The Portuguese force is said to have consisted of fifteen hundred Portuguese and six hundred Indian soldiers; this took place in 1514. Panorama or Univers Pittoresque. According to San Roman Hist. de

city, and at once gave him permission and a place in which to built the fortress, which on a former occasion the Portuguese had begun to build: and he ordered it to be built at once, very large and magnificent. At this time the king, who was a Moor, and very young, and in the power of the governors, and so ruined that he did not dare do anything of himself, found the means to inform the captain-major secretly of the little liberty he enjoyed, and that the governors kept him like a prisoner, and that they had forcibly taken the government which belongs to others who were accustomed to exercise it, and that it appeared that they were exchanging letters with Sheikh Ismail in order to give him the kingdom. The captain-major kept this very secret, and determined to have an interview with the king; and they agreed that this interview should be in some large houses near the sea. On the day on which the interview was to take place, the captain-major entered the houses with ten or fifteen captains, leaving his people well arranged, and all concerted as was most convenient. So the king and his principal governor came there with many people, and the king and the governor entered the houses with ten or twelve honourable Moors, and the door was well shut and guarded. Then the captain-major ordered them to kill the governor[1] with their daggers in his presence and that of the king: and he said to the king, "Have no fear, Sir, for I do this to make you absolute king." However those who were without heard the noise, and began to raise a disturbance, that it to say, the relations, servants, and friends of the said governor, who were many in number, and all came armed, so that it was necessary for the captain-major

la India Oriental in the beginning of 1515, Albuquerque's force consisted of 26 sail, 1500 Portuguese, and 600 Malabars.

1 This governor's name was Rais Hamid; one account says so many daggers were drawn against him that the Portuguese wounded one another's hands: the other governor mentioned later was named Rais Nordim, i.e., Nureddin.

to take the king by the hand; they went up on to the roof, both of them armed, in order that the king might speak thence to the Moors, and might pacify them; so he spoke to them, but could do nothing with them. They, on the contrary, required that he should confide to them his brother and lord: and they went thence to establish themselves in the king's palace, saying they would make another king. The captain-major wished to lay hands upon them, and thus they remained a great part of the day, and the king sought how to turn them out, and the captain-major determined to kill them by force or to drive them out, as they did not choose to go out of the fortress. So when the Moors saw that the captain-major, with the king, was determined to attack them, they resolved to give the fortress to the king; and when they gave it up, the king commanded that they should be banished immediately, they and their families; and this was done, and they went to the mainland.

The captain-major conducted the king from these houses to the palace in triumph and honourably, and with many people, both of ours and of his, and entrusted him to the other governor who was so before. He then committed to him his palaces and the city very freely, and told the governor to serve the king very honourably, and to leave him to govern his country at his pleasure, and only give him advice, as happens with other Moorish kings: and thus he put him at liberty. He then left in the fortress that was built a captain and many men of Portugal, and ships, in order to favour this king, who does nothing without the advice of the captain of the fort. And he is in submission to the King of Portugal, with all his kingdoms and territories.

After the captain-major had put everything in quiet and order, and under his command, he then had banished by the public crier, and turned out of the island all the paiderastoi, with a warning that if they returned there again they would he burned, at which the king showed great satisfaction. He likewise ordered all the blind kings who were in the city to be taken, and there were thirteen or fourteen of them, and put in a large ship, and he sent them to India, and they were landed at Goa, where he gave orders for them to be maintained at the expense of his revenues, so that they might end their days there, and not cause any disturbance in the kingdom of Ormuz, and be in peace and quietness.

DIULCINDI.

Leaving the kingdom of Ormuz, from the mouth of the Sea of Persia the coast goes to the south-east for a hundred and seventy-two leagues as far as Diulcinde,[1] entering the kingdom of Ulcinde,[2] which is between Persia and India. It is a kingdom, and has a Moorish king over it, and most of the inhabitants of the country are Moors, and there are some Gentiles subject to the Moors. This king has an extended rule over the country in the interior, and few sea-ports. They have many horses. On the eastern side this country is bounded by the kingdom of Cambay, and on the west by Persia. It is in obedience to Sheikh Ismail. The Moors are white and coloured; they have a language of their own, and also speak that of the Persians and of Arabia. There is much wheat and barley in this country, and plenty of meat. It is a level country, with little timber. They make little practice of navigating the sea; they possess extensive sea-beaches, where there are great fisheries, and they catch large fish, which they dry and salt, both for consumption in the country and for exportation in small vessels to other kingdoms. In this country they give dried fish to their horses to eat. A few ships which sail to this country from India, bring rice, sugar, and some spices, timber, planks, and Indian

[1] In Ortelius's Map of Asia Dulcinda is some way up a river; in the German Atlas of 1753 no trace of it appears.

[2] Ulcinde, Camoens, canto x, stanza 106.

canes, which are as thick as a man's leg. And in all this trade they make much money; and from this place they carry away cotton, horses, and cloth. A great river comes into the sea through this kingdom; it comes through the middle of Persia, and they say that it comes out of the river Eufrates. Along this river there are many large and rich towns of Moors. It is a very fertile and fruitful land, and very abundant in provisions.

KINGDOM OF GUZERAT, IN INDIA.

Leaving the kingdom of Ulcinde, in the same direction, at a distance of fifty leagues, the traveller enters the first[1] India, in the great kingdom of Guzarat, which kingdom had belonged to King Darius. And the Indians have long histories of him and of King Alexander. This kingdom has many cities and towns in the interior of the country, as well as ports along the sea; and very much shipping. It has many merchants and shipowners, both Moors and Gentiles.

The king, and the men-at-arms, and nobles of the country were all Gentiles formerly, and now they are Moors, since the Moors conquered the country in war, and hold the Gentiles subject to them, and molest them and treat them ill. There are three qualities of these Gentiles, that is to say, some are called Razbutes, and they, in the time that their king was a Gentile, were knights, the defenders of the kingdom, and governors of the country; they used to carry on war, and even now there remain some towns of them in the mountains, which have never chosen to pay obedience to the Moors, but, on the contrary, make war upon them; and the King of Cambaya is not sufficiently powerful to destroy them or subject them. They are very good knights and great archers, and they have many other kinds of arms with which they defend themselves from the Moors, without owning any king or lord to govern them. The others are called

[1] Or hither.

Banians, and are merchants and traders. These live amongst the Moors, and trade with them in their goods. They are men who do not eat meat nor fish, nor anything that has life ; neither do they kill anything, nor like to see it killed, because their idolatry forbids it them ; and they observe this to such an extreme that it is something marvellous. For it often happens that the Moors bring them some worms or little birds alive, saying they intend to kill them in their presence ; and they ransom them, and buy them to set them flying, and save their lives for more money than they are worth. And in the same way, if the governor of the country has got a man to be executed, these Banians unite together and buy him from the officers of justice, that he may not die ; and frequently they sell him to them. And in the same manner the Moors who beg for alms, when they want alms from these people, take great stones and strike themselves with them on the shoulders and the breast, and on their stomachs, as if they were going to kill themselves with them, and they receive alms not to do it, and to go away in peace. And others bring knives and stab themselves in the arms and legs before them, in order to extract alms ; and others come to their doors to decapitate rats and snakes and other reptiles, and they give them money not to do it, so that they are very ill-treated by the Moors. If these people meet with a band of ants in the road, they hasten out of the road, and go and look for a place to pass without treading upon them. They likewise sup in the daytime because they do not light candles at night, in order that the mosquitoes and other insects may not come and die in the flame ; and if of necessity they must have a candle, they keep them in lanterns of paper, or of stuff dipped in gum, so that no living thing can get there to suffer. If these people have lice they do not kill them, and if they worry them very much, they send to fetch some men whom they have amongst them, also Gentiles, whom they esteem of holy lives, like hermits, and who live in much abstinence for the love of their idols, and these people pick out their insects, and all those that they extract they put in their own heads, and they nourish them on themselves and on their flesh for the service of their idols. And so this law of not killing anything is held in great observance. On the other hand, they are great usurers and falsifiers of weights and measures, and merchandise, and coin; and liars and cheats. These Gentiles are brown people, well built and of good proportions, smart in their dress, and delicate and temperate in their food. Their victuals are milk, butter, sugar, rice, preserves of many kinds, many fruits, bread, vegetables, and field herbs; they all have gardens and orchards wherever they live, and many pools of water where they bathe twice every, day, both men and women; and having ended their washing, they hold the belief that they are pardoned for all the sins which they have committed up to that time. They wear the hair very long like the women in Spain, and they wear it gathered on the top of the head, and made into a band which is much adorned, and upon this a cap to fasten it; and they always wear many flowers stuck into their hair, and sweet smelling things. They also anoint themselves with white sandal mixed with saffron and other scents; they are much given to fall in love. They go bare, only covering themselves from the waist downwards with very rich silk stuffs; they wear embroidered shoes of very good leather, well worked, and some short silk skirts, and other short ones of cotton, with which they cover their bodies. They do not carry arms, only some small knives garnished with gold and silver, for two reasons: one because they are persons who make little use of arms, the other because the Moors forbid it to them. They use many earrings of gold and jewellery in the ears, and many rings, and belts of gold and jewellery upon the cloths with which they gird themselves. The women of these Gentiles have very pretty, delicate faces, and well made bodies, a little dark.

Their dress is silk stuff like their husbands' as far as the feet, and jackets[1] with narrow sleeves of silk stuff, open at the shoulders, and other silk cloths with which they cover themselves in the manner of morisco almalafas; their heads bare, the hair gathered up upon the head; they wear thick ankle rings of gold and silver on the legs, and rings on their toes, and large coral beads on their arms, with beads of gold filigree, and gold and silver bracelets; and round their necks, necklaces of gold and jewellery, fitting closely; they have large holes pierced in their ears, and in them rings of gold or silver large enough for an egg to pass through them. They are modest women, and when they go out of their houses they are much covered up with their wraps over their heads. The other set of people are called Bramans, and are priests and the persons who administer and direct the idolatry; they have very large houses of prayer, some of them with revenues, others are maintained by alms. In these they keep many idols: some of stone, some of wood, and other of copper. In these houses and monasteries they always perform many ceremonies to their gods; they make feasts for them magnificently, with instruments and songs, and with many lights of oil, and they have bells in our fashion. These Bramans have got images which represent the Holy Trinity: they pay much honour to the number three, and in trine make their adoration to God, whom they confess to be the true God, Creator, and Maker of all things, which are three things in one sole person; and they say that there are many other gods governed by him, in which they also believe. These Bramans, wherever they find our churches, enter willingly into them, and adore our images; and they always ask for Santa Maria, our Lady, like men who have some knowledge of her. And as they see our manner of honouring the churches, they say that there is no great difference between them and us. These Bramans go

[1] Cogecillos.

bare from the waist upwards; they wear upon their shoulder a thread of three threads, which is a sign by which they are known to be Bramans. They are men who also do not eat anything which receives death, nor do they kill anything. They hold it to be a great ceremony to wash their bodies, and say that they wash on that account. These Bramans, and also the Banians, marry in our fashion, with one woman only, and only once. They make great feasts at their weddings, which last many days, and there are many people assembled at these very well dressed and decked out. These festivities are magnificent. For the most part they are married when very young, both men and women, and on the day of the betrothal, and of the wedding, the couple are both of them seated on a platform,[1] very much bedizened with gold and jewellery and precious stones, and in front of them is a small table with an idol covered with flowers, and many lighted oil lamps all round it; and both of them have to remain there with their eyes fixed on that idol from the morning until the evening, without eating or drinking, or speaking to anybody during that time. The people make great rejoicings over them with their instruments and songs and dances; they let off many cannons, rockets and other fireworks to divert themselves. And if the husband dies the woman does not marry again, and so also does the husband should the wife die. And the children are his rightful heirs; and Bramans must be sons of Bramans, amongst whom there are some of a lower rank who serve as messengers and travellers, and they go in security to all parts without any one vexing them in any way. Even if there should be war or thieves, they always pass safely. These are called *pater*.

[1] Or gallery.

OF THE KING AND THE LORDS OF GUZARAT, WHICH IS OF THE KINGDOM OF CAMBAY.

The King of Guzarat is a great lord, both in revenue and people, and extensive and rich territory. He is a Moor, as also are his men-at-arms, as has been said. He has a large court of many knights, and he is the lord of many horses and elephants, which are brought for sale to this kingdom from the country of Malabar and Ceylon. And with the horses and elephants he makes war upon the Gentiles of the kingdom of Guzarat who do not pay obedience to him, and upon some other kings with whom at times he is at war. And they make wooden castles on the top of the elephants, which hold four men, who carry bows and guns, and other weapons, and fight thence with the enemy. And the elephants are so well trained, that they know how to take part in the battle, and with their tusks wound the men and horses so severely, that in a very short time they put any array into confusion. But they are so timid, and subject to pain when wounded, that they take to flight at once, and put one another into confusion, and rout their own side. This king has four or five hundred of these at his residence, very large and fine. They buy them for one thousand five hundred ducats each, at the seaports where the Malabars bring them for sale. And they make war much with the horses bred in the country, for it has a wonderful quantity; and the Moors and Gentiles of this kingdom are bold riders, ride small saddles,[1] and use whips. They carry very thick round shields, edged with silk, and two swords each man, a dagger, and a Turkish bow, with very good arrows; and some carry steel maces, and many of them coats of mail, and others tunics quilted with cotton. And the horses have housings and steel head pieces, and so they fight very well and are light in their movements; and they are so supple in

[1] A la bastarda.

their saddles that they can play on horseback at the choga[1] or at any other game. They have amongst them the game of the jerid, as in Spain. These Moors are white, and of many countries: both Turks and Mamelukes, Arabs, Persians, Khorasanys, Turkomans, and from the great kingdom of Dily, and others born in the country itself. These people come together there on account of the country being very rich, and well supplied; and the king gives good pay and rations, and regularly paid. These people are very well dressed, with very rich stuffs of gold, silk, cotton, and goats' wool, and all wear caps on their heads, and their clothes long, such as morisco shirts and drawers, and leggings to the knee of good thick leather, worked with gold knots and embroidery; and their swords are borne in their girdles, or in the hands of their pages. They are richly ornamented with gold and silver. Their women are very white and pretty, also very richly decked out. They may marry as many as they like and are able to maintain, to honour the sect of Mahomed; and so there are many of them who have three or four or five wives, and of all of them they have sons and daughters. And these Moors of Cambay speak many languages, that is to say, Arabic, Persian, Turkish,[2] and Guzaraty. They eat wheaten bread, rice, meat of all kinds, leaving aside pork, which is against their law. They are luxurious people, who live well and spend much money. They always go with their heads shaved, and the women with very fine hair. When they go out of their houses, they go on horses, or in cars, and so covered up that nobody can see them. They are very jealous men, and can unmarry themselves when they please, on paying to the wife a certain sum of money (which is promised when they marry them), if at any time they repent of it; and the women have also the same liberty.

[1] The Chaugan, Persian game of hockey on horseback.

[2] Urdu perhaps is meant by the writer.

This King of Cambay has been king since a short time only, and his father was called Sultan Mahomed, who was brought up from a child and nourished with poison, for his father desired that he should so be brought up in order that it should not be possible to kill him with poison; for the Moorish kings of these parts often have one another killed by poison. And this king began to eat it in such a small quantity that it could not do him any harm, and from that he went on increasing this kind of food in such manner that he could eat a great quantity of it; for which cause he became so poisonous that if a fly settled on his hand it swelled and immediately fell dead. And many wives with whom he slept died at once of his poison, which he was unable to leave off eating, for he feared if he did not use it, to die soon after; as we see by experience with the opium which the Indians eat, for if they leave off eating it they die immediately, that is, if they begin as children to eat it in such a small quantity that it can do them no harm, for some length of time, and then increasing the quantity by degrees until they remain accustomed to it. This anfion is cold in the fourth degree, and on account of being so cold it kills. We call it opio, and the women of India when they wish to kill themselves in any case of dishonour or of despair, eat it with oil of sesame, and so die sleeping without feeling death.

CITY OF CHAMPAVER.[1]

This King possesses great cities in his kingdom, and especially the city of Champaver, where he resides continually, with all his court. This city is to the north of Guzerat, eighty leagues inland. It is a very fertile country: of abundant provisions, wheat, barley, millet, rice, peas and other vegetables, and many cows, sheep, goats, and plenty of fruit, so that it is very full of all things; and it has in its neighbourhood many hunting grounds, and deer and

[1] Campanero in Ramusio, Champanel in Portuguese edition.

other animals, and winged game. And this country possesses dogs and falcons for the chase, and tame leopards for hunting all sorts of game. And the King for his pastime keeps many animals of all kinds, which they send to find and bring up. This King sent a Ganda[1] to the King of Portugal, because they told him that he would be pleased to see her.

ANDAVAT.

Leaving this city and going further inland there is another city called Andavat, which is larger than the said city of Champaver, and it is very rich, and well supplied. The former kings used always to reside in this city. These towns are walled, and embellished with good streets and squares, and houses of stone and whitewash, with roofs in our fashion; and they have large courts, and much water in wells and pools. They make use of horses, donkeys, mules, camels and carts, and have fine rivers, with plenty of fresh water fish, and many orchards and gardens. There are also in this kingdom, inland, many cities, towns and villages, in which the king keeps his governors and collectors of his revenue. If these commit a fault he summons them, and after having heard them he bids them drink a cup of poison, with which anyone dies immediately; and in this way he chastises them, so that they are in great fear of him.

PATEMXI.

The places which this king has on the sea coast are these. Firstly, leaving the kingdom of Ulcinde for India at a dis-

[1] Gandos, people of Hindustan, established in the mountainous parts of the province of Ganduana: they live by the chase and the produce of their flocks, and, contrary to the custom of other Indians, eat fowls and bury their dead. The women are obese, and stronger than the men; they wear a dress all of one piece, paint all their body, and become bald in the prime of life. Ganduana, between 17 deg. and 24 deg. N. lat. and 81 deg. and 88 deg. E. long. Diccionario Encic., Madrid, Gaspar y Roig. 1855.

tance of thirty-seven leagues, is a river, on the shore of which there is a great city called Patemxi, a good seaport, very rich, and of great trade. In this city many silk stuffs are made, coloured with much embroidery, which are used over the whole of India, Malacca, Bengal, and also many cotton stuffs. To this port come many Indian ships laden with cocoa nuts, sugar of palms which they call xagara,[1] and from there they carry away a great quantity of cloth and much cotton, horses, wheat, and vegetables, by which much money is made. Their voyage, with the delays, is of four months.

SURATIMANGALOR.

Passing by this city, further on the coast to the east and south, at fifteen leagues distance, there is another town of commerce, which has a very good port, and is called Suratimangalor, where also many ships from Malabar touch, for horses, wheat, rice, cotton cloths, vegetables and other goods which are of use in India. And they bring cocoa nuts, hurraca[2] (which is something to drink), emery, beeswax, cardamums, and all sorts of spices, in which trade and voyage great profit is made in a short time.

DUY.

Fifty leagues further along the coast, towards the south, there is a promontory, and joining close to it is a small island, which contains a very large and fine town, which the Malabars call Diuixa,[3] and the Moors of the country call it Diu. It has a very good harbour, and is a port of much trade in merchandise, and of much shipping from Malabar, Baticala, Goa Dabul and Cheul; and the people of Diu sail to Aden, Mekkah, Zeyla, Barbara, Magadoxo, Brava, Melinde, Mombaza, Xer,[4] Ormuz, and all parts of the king-

[1] Jagri.

[2] Arrak.

[3] This name might also be read Dvuxa or Dimxa.

[4] Shehir.

dom. And the Malabars bring hither rice, cocoa nuts, jagara, wax, emery, iron, and sugar from Baticala, and all the spices that can be got in India and Malacca; and from Chaul and Dabul they bring a large quantity of cotton stuffs, which they call *beyranies*, and caps for women, which are carried from this place to Arabia and Persia. And they load at this port for the return voyage cotton cloths of the country and silk stuffs, horses, wheat, vegetables, sesame, cotton, oil of sesame, and opium, both that which comes there from Aden, and that which is made in the kingdom of Cambay, which is not so fine as that of Aden; and they export many coarse camlets and silk stuffs made in this kingdom of Cambay, and thick carpets,[1] taffeta, scarlet cloth, and of other colours. They also export the spices and things brought to them from India, by the people of the country, to Aden, Ormuz, and all parts of Arabia and Persia, so that this town is the chief emporium of trade which exists in all these parts. This town gives such a large sum of money as revenue to the king, for the loading and unloading of such rich goods, that it is a subject of marvel and amazement; for they also bring to it from Mekkah much coral, copper, quicksilver, vermillion, lead, alum, madder, rose-water, saffron, and much gold and silver coined and uncoined. The king keeps a Moorish governor in this place called Melquiaz; an old man, and a very good gentleman, discreet, industrious, and of great information, who lives with great order and regularity in all his affairs. He makes much artillery, and has many rowing barges, very well arranged, small and very light, which are called Talayas.[2] He has had constructed in the port a very strong and fine bulwark, in which he has very good artillery, with many lombards,[3] and he always

[1] This word alcatifa might also mean velvets, at least that is its meaning in Arabic and Wallachian; in modern Spanish it means a fine carpet.

[2] Coast guards, watch boats.

[3] Kind of artillery.

keeps with him many men-at-arms, to whom he pays very good appointments. They are very well armed. He is always on his guard, and is very apprehensive of the power of the King of Portugal.[1] He shows great honour and attention to the ships and people of Portugal who come to his port. The people of his country are kept in very good order, and governed with much justice and good treatment; he dispenses many favours and presents to voyagers and strangers in his country.

A large fleet of the Great Sultan[2] of sailing ships and row galleys arrived at this port, well equipped, with large crews and a good armament; its captain was Emir Hussein. He came to reinforce himself in this port with the assistance of the king of Cambay and the before-mentioned governor Meliquiaz, and from thence to go to Calicut, to fight with the Portuguese, and turn them out of India. He was for some time in the port making many preparations, and the Portuguese fleet came there to seek for them, of which Don Francisco de Almeyda, viceroy of India, was the captain major. And the Moors put out to sea to meet them, and the two fleets fought in the entrance of the roadstead vigorously, and many people were killed and wounded on both sides; and at the end the Moors were beaten and captured with great slaughter, and the Portuguese took their ships and galleys, with all their arms and heavy artillery. They captured there many Moors, and the said Emir Hussein escaped, and left his fleet to suffer as has been told; and when Meliquiaz, who assisted and favoured them with his guard-boats and forces, saw the havoc, he at once sent messengers to the before-mentioned viceroy to seek peace of

[1] This passage seems to fix the date of this work as previous to 1515, since in that year the Portuguese made themselves masters of Diu, in which they built a fortress in 1536. (Diccion. Geog. Universal, Barcelona, 1831.)

[2] Of Egypt.

him, and he sent many provisions and refreshments and other presents as a sign of peace.[1]

[1] This author seems to have confused the account of two naval battles, reducing them to one; the above account, as far as the description of the meeting of the hostile fleets, refers to the battle in 1507, in which the Portuguese, commanded by Lorenzo son of Francisco de Almeyda, were routed and Lorenzo slain. Melik Az saved twenty prisoners alive from Lorenzo's ship, which would not strike, treated them well, and wrote to condole with the father, Francisco de Almeyda, for the death of his son. Almeyda prepared a fleet of nineteen sail to avenge his son's death, when Albuquerque arrived to supersede him; he had been sent from Europe in 1506. In spite of this Almeyda sailed for Diu, where Emir Hussein, instead of waiting for him, put out to sea against the advice of Melik Az and was defeated. Vasco Pereyra, captain of the ship that carried Admiral Hussein's ship by boarding, was killed, and his lieutenant, Tavora, took Emir Hussein's ship, killing or capturing all those who did not save themselves by swimming ashore. The captured ships were richly laden, and Almeyda distributed all the spoil amongst his crews. (This action was fought on the 3rd February, 1509.) Melik Az sued for peace after this defeat. His proposals were received with arrogance and a demand for the surrender of Emir Hussein: this Melik Az refused, but gave up all his Portuguese prisoners. Almeyda accepted this, but cut the heads off all his Moorish prisoners in cool blood at Cananor. Panorama, India, pp. 358-360, Barcelona, 1845; Translation of the Univers Pittoresque. The same work in the volume on Portugal, speaking of the first battle of Diu, merely says, "Mir Hosein routed the Portuguese, and Don Lorenzo lost his life," p. 121.

Camoens thus describes the second battle of Diu, in his 10th canto, stanzas 35, 36.

E logo, entrando fero na enseada
De Dio, illustre em cercos e batalhas,
Fará espalhar a fraca e grande armada
De Calecut, que remos tem por malhas:
A de Melique Yaz acautelada,
Co 'os pelouros que tu, Vulcano, espalhas,
Fará ir ver o frio e fundo assento,
Secreto leito do humido elemento.

Mas a de Mir-Hocem, que, abalroando,
A furia esperará dos vingadores,
Verá braços, e pernas ir nadando,
Sem corpos, pelo mar, de seus senhores:
Raios de fogo irão representando
No cego ardor os bravos domadores:
Quanto alli sentirão olhos, e ouvidos,
He fumo, ferro, flammas e alaridos.

The last speech of Don Lorenzo d'Almeida is given in the following

GOGARI.

Further on after this the coast begins to make a bend into Cambay towards the north, in which bend are several sea-ports of the same king, and towns of great trade. One of these is Guogari, at a distance of twenty-five leagues (from Diu), which is a very large town and a good port, where they always load many ships from Malabar and other parts of India; and many other ships bound for Mekkah and Aden. At this place all sorts of merchandise are dealt in, as at Diu.

BARBESY.

Another is called Barbesy, a sea-port twelve leagues further on to the north, in which stretch of coast are several sea-ports of the King of Cambay. All sorts of goods are traded in for all parts, and the dues upon them produce very much to the king, who has in each of these two places his custom houses, and all are well supplied with provisions.

words in a MS. belonging to the Duke of Gor, at Granada, which describes the voyages to India from 1497 to 1509; it differs a little from that given in the second decade:

"Dom Lourenzo lhe disse Snõres companheiros e irmaos, minha vida he acabada que este mundo me tinha emprestada e minha alma ira dar conta ao Snõr Deos que a fez. En vos mando, e muito rogo que tomandonos Meliquiaz sobre si como diz aventureis as vidas em sua palavra, porque de o nõ fazerdes tao certas aqui tendes as mortes se Ds' nõ acodir cõ sua mĩa (misericordia) que lhe pezo que aja cõ minha alma, que em suas sanctas mãos encomendo: e deu a alma," f. 406 v.

Don Lorenzo said to them: "Gentlemen, companions and brothers, my life which this world had lent me is ended, and my soul will go to give an account to the Lord God who made it. I charge you, and beg much of you, that as Melikiaz will take us on his own responsibility, as he says, that you adventure your lives upon his word, because if you do not do so, you have before you certain death, unless God succour you with his mercy: which I pray him to have with my soul, which I commend into his holy keeping." And he gave up his spirit.

BUENDARI.

Further on, to north-west by north, there is another place in the mouth of a small river which is called Guendari, twenty leagues distant from Barbesy. And it is a very good town, a seaport of the same trade, because further up that river is the great city of Cambay. There arrived there many zambucos,[1] which are small vessels of the Malabar country, with areca (nuts), spices, wax, sugar, cardamums, emery, ivory, and elephants:[2] and these goods are sold there very well. And from there they carry away cotton, sesame, thread, wheat, peas, horses, alaquequas, and many other goods. The navigation of these places is very dangerous, especially for ships with keels which draw much water, because in this gulf which the coast here makes, the ebb and flow is so great, that in a very short space of time the sea leaves uncovered four or five leagues of dry land, and in some places less; and it is expedient for those who go in there to take country pilots, because, when the tide runs down, they may know how to remain in pools of deep water[3] such as there are there, and sometimes they make mistakes and remain upon rocks, where they are lost.

CITY OF CAMBAY.

Entering this river of Guendari, to the north-east is the great city of Cambay, inhabited by Moors and Gentiles. It is a very large city of handsome houses of stone and whitewash, very lofty, with windows, and covered with roofs in the Spanish fashion; it has very good streets and squares, and is situated in a rich, fertile, and pretty country, full of abundant provisions. There are in it rich merchants and

[1] Sambuks, Arab undecked boats.

[2] This may have been intended for ivory of elephants, it would seem difficult to get an elephant into a sambuk.

[3] *Pozos*, wells, hollows.

men of great property, both Moors and Gentiles; and there are many workmen and mechanicians of subtle workmanship of all sorts, after the fashion of Flanders, and all very cheap. They make there many cloths of white cotton, fine and coarse, and other woven and coloured fabrics of all kinds; also many silk fabrics, of all kinds and colours; and camlets of silk and velvets of all colours, both smooth and fluffy, coloured tafetans, and thick alcatifas. The inhabitants of this city are all white, both men and women, and there are many people from outside living in it who are very white and very well dressed, and of luxurious lives, much given to pleasure and amusement. They are very much accustomed to wash themselves; they eat very well, and always go perfumed and anointed with sweet smelling things. They wear in their hair, both men and women, many jessamine and other flowers that grow amongst them. They have many musicians, and various kinds of instruments and songs. There are always carts with oxen and horses going about the city, of which they make use for everything; and they go in these with rich mattrasses, shut up and well fitted up with their windows, after the manner of cabins; furnished and ornamented with silk stuffs, and the seats within with cushions and pillows of silk and stamped kid skins:[1] and with their waggoners. Men and women go in these to see amusements and diversions, or to visit their friends, or wherever they wish, without being known, and they see all that they wish. And they go singing and playing on instruments in these same waggons for their amusement. And these people possess many orchards and gardens, where they go to take their ease, and where they grow much fruit and vegetables for the sustenance of the gentiles, who do not eat meat nor flesh. In this city a very large quantity of ivory is employed in very delicate works, well known in commerce, like inlaid works of gold,

[1] Guadamecil, *aluta celata.*

and things made by turning, and handles of knives and daggers, bracelets, games of chess and chess-boards. There are also great artists with the turning lathe, who make large bedsteads, and they make beads of great size, brown, yellow, blue and coloured, which they export to all parts. There are also great lapidaries, and imitators of precious stones of all kinds, and makers of false pearls which seem real. So also there are very good silversmiths of very skilful workmanship. In this city they make very delicate cushions, and pretty ceilings (or canopies) of bedsteads, of delicate workmanship and paintings, and quilted clothes for wearing. There are many Moorish women who produce very delicate needlework. They work there too in coral alaquequas and other stones.

LIMADURA.

Leaving this city of Cambay there is a town inland called Limadura, where there is a stone with which they make aquequas, for making beads for Berberia. It is a stone white as milk, and has some red in it, and with fire they heighten the colour, and they extract it in large blocks. In these places there are great artists who manufacture and pierce these beads in various fashions, oval, octagonal, round, and of other shapes; and with this stone they make rings, buttons, and knife handles. And the Cambay merchants go there to buy them, and they harden[1] them to take them away to sell in the Red Sea, from whence they are in the habit of arriving in our parts by way of Cairo or Alexandria: and they also carry them throughout all Arabia, Persia, and Nubia, and now they take them to India, because our people buy them. They also find in this town much chalcedony,

[1] This word is very clearly *enyertan*, which is an old word meaning to freeze, to congeal, to make *yerto*—hard: so that this stone would be like the Chinese soap stone, which is soft and easily carved when first extracted. *Ensartan* would apply, meaning to string beads, but the writing does not admit of it.

which they call *babagore.* They make beads with it, and other things which they wear about them, so that they touch the skin, as they say that it is good for chastity. These stones are of little value there, for there are many of them.

RAVEL.

Returning to the towns on the sea, and passing Gandar, to the east there is a good river twenty leagues further along the coast, and on this side of it there is a good town of the Moors, called Ravel,[1] built of very pretty houses and squares. It is a rich and agreeable place, because the Moors of this town trade with their ships at Malacca, Bengal, Tarvasery, Pegu, Martaban, and Samatara, in all sorts of spices, drugs, silks, musk, benzoin, porcelain, and all other valuable merchandise. They possess very large and fine ships, so that those who would wish to get Chinese articles, will find them there more completely than in any other part, and at very fair prices.

The Moors of this place are white and well dressed, and very rich. They have very pretty wives, and in the furniture[2] of their houses they have many china vases of different shapes, and they keep them in glass cupboards very well arranged. These women are not secluded like those of other Moors and other places, but go about the city in the daytime attending to their business, with the face uncovered as in our parts.

SURATI.

Having passed this river of Ravel, at twenty leagues to the south is a city called Surat, at the mouth of a river. This also is a city of very great trade, in all classes of merchandise. Many ships of Malabar and all other parts sail thither continually, and discharge and take in goods, because this is a

[1] Ravel in Ortelius's map of India, 1570.

[2] Axuar, the household furniture which a wife has to bring to her husband on her marriage.

very important seaport, and there are in it very vast quantities of merchandise. Moors, Gentiles, and all sorts of people live in this city. Its custom-house, which they call the Divana,[1] produces a very large revenue for the King of Guzarat: and until now Malaguioy, a Gentile, commands in, and governs it, as lord of it. And he is the greatest nobleman in all India, and he gave orders to kill the King of Guzerat for some gossip which they reported respecting him.

DENVY.[2]

After leaving the town of Surat, at ten leagues along the coast to the south, there is place called Denvy, of Moors and Gentiles, also of great trade, where many merchant ships from Malabar and many other parts always take in cargo.

BAXAY.

Having passed this town of Dendi, twenty leagues further on to the south[3] is another town of Moors and Gentiles, a good seaport, which also belongs to the King of Guzarat, in which much goods are exchanged; and there is a great movement of the shipping which comes there from all parts, and many Zambucs from the Malabar country laden with areca, cocoas, and spices, which they delight in, and they take thence others which are used in Malabar.

TANAMAYAMBU.

Twenty-five leagues further on the coast is a fortress of the before named king, called Tanamayambu, and near it is a Moorish town, very pleasant, with many gardens, and very fertile—a town of very great Moorish mosques, and temples of worship of the Gentiles. It is nearly at the ex-

[1] The writer had forgotton that *aduana* (custom-house) and *divan* are the same word.

[2] Or Denby.

[3] Mezzo giorno, the Italian, instead of medio dia, a slip of the writer, the Genoese envoy.

tremity of the kingdom of Cambay or Guzarat, and it is likewise a seaport, but of little trade. And there are in this port small vessels of rovers like watch boats, which go out to sea, and if they meet with any small ship less strong than themselves, they capture and plunder it, and sometimes kill their crews.

KINGDOM OF DACANI.

On coming out of this kingdom of Guzarat and Cambay, towards the south and the inner parts of India, is the kingdom of Dacani, which the Indians call Decani. The king is a Moor, and a large part of his people is Gentile. He is a great lord, and possesses many subjects and an extensive territory, which stretches far inland. It has very good seaports, of great trade in the goods used on the mainland, and they are the following places:

CHEUL.

Leaving the kingdom of Cambay, along the coast towards the south, at eight leagues distance, there is a fine large river, and on it is a place called Cheul,[1] not very large, of handsome houses, which are all covered with thatch. This place is one of great commerce in merchandise, and in the months of December, January, February and March there are many ships from the Malabar country and all other parts, which arrive with cargoes. That is to say, those of Malabar laden with cocoa nuts, arecas, spices, drugs, palm sugar, emery, and there they make their sales for the continent and for the kingdom of Cambay; and the ships of Cambay come there to meet them laden with cotton stuffs, and many other goods which are available in Malabar, and these are bartered for the goods which have come from the Malabar country. And on the return voyage they fill their ships with wheat, vegetables, millet, rice, sesame, oil of sesame, of which there is

[1] Chaul, Ortelius, 1570.

much in this country; and these Malabars also buy many pieces of fine muslin[1] for women's head dress, and many beyranies, of which there are plenty in this kingdom. A large quantity of copper is sold in this port of Cheul, and at a high price, for it is worth twenty ducats the hundred weight, or more, because in the interior money is made of it, and it is also used throughout the country for cooking pots. There is also a great consumption in this place of quicksilver and vermilion for the interior, and for the kingdom of Guzarat, which copper, quicksilver and vermilion is brought to this place by the Malabar merchants, who get it from the factories of the King of Portugal; and they get more of it by way of the Mekkah, which comes there from Diu. These people wear the beyranies put on for a few days nearly in the raw state, and afterwards they bleach them and make them very white, and gum them to sell them abroad, and thus some are met with amongst them which are torn. In this port of Chaul there are few inhabitants, except during three or four months of the year, the time for putting in cargo, when there arrive merchants from all the neighbourhood, and they make their bargains during this period, and despatch their goods, and after that return to their homes until the next season, so that this place is like a fair in those months. There is a Moorish gentleman as governor of this place, who is a vassal of the King of Decani, and collects his revenues, and accounts to him for them. He is called Xech, and does great service to the King of Portugal, and is a great friend of the Portuguese, and treats very well all those that go there, and keeps the country very secure. In this place there is always a Portuguese factor appointed by the captain and factor of Goa, in order to send from this place provisions and other necessaries, to the city of Goa, and to the Portuguese fleets; and at a distance of about a league inland from Cheul is a place where the Moors

[1] Beatilla, bétille in French.

and Gentiles of the cities and towns throughout the country come to set up their shops of goods and cloths at Cheul during the beforementioned months; they bring these in great caravans of domestic oxen, with packs like donkeys, and on the top of these long white sacks placed crosswise, in which they bring their goods; and one man drives thirty or forty beasts before him.

DAMDA.

Having passed this place, Cheul, at twelve leagues further on along the coast to the south towards Malabar is another town and seaport, also belonging to the kingdom of Dacani, called Damda; where there enter and go out many Moorish ships, both Guzaratis and Malabaris, with cloth and other goods, as at Cheul.

MANDABAD.

Five leagues further on is a river called Mandabad, on which is a town of Moors and Gentiles, of the same kingdom of Decani; likewise a seaport. Many ships from various parts congregate at this harbour to buy stuffs, particularly from the Malabar country. And they bring there many cocoanuts, arecas, and also a few spices, copper and quicksilver: for the merchants of the country buy all these goods.

DABUL.

Having left this place, Mandabad, and going along the coast to Malabar and the south, at eight leagues distance is another fine large river, at the mouth of which is a large town of Moors and Gentiles, belonging to the same kingdom of Decani. It is called Dabul,[1] and in the mouth of the river near this same town there is a rampart, with artillery to defend the entrance of the river. This town of

[1] Dabul, Ortelius, 1570.

Dabul has a very good harbour, where there always congregate many Moorish ships from various parts, and especially from Mekkah, Aden, and Ormuz with horses, and from Cambay, Diu, and the Malabar country. It is a place of very great trade in all sorts of merchandise; there are in it very respectable Moors and Gentiles, and Guzarati merchants. Much copper, quicksilver, and vermilion is sold here for the interior of the country: a great quantity of country fabrics are brought to this town down the river for embarcation in the ships, and also much wheat and vegetables of all sorts. The custom-house of this port produces much money, and the collectors take the dues there for the lord of the town. And this town is pretty and well situated, but its houses are covered with thatch, and it also has very beautiful mosques. Higher up this river, on either bank there are many pretty towns, plentifully supplied, and owning much cultivated land and flocks. A fleet of the King of Portugal arrived at this city, of which the viceroy was the captain, and landed his people on the shore for the purpose of taking and destroying this town.[1] And the Moors put themselves on the defensive, and fought very courageously with the Portuguese. In the fight many Moors and Gentiles died, and at last the Portuguese took this city by assault, making a great slaughter of the inhabitants, and plundering and burning the city, in which much wealth and merchandise were burned, and at the same time several ships which were lying in the river. And those who escaped thence returned later to restore this city, so that now it is already inhabited as before.

SINGUYCAR.

Ten leagues further on from this river, along the coast southwards, is another river called Singuycar, upon which is a town of much commerce and merchandise. And many

[1] This was done by Don Francisco de Almeyda on his way to Diu, in the beginning of 1509.

ships from divers parts put in there; and it is a town of Moors and Gentiles, and belongs to the kingdom of Dacani.

RIVER DOBETALA.

Twelve leagues further along the coast, to the south, is another river called Dobetela; and there are along its course several small places, with very pretty gardens and orchards, where they gather a great quantity of betel; this is a leaf which they eat, and it is put on board small vessels, and carried away for sale in other towns and seaports. We call this betel Indian leaf, and it is as large as a leaf of the plantain,[1] and about of the same pattern; and it grows like ivy, and climbs up other trees by means of poles placed for that purpose: it does not give any fruit or seed. It is a very favourite leaf, and all the Indians both men and women eat it both day and night in their houses, in the streets, and on the road, and in their beds. They always go about eating this leaf, which they mix with some small fruits called arecas, and the leaf is smeared with moistened lime, which is made with sea-shells, and the shells of oysters and *albejas*. And these three things being added together, they eat this betel, not swallowing more than the juice; and it colours the mouth and makes the teeth brown: and they say that it is good for drying and purging the stomach, and for preserving the brain, and it drives out flatulence, and quenches thirst: so that it is very much esteemed among all Indians, and in general use from this place further on throughout India. There are great quantities of it, and it is one of the principal revenues which the kings of the country possess. The Moors and Arabs and Persians call it tanbul. After passing this river of Betala, further along the coast are other small places and seaports, likewise belonging to the kingdom of Dacani, in which small vessels from Malabar enter to take

[1] Llanten, *plantago*. The leaf is chewed, not eaten, and assists the digestion.

on board inferior rice and vegetables which are found there: and one of them is called Arapatani, and another Munaryni.[1]

BANDA.

After leaving these places, about six leagues along the coast southwards is a river, upon which is a town of Moors and Gentiles called Banda, in which there are many merchants who trade on the continent with the merchants whom the Malabars bring thither. And many ships come there from many parts on account of its being a good harbour, and there is a great exportation of goods and provisions from the interior of the country. Many ships fill here with rice, coarse millet, and other vegetables that are profitable to them; and they bring to this place cocoa-nuts, pepper, and other spices and drugs which have a good sale there, because thence they ship them for Diu, Aden, and Ormuz. And leaving this place, between it and Goa there is another river called Bardes, on which there are other towns which are not of much trade.

GUOA.

Leaving these places, there are twenty leagues of coast southwards as far as a cape, which must be doubled to enter Goa; and after that ten leagues to the north-west, then ten more to the east, and south-south-west twenty leagues, then seventeen leagues to the north-west, as far as the Cape Rama. And in this gulf there are many small islands, the chief of which is Goa. There is a large river which issues by two branches into the sea, between which is formed the island of the city of Goa, which belonged to the kingdom of Decani, and was a lordship of itself along with other towns in the neighbourhood; and the king gave it to a vassal of his, a great lord called Vasabaxo, who was a very good knight, and on account of his being very distinguished and skilful in warlike matters, this lordship of Goa was given him, in order

[1] Munacem in Ramusio, and Muruary in the Portuguese edition.

that he might carry on war thence with the King of Narsinga, as he always did until his death. This city then remained to his son, Sabaym Delcani, and it was inhabited by many Moors, respectable men, and foreigners, white men and rich merchants, and several of them are very good gentlemen. There are also many great Gentile merchants, and others, gentlemen and cultivators, and men-at-arms. It was a place of great trade in merchandise. It has a very good port, to which flocked many ships from Mekkah, Aden, Ormuz, Cambay, and the Malabar country. And the before mentioned Sabaym Delcani resided much in this place, and he kept there his captain and men-at-arms, and no one entered or went out of this island and city, either by sea or by land, without his permission; and all those who entered there were registered with all their signs and particulars, and from whence they came; and so, with this precaution and arrangement, they allowed them to return. This town was very large, with goodly edifices and handsome streets and squares, surrounded by walls and towers. There is a very good fortress in it, and in the environs many gardens and orchards of fine trees and fruits, and many pools of good water. There were many mosques and houses of worship of the Gentiles. The country all round was very fruitful and well cultivated, and enjoyed much produce both from sea and land. This Sabaym, as soon as he knew that the Portuguese viceroy had routed the Rumes[1] and the fleet of the great sultan before Diu, immediately sent to call the Rumes, knights, and other people of the sultan, who having escaped thence, arrived, leaving their captain in the kingdom of

[1] *Rumys.* Turks are so called east of Turkey. These Turks may have served in the Egyptian fleet, but did not belong to the Ottoman forces, as Egypt was not united to the Ottoman Empire till later in 1517.

> Traz este vem Noronha, cujo auspicio
> De Dio os Rumes feros affugenta,
> Dio, que o peito e bellico exercicio
> De Antonio da Sylveira bem sustenta.
>
> Camoens, canto x, stanza 72.

Guzarat. And this Sabaym Delcani received them very well, and determined on putting all India at their disposition for their assistance, and to refit them again with the aid of all the Moors and kings of India, in order to again carry on war against the Portuguese. They then collected together much money and began to build in this city of Goa very large ships, and handsome galleys and brigantines, all after the manner and fashion of ours, and likewise to prepare much artillery of brass and iron, and all other munitions of maritime war. And the Moors were so expeditious in this that they had got a large part of the fleet made, and vast magazines of munitions for the fleet; and they already went out with guard boats and rowing galleys, to take the Sambuks which passed by, because they carried Portuguese safe-conducts. And Alfonso de Albuquerque, who was then captain-major in India, had information of all this, and determined to go and seek them, and drive them from their design. He therefore collected the most that he could of a fleet of ships, caravels, and galleys, and with these entered the before mentioned river, and attacked the city of Goa[1] and took it. Upon which many great things occurred, which I say nothing about, in order not to be more prolix. He captured many people, and all the ships and galleys of the Rumes, and he burned some of them; and the city submitted to the commands of the King of Portugal, as it now is. And he fortified it with several castles. This city is inhabited by Portuguese, Moors and Gentiles; and the fruits of the earth and provisions now produce a yearly revenue to the King of Portugal of twenty thousand ducats, without the port, which has much trade in merchandise of Malabar, Cheul, Dabul, Cambay and Diu. They sell there many horses for other parts, at two, three and four hundred ducats each, according to their quality, and upon each the King of Por-

[1] February 25th, 1510, or on the 17th February according to San Roman; Albuquerque was driven out of Goa, and reconquered it on the 25th November 1510.

tugal levies forty ducats as duty; and although they pay less dues than in the time of the Moors, this harbour produces much revenue to the King of Portugal.[1]

In this kingdom of Decani there are many great cities, and many other towns within the country inhabited by Moors and Gentiles. It is a country very well cultivated, and abundantly supplied with provisions, and it has an extensive commerce, which produces much revenue to the king, who is called Mahamuza, and is a Moor; and he lives very luxuriously, and with much pleasure, in a great city inland, which is called Mavider. This king holds the whole of his kingdom, divided amongst Moorish lords, to each one of whom he has assigned cities, towns, and villages; and these lords govern and rule, so that the king does not give any orders in his kingdom, nor does he meddle except in giving himself a pleasant life and amusement. And all these lords do obeisance to him, and bring him the revenue, with which they have to come into his presence. And if any one of them were to revolt or disobey, the others go against him and destroy him, or reduce him again to obedience to the king. These lords frequently have wars and differences among one another, and it happens that some take villages from others; but afterwards the king makes peace, and administers justice between them. Each one has many horsemen, very good archers with the Turkish bow, white people, of good figures. Their dress is of cotton stuffs, and they wear caps on their heads. They give large pay to the soldiers: they speak Arabic, Persian and the Decani language, which is the natural language of the country. These Moorish lords take tents of cotton cloth into the field, in which they dwell when going on a journey, or to war.

They ride a small saddle, and fight tied to their horses. They carry in their hands very long light lances, with four-

1 San Roman says that the revenue of Sabayo was five hundred thousand ducats; and that Goa produced much more in the hands of the King of Portugal (p. 183).

sided iron points, very strong, and three palms in length. They wear tunics quilted with cotton, which they call *laudes*, and some wear tunics of mail, and their horses caparisoned; some carry iron maces and battle-axes, two swords and a buckler, Turkish bows supplied with many arrows, so that each man carries offensive weapons for two persons. Many of these take their wives with them to the wars; they make use of pack oxen, on which they carry their chattels when they travel. They are frequently at war with the King of Narsinga, so that they are at peace but for a short time. The Gentiles of this kingdom of Decani are black, well made and courageous; most of them fight on foot, and some on horseback: and these foot soldiers carry swords and shields, bows and arrows, and are very good archers. Their bows are long, after the fashion of Englishmen. They go naked from the waist upwards, and wear small caps on their heads; they eat all meats except cow; they are idolaters, when they die their bodies are burned, and their wives burn themselves alive with them voluntarily, as will be related further on.

CINTACOLA.

Seventeen leagues further along the same coast to the south-east, and towards Malabar, there is another river called Aliga,[1] which separates the kingdom of Decani from the kingdom of Narsinga, and at the mouth of the river on the top of a hill is a fortress, Cintacola;[2] and it belongs to the Zabayo, for the defence of his country. In it he continually keeps horse and foot soldiers. Here the said kingdom of Decani comes to an end at its southern portion, and the northern part ends at Cheul; and from one place to the other along the coast there are eighty leagues.

KINGDOM OF NARSINGA.

Beyond this river commences the kingdom of Narsinga,

[1] Aliga R., German Atlas, 1753.

[2] Cintacola, Ortelius, 1570.

which contains five very large provinces, with a language of their own. One province is along the coast, and is called Tulinat; another has the name of Legni, which confines with the kingdom of Tisa; another is Canari, in which is the great city of Visenagar,[1] and the other is Chomendel,[2] a kingdom which they call Tamul. This kingdom of Narsinga is very rich and well supplied with provisions, and is very full of cities and large townships; and all the country is very fertile and brought into cultivation. The province of Tulinat contains many rivers and sea-ports, in which there is much trade and shipping bound for all parts, and many rich merchants dwell in them. Between the others there is a very large river called Mergeo, from which is produced a large quantity of inferior rice for the common people, which the Malabars come here to buy, with their sambuks, in exchange for cocoa nuts, oil, and jagra, which are much used in this country.

HONOR.

Having passed this river Aliga,[3] and going along the coast to the south-east, there is another river, at ten leagues distance, with a good town near the sea, called Honor,[4] and the Malabars call it Povaran; many of them come to this place to fetch cargoes of inferior brownish rice, which is their peculiar food: and they bring cocoa nuts, oil and jagra, and wine of the palm trees, from which grow the cocoa nuts.

BATECALA.

Ten leagues further along this coast to the south is another small river, with a large town called Baticala,[5] of very great trade in merchandise, inhabited by many Moors and Gentiles, very commercial people. And at this port congregate many ships from Orguz, to load very good white

[1] Bisinagar, Ortelius.
[2] Cholmandel, Ortelius.
[3] In the Italian and Portuguese editions Mergeo.
[4] Onor, Ortelius.
[5] Batticalla, Ortelius.

rice, sugar in powder, of which there is much in this country, for they do not know how to make it in loaves; and it is worth at the rate of two hundred and forty maravedis the arroba.[1] They likewise load much iron, and these three kinds of goods are what are chiefly shipped at this place: and also some spices and drugs, which the Malabars import. There are many myrobalans of all sorts, and very good preserves are made with them, which the ships of Ormuz, which traffic at this place, export for the Arabs and Persians. They used each year to bring to this port many horses and pearls, which were there sold for the whole kingdom of Narsinga, and now they take them all to the city of Goa, on account of the Portuguese. Some ships are also laden at this place for Aden, risking themselves, although it is forbidden them by the Portuguese. Many Malabar ships and sambuks also come to this port to take in rice, sugar, and iron; and they bring cocoa nuts, palm sugar, cocoa nut oil, and palm wine, in return for these things, and spices and drugs, concealed from the Portuguese who prohibit them. This town produces much revenue to the king. Its governor is a Gentile; he is named Damaqueti. He is very rich in money and jewels. The king of Narsinga has given this place and others to a nephew of his, who rules and governs them, and lives in great State and calls himself king, but he is in obedience to the king his uncle. In this kingdom they make a great practice of duelling, for on account of anything they at once challenge one another, and the king at once grants them a field and arms, and appoints a time for killing each other, and gives them seconds, who back up each his own man. They go to fight one another bare from the waist upwards, and from the waist downwards wrapped in cotton cloths drawn tightly round, and with many folds, and with their arms, which are swords, bucklers and daggers.[2] And

[1] Quarter of a hundredweight.

[2] Gomio, this word is intended, perhaps, for gumia, a kind of dagger,

the king appoints them of equal length. They enter the lists with great pleasure, first saying their prayers, and in a very few passes they kill each other in the presence of the king and many people, without any one speaking except the seconds, of whom each encourages his own man. This town of Baticala pays a yearly tribute to the king of Portugal; much copper is also sold in it each year, which is taken into the interior of the country to make money, and cauldrons and other pans which they use. There is also sold there much quicksilver, vermilion, coral, alum and ivory. This town is situated in level country, it is very populous, and not walled; it is surrounded with many gardens, very good estates, and very fresh and abundant water. There is in this place gold coin called Pardan,[1] and it is worth three hundred and twenty maravedis; and there is another silver coin called *dama*, worth twenty. The weights are called bahars, and each bahar is equal to four quintals of Portugal.[2]

MAYANDUR.

Having passed Baticala, at ten leagues towards the south is another small river, on which there is a town called Mayandur, under the jurisdiction of Baticala, in which much rice is gathered of a good quality, which is shipped at Baticala. The people of this town sow it principally in certain watery valleys, which they plough with oxen and with buffaloes, two and two, in couples, with their ploughs after our fashion, and they put the rice for seed in some hollow irons placed in the ploughshare, which entering the earth ploughing it and

a Marocco word not Arabic; these words are neither of them to be found in the old dictionaries. The dagger is not mentioned in the Italian or Portuguese editions.

1 Pardao, an Indian coin worth 300 reis coined at Goa by the Portuguese, with the figure of King Sebastian. Dict. of P. Raphael Bluteau, Lisbon, 1720.

2 Bahar, an Indian weight varying from 4½ quintals to 5 quintals 3½ arrobas.

making a furrow, leave behind the seed in it, because otherwise they would not be able to sow it on account of the quantity of water; and on dry land they sow it by hand. They gather the harvest twice every year from this watery land, and it is of four sorts of rice. The first they call girazat, which is the best; the second jani bazal,[1] the third camagar, and the fourth pachari: each one has its price, and there is a great difference between one and the other.

BACAVOR BAZALOR.

There are two small rivers ten leagues further along the coast to the south, and on both of them towns, one of which is called Bacavor, and the other Basalor;[2] both belong to the kingdom of Narsinga. In these also there is much rice of good quality, which is there shipped for all parts: and many ships come from Malabar, and sambuks great and small, which take this rice on board in sacks of a fanega[3] each, which is worth from one hundred and fifty to two hundred maravedis each fanega, according to its goodness. Ships also put in here from Ormuz, Aden, Xeher, and many other places, to take in cargo for Canaor and Calicut. They also ship there much rice in exchange for copper, cocoa nuts, jagra, oil of cocoa nuts, for the Malabars maintain themselves with scarcely anything else but rice, since the country of Malabar is small and very populous: so full of inhabitants, that it may almost be said that all the country is one single city from the mountain Deli to Coulam.

MANGALOR.

Having left these places, at ten leagues distance there is another large river towards the south, along the sea-shore, where

[1] Or Jauibasal, these names are variously spelled in the Italian and Portuguese editions.

[2] Bacanor and Barsalor, German Atlas.

[3] Fanega—4 bushels or 84 lbs. French.

there is a very large town, peopled by Moors and Gentiles, of the kingdom of Narsinga, called Mangalor.[1] There many ships always load brown rice, which is much better and more healthy than the white, for Malabar, for the common people, and it is very cheap. They also ship there much rice in Moorish ships for Aden, also pepper, which henceforward the earth begins to produce, but little of it, and better than all the other which the Malabars bring to this place in small vessels. The banks of this river are very pretty, and very full of woods and palm trees, and are very thickly inhabited by Moors and Gentiles, and studded with fine buildings and houses of prayer of the Gentiles, which are very large, and enriched with large revenues. There are also many mosques, where they greatly honour Mahomed.

CUNBALA.

Ten leagues further along the same coast to the south, is another town of the Gentiles, of the kingdom of Narsinga, which is called Cunbala. In it also much brown and very bad rice is harvested, which the Malabars go to buy there, and load it in their vessels for the lowest people amongst them, and of the Mahaldiu islands, which are across from Malabar, because it is very cheap, and the people poor; and they sell it there in exchange for thread for making cordage for ships. This thread is made of a covering and integument which grows upon the cocoa nuts of the palm trees, and a great quantity of it is produced; and in that place it is a great article of commerce with all parts. This town of Cunbala has a lord to rule and govern it for the kingdom of Narsinga, and it is frontier to the kingdom of Cananor: because here the kingdom of Narsinga comes to an end along the coast of this province of Tulinat.

[1] Mangalor, Ortelius.

OF THE CUSTOMS AND GREATNESS OF THIS KINGDOM OF NARSINGA IN THE INTERIOR OF THE COUNTRY.

Leaving this sea coast, and going inland into the kingdom of Narsinga, at twelve or fifteen leagues distance there is a very high mountain range, precipitous and difficult of ascent, which stretches from the beginning of this kingdom to Cape Comeri,[1] which is beyond the Malabar country; and the before-mentioned province of Tulinat is at the foot of this range, between it and the sea. And the Indians say that in former times all these low grounds were sea, which reached to the said range, and that in process of time the sea uncovered it, and swelled it up in other parts, and to the foot of those mountains. There are many traces of things of the sea, and all the low ground is very level like the sea, and the mountain chain is very craggy, and seems to rise to the heavens; and it is not possible to ascend, except in a few parts, and with difficulty, which is a cause of great strength to the Malabars, for were it not for the difficulty of entering their country on account of the roughness of these mountains, the King of Narsinga would already have conquered them. This range is peopled in several parts, with good towns and villages, very luxuriant in water and delicious fruit: and in it there are many wild boars, and large and fine deer, many leopards, ounces, lions, tigers, bears, and some animals of an ashy colour, which look like horses, very active, and which cannot be caught.[2] There are serpents with wings, which fly, very venomous, so that their breath and looks kill whatever person places himself very near them, and they always go amongst the trees. There are also many wild elephants, and many stones of gegonzas,[3] amethysts, and soft sapphires, are found in the rivers where they are deposited. They

[1] Cape Comori, Ortelius.

[2] The Nil Gau or Blue Cow.

[3] Ramusio coincides with this MS. in writing giagonzas on a former occasion, and on this gegonzas.

carry them from the mountains to sell them in the Malabar towns, where they are wrought. After passing this mountain range, the country is almost entirely plain, very fertile and abundantly supplied in the inland districts, which belong to the kingdom of Narsinga, in which there are many cities and villages and forts, and many large rivers run through it. There is in this country much cultivation of rice and other vegetables, with which they maintain themselves, and many cows, buffaloes, pigs, goats, sheep, asses, and diminutive ponies, all of which they make use of; and they carry their goods by means of buffaloes, oxen, asses, and ponies, and do their field work with them. Almost all the villages are of Gentiles, and among them are a few Moors; some of the lords of these villages are of these last, to whom the king of Narsinga has granted the villages, and others are his, and he keeps his governors and tax collectors in them.

BIJANAGUER.

Forty-five leagues from these mountains inland, there is a very large city which is called Bijanaguer, very populous and surrounded on one side by a very good wall, and on another by a river, and on the other by a mountain. This city is on level ground, the King of Narsinga always resides in it. He is a Gentile and is called Raheni: he has in this place very large and handsome palaces, with numerous courts in which are many mounds, pools of water with plenty of fish, gardens of shrubs, flowers, and sweet-smelling herbs. There are also in the city many other palaces of great lords who live there. And all the other houses of the place are covered with thatch, and the streets and squares are very wide: they are constantly filled with an innumerable crowd of all nations and creeds; for, besides many Moorish merchants and traders, and the Gentile inhabitants of the country who are very rich, an infinite number of others flock there from all parts, who are able to come, dwell, trade, and live very freely and in security, without anyone molesting them, or asking or requiring of them any account of whence they come, or in what creed they live, whether they be Moors, Christians, or Gentiles; and each one may live according to any creed, or as he pleases. There is an infinite trade in this city, and strict justice and truth are observed towards all by the governors of the country. In this city there are very many jewels which are brought from Pegu and Celani, and in the country itself many diamonds are found, because there is a mine of them in the kingdom of Narsinga and another in the kingdom of Dacani. There are also many pearls and seed-pearls to be found there, which are brought from Ormus and Cael; and all these jewels and pearls are much esteemed among them, because they adorn themselves much with them, and on that account a great quantity are poured in. In this city they wear many silks and inferior brocades, which are brought from China and Alexandria, and much scarlet cloth, and of other colours, and much coral worked into round beads; and they import copper, quicksilver, vermilion, saffron, rosewater, much anfiani which is opium, sandal and aloes wood, camphor, musk, because the inhabitants of this country are much in the habit of anointing themselves with these perfumes.

There is also a great consumption in this place, and in the whole kingdom, of pepper, which is brought from Malabar on oxen and asses. The money is of gold, and is called parda, and is worth three hundred maravedis;[1] it is coined in certain cities of this kingdom of Narsinga, and throughout all India they use this money, which passes in all those kingdoms; its gold is a little inferior. This coin is round, and made in a mould. Some of them have some Indian letters on one side, and two figures on the other of a man and a woman, and others have nothing but the lettering on one side.

[1] The abbreviation is $\overline{m}$ $\overline{mrs}$; this might stand for ccc or three hundred, the value given by Ramusio.

CUSTOMS OF THIS KINGDOM OE NARSINGA AND OF ITS INHABITANTS.

This king constantly resides in the before-mentioned palaces, and very seldom goes out of them: he lives very luxuriously and without any labour, because he discharges it all upon his governors. He and all the dwellers in this city are Gentiles, coloured men and nearly white, of long and very smooth black hair; they are well proportioned men, of features and . . . .[1] similar to our own, and so likewise are the women. The costume of the men is from the waist downwards with many folds and very tight, and a short shirt which reaches half way down the thigh, made of white cotton stuff, silk, or brocade, open down the front, small caps on their heads, and the hair gathered up on the top, some caps of silk or brocade, and their sandals on their bare feet, cloaks of cotton stuff or silk on their arms, and their pages with their swords behind them, and their bodies anointed with white sandal, aloes-wood, camphor, musk, and saffron; all ground together with rosewater. They bathe every day, and after bathing, anoint themselves. They wear small gold chains and jewels round their necks, and bracelets on their arms, and rings on their fingers of very valuable jewels, and also many jewels in their ears of pearls and precious stones. And they take a second page who carries for them a slender canopy with a long handle with which to shade them and protect them from the rain. These shades are of silk stuff, much ornamented with gold fringes, and some of them have jewels and seed-pearls, and made in such a manner that they shut up and open; and some of these cost three or four hundred gold pieces, according to the quality of the persons. The women wear a cloth of very fine white cotton, or of silk of pretty colours, which may be about six cubits long; they gird themselves with

[1] Filosañias, may be intended for physiognomy. It is so translated by Ramusio.

part of this cloth from the waist below. and the other end of the cloth they cast over the shoulder and the breasts, and one arm and shoulder remain uncovered; on their feet sandals of gilt and well-worked leather; their heads bare, only their hair combed, and they put a plait of it over their heads, and in this many flowers and scents; and in the nostrils a small hole on one side, and in it a gold thread with a drop, either a pearl, or a ruby, or a sapphire drilled with a hole; their ears also are bored and in them they wear many gold rings with pearls and precious stones; and jewel necklaces round their throats, bracelets on their arms of the same fashion, and also strings of fine round coral on their arms, many rings with precious stones on their fingers; and girt over their clothes with belts of gold and jewels; and rings of gold on their legs; so that for the most part these are very rich and well-dressed people. They are great dancers; they sing and play on various instruments; they are taught to tumble and to perform many feats of agility. They are pretty women, and of a grand presence. These people marry in our manner; they have a marriage law, but the great men marry as many women as they can maintain, and the king has with him in his palaces many wives, daughters of the great lords of his kingdom; and, besides these, he has many others as concubines, and others as serving women who are chosen throughout the kingdom as the most beautiful. And all the attendance on the king is done by women, who wait upon him within doors; and amongst them are all the employments of the king's household: and all these women live and find room within these palaces, which contain apartments for all. They bathe every day in the pools of water, they sing and play on their instruments, and in a thousand ways amuse the king: and he goes to see them bathe, and from thence sends to his chamber the one that pleases him most; and the first son that he has from any of these, inherits the kingdom. Amongst them there is so much envy and rivality for the preference of the king, that sometimes they kill themselves with poison. This king has a house in which he meets with the governors and his officers in council upon the affairs of the kingdom; and there all the great men of the realm go to see him with great gifts; and he dispenses great favours and likewise great punishments to those that deserve them. These great men, his relations and those of great lineage, when they do anything ill-done or prejudicial to his service, are summoned to him; and they have to come immediately: and they come in very rich litters on men's shoulders, and their horses are led by the bridle before them, and many horsemen go in front of them. They get down at the door of the palace and wait there with their trumpets and musical instruments, until word is brought to the king, and he commands them to come to his presence; and if they do not give a good excuse and account of themselves and of the evil of which they are accused, he commands them to be stripped and thrown on the ground, and there bids them to receive many stripes. If such a person were a near relation of the king's or a very great personage, the king himself scourges him with his own hand, and after he has been well beaten, the king orders very rich garments to be given him from his own clothes chests, and then directs him to be reconducted to his litter, and carried with great honour and great clang of musical instruments and festivity to his abode. Many litters and many horsemen always stand at the door of this palace: and the king keeps at all times nine hundred elephants and more than twenty thousand horses, all which elephants and horses are bought with his money: the elephants, at the price of fifteen hundred to two thousand ducats each, because they are very great and well-fitted for war, and for taking about with him continually for state. And the horses cost from three to six hundred ducats each, and some of the choicest for his personal use, nine hundred or a thousand ducats. These horses are distributed amongst the great lords who are responsible for them, and keep them for the gentry and knights to whom the king bids them to be given: and he gives to each knight a horse and a groom and a slave girl, and for his personal expenses four or five pardaos of gold per month, according to who he is; and, besides that, each day's provisions for the horse and groom; and they send to the kitchen for the rations both for the elephants and horses. The kitchens are very large and numerous, they contain many cauldrons of copper, and several officials who cook the food of the elephants and horses; which, it must be said, is rice, chick-peas, and other vegetables. In all this there is much order and arrangement, and if the knight to whom the king has given a horse cares for it and treats it well, they take away that one and give him another and a better one; and if he is negligent, they take his away and give him another that is worse. And thus all the king's horses and elephants are well fed and cared for, at his cost: and the grandees, to whom he gives a great quantity of them, act in the same manner with their knights. These horses live but a short time; they are not bred in this country, for all of them are brought there from the kingdom of Ormuz and that of Cambay, and on that account, and for the great need of them, they are worth so much money. This king has more than a hundred thousand men, both horse and foot, to whom he gives pay: and fully five or six thousand women, to whom also he gives pay. And wherever there is war, according to the number of men-at-arms whom he sends there, he likewise sends with them a quantity of women; because they say that it is not possible to bring together an army, nor carry on war well, without women. These women are like enchantresses, and are great dancers; they play and sing, and pirouette. And whenever the king's officers take and enrol any man, they strip him and look what marks he has got on his body, and measure what his stature is, and set it all down in writing, and from whence he comes, and the names of his father and mother: and so he remains enrolled with all these particulars in the pay books. And after being enrolled, it is with difficulty that he can again obtain permission to go to his country; and if he flies and is taken, he runs great danger, and is very ill treated. Among these men-at-arms there are many knights, who arrive there from many parts to take service, and these do not cease to live in their creeds. In this kingdom there are three sects of Gentiles, and each one of them is distinguished from the others, and their customs are different. In the first place, the king and the grandees, and lords and chief people of the men-at-arms, can marry more than one wife, especially the grandees, who can maintain them: their children are their heirs. The wives are bound to burn themselves and to die with their husbands when they decease, because when the people die, their bodies are burned, both of men and women. And the wives burn themselves alive with them to honour them, in this manner: that is to say, if she is a poor woman of little rank, when the body of the husband is borne out to be burned in an open space outside the city, where there is a great fire, and whilst the body of the husband is being consumed, the wife casts herself, of her own will, into the fire, and burns there with him. And if she is some honourable woman, and of much property, and whether she be a young woman of beautiful presence, or old, when her husband dies, the relations all go to the before mentioned open space, and make a wide grave as deep as a man's height, and fill it with sandal and other wood, and place the dead body within and burn it; and his wife, or wives, weep for him, and then, should she desire to honour her husband, she asks for a term of a certain number of days to go and be burnt with him. And they bid all her relations, and those of her husband, come and do her honour, and give her a festal reception. And in this manner all collect together, and entertain and pay court to her, and she spends what she possesses among her relations and friends, in feasting and singing, in dances and playing on musical instruments, and amusements of jugglers. And when the term fixed has ended, she dresses herself in her richest stuffs, and adorns herself with many precious jewels, and the rest of her property she divides amongst her children, relations, and friends. and then mounts a horse, with a great sound of music, and a large following. The horse must be grey, or very white if possible, for her to be seen better. And so they conduct her through the whole city, paying court to her as far as the place where the body of her husband was burned; and in the same grave they place much wood, with which they light a very great fire, and all round it they make a gallery with three or four steps, whither she ascends with all her jewels and robes; and when she is upon the top she takes three turns round it, and raises her hands to heaven, and worships towards the east three times. And having ended this, she calls her relations and friends, and to each she gives a jewel of those which she wears: and all this with a very cheerful demeanour, not as though she were about to die. And after she has given them away, and there only remains a small cloth with which she is covered from the waist downwards, she says to the men, "See, gentlemen, how much you owe to your wives, who, whilst enjoying their freedom, burn themselves alive with their husbands." And to the women she says, "See, ladies, how much you owe to your husbands, for in this manner you ought to accompany them even in death." And when she has concluded uttering these words, they give her a pitcher full of oil, and she places it on her head and says her prayer, and takes three more turns and worships to the east, and casts the pitcher of oil into the pit where the fire is: and she springs into it, after the pitcher, with as much good will as though she were jumping into a pool of water. And the relations have ready for this occasion many pitchers and pots full of oil and butter, and dry wood, which they immediately throw in, so that so great a flame is at once kindled, that she is suddenly reduced to ashes. And afterwards they collect these ashes, and cast them into flowing rivers. All perform this in general, and if any women do not choose to do this, their relations take them, shave their heads, and turn them out of their houses and families with disgrace. And so they wander through the world as lost ones. And those of this sort to whom they may wish to show favour, are sent to the houses of prayer of the idols, to serve and gain for that temple with their bodies, if they are young women. And of these houses there are many, which contain fifty or a hundred women of this sort; and others, who of their own accord, being unmarried, place themselves there.[1] These have to play and sing, for certain hours of the day, before their idols, and the rest of the time they work for themselves.

So also when the king dies, four or five hundred women burn themselves with him in the same manner, and they throw themselves suddenly into the pit and fire where they burn the body of the king: for the pit and fire are very large, and a great quantity can be burned in it, with great abundance of wood, sandal, brasil, eagle wood, aloes wood, and much oil of sesame and butter to make the wood burn well. So great is the haste of those who wish to burn themselves first, that it is something wonderful, and many men, confidants of the king, burn themselves with him. These people eat meat, fish, and all other viands, only cow is forbidden them by their creed. There is another sect of Gentiles who are called Bramans, who are priests and directors of the houses of prayer. These do not eat meat or fish, they marry only one wife, and if she dies they do not marry again: their children inherit their property. They

[1] The Arab travellers of the ninth century mention this.

wear over the shoulder three threads as a sign of being Bramans. These do not die for any cause, or crime which they may commit; they are very free and easy, and are very much venerated amongst the people. They enjoy amongst them large alms from the kings, lords, and honourable people, with which they maintain themselves; and many of them are rich, and others live in the houses of prayer which there are about the country, after the manner of monasteries. These temples also have great revenues. These people are great eaters, and do no work except in order to eat: and they at any time go eight leagues to satisfy themselves with food, which they can eat on the road. Their food is rice, butter, sugar, vegetables, and milk. In this country there is another sect of people, who are like Bramans: they wear round their necks hung with silk cords and wrapped in coloured cloth, a stone of the size of an egg, and they say that it is their god. These people are much venerated and honoured in this country; they do them no harm for any offence which they may commit, out of reverence for that stone, which they call tabaryne.[1] Neither do these people eat flesh nor fish; they go safely in all countries, and they transport from one kingdom to another much merchandise and money of the merchants, on account of their greater security from thieves. And there are some of them who deal in merchandise with their tani bar ine round their necks. These likewise marry only one woman, and if they die before their wives, they bury these alive in this manner.[2] It must be said, that they make a grave for her a little deeper than she is tall, and put her in it standing, and while she is quite alive they throw in earth all around her, and press it down with their feet until she is walled in with earth much pressed

[1] Tambarme in Ramusio.

[2] This is the probable origin of the story in Sinbad the Sailor. The Arabian Nights are not entirely fiction, as is usually supposed: the story of Seif el Muluk refers to facts in the Malay Annals, and describes the people, country, and winds about Sumatra.

down, which reaches to her neck, and then they put some large stones above her, and leave her there alive covered with earth until she dies; and on this occasion they perform great ceremonies for them. The women of this country are so enterprising and idolatrous, that they do marvellous things for the love of their idols, in this manner. There are amongst them young girls who desire to marry some man for whom they have a liking, and one of these will promise her idol to do it a great service if she should marry such a one whom she wishes for. And if she marries that one, she then says to him, I have to make a feast for such a god, and I have to offer my blood before I deliver myself to you. And so they appoint a day for celebrating that feast. And she takes a large waggon with oxen, and they fix it in a very high crane, such as those with which they draw water, and they fasten it to an iron chain with two iron hooks, and she comes out of her house with great honour, accompanied by all her relations and friends, men and women, with much singing and playing of instruments, and many dancers and jesters; and she comes wrapped very tightly round the waist with her white stuffs, covered from the waist to the knees, the rest bare, and at the door of her house, where the car stands, they lower the crane, and stick the two hooks into her in the loins between the skin and the flesh, and put into her left hand a small round shield, and a little bag with lemons and oranges. They then raise the crane with great shouting and sound of instruments, firing guns, and making other festal demonstrations: and in this manner the car begins its march on the way to the house of the idol to which the promise was made, and she goes suspended by those hooks fastened into her flesh, and the blood runs down her legs. And she continues to sing and shout for joy, and to strike upon the shield, and to throw oranges and lemons to her husband and to her relations, who go with her in this manner to the door of the said house of prayer, where they take her down, and cure, her, and deliver her to her husband; and she gives at that place great alms to the Bramans and offerings to the idols, and a great feast to as many as accompanied her.

There are other persons also who offer the virginity of their daughters to an idol, and as soon as they are ten years of age they take her to a monastery and the house of prayer of that idol, with great honour, and accompanied by her relations, entertaining her like one that is going to be married. And outside of the monastery, at the door, there is a bench of hard black stone, square, of half a man's height, and surrounded with wooden steps, with many oil lamps laced on the steps, which are lit at night.[1] * *

* * * * *

* * * * *

This King of Narsinga is frequently at war with the King of Dacani, who has taken from him much of his land; and also with another Gentile King of the country of Otira,[2] which is the country in the interior. And he always sends his captains and troops to this war, and on some occasions, if of necessity, he goes to the war in person; and as soon as it is determined on, he goes out to the country, on a certain day, on an elephant or in a litter, very richly adorned with gold and jewels, accompanied by many knights and horse and foot-men: and many elephants go before him, all covered with scarlet cloth and silk, and much bedizened and dressed out as for a feast. And as they go through the fields they bring the king a horse, on which he rides, and a

[1] "Y sobre el dicho palo esta una piedrá de altura de un cobdo y en el medio un agujero en el qual meten un palo agudo y arman las gradas paramentadas con paños de seda para que la gente de fuera no vea el secreto de dentro y la madre de la moza con algunas otras mugeres entran en aquel lugar despues de hechas muchas cerimonias y alli sobre aquel palo agudo rompen la moza su virginidad y deraman la sangre sobre aquella piedra."

[2] Apparently Orissa.

bow and an arrow, which he shoots towards the part where he intends to go and make war. And they name the day of his setting out, and this news immediately runs throughout all the kingdom. He then pitches his tents and camp in the country, and there remains until the appointed term of days is accomplished for his departure. When this is concluded he orders the city to be set on fire, and directs it all to be burned except the royal palaces, castles, houses of prayer, and those of some of the grandees which are not covered with thatch, in order that all may go to the war to die with him, and with his wives and children, whom he has with him in the wars. In order that these may not take to flight he directs large pay to be given to all: in the first place, to the enchanting single women, who are numerous, and who do not fight, but their lovers fight for love of them very vigourously. And it is also said that many men come from all the other kingdoms to this king's camp for the love of these women,[1] amongst whom there are many very honourable ones, great confidantes of the king, who come of great houses, and are very rich. Each one of them keeps seven or

[1] Compare Plato's views on this subject :—"But if a soldier highly distinguishes himself and gains himself credit, ought he not, think you, in the first place, while the army is still in the field, to be crowned with a garland by each of the youths and children in turn among his comrades in arms?" "Yes, I think so." "But I suppose you will hardly extend your approbation to my next proposition?" "What is that?" "That he should kiss and be kissed by them all." "Most certainly I do; and I would add to the law, that during the continuance of the campaign, no one whom he has a mind to kiss be permitted to refuse him the satisfaction; in order that, if any soldier happens to entertain an admiration for either a male or female comrade, he may be the more stimulated to carry off the meed of valour." "Good, I replied; and we have already said that a brave man will be allowed to enter into marriage relations more frequently than others will, and to exercise more than the usual liberty of choice in such matters, so that as many children as possible may be obtained from a father of this character."—Republic of Plato, book v, § 468, p. 201. Translation by Davies and Vaughan, Cambridge, 1858.

eight pretty waiting women, who are given to them by their mothers to bring them up, and put them in the court enrolled on the pay list. They hold this service in great honour, and it is but a short time since one of them died who had no son nor heir, and left the king for her heir; and he gathered from the inheritance sixty thousand gold pardaos, besides twelve thousand which he gave to a waiting woman of his, whom he had brought up from a girl: which is not to be wondered at for the great wealth of the kingdom..

In this kingdom jewels are esteemed as treasure by the king and also by the rich, who buy them at large prices. The people of this kingdom are great hunters both of flying game and wild beasts. There are many small hacks, and very good ones to go.

HOTISA.

Having passed the said kingdom of Narsynga inland, there is next another kingdom called Hotisa,[1] which confines with it on one side, and on another with the kingdom of Bengal, and on the other with the kingdom of Dely: and it is inhabited by Gentiles. The king is also a Gentile, very rich and powerful, who has many foot soldiers; he is frequently at war with the kingdom of Narsinga, from which he has taken lands and villages; and the King of Narsinga has taken others from him: so that they are rarely at peace. Of the customs of these people I have little information, on account of their being placed so much in the interior of the country. It is only known that in that country there are very few Moors, and that they are almost all Gentiles and very good fighting men.

KINGDOM OF DELY.

Having passed this kingdom of Otisa, more inland there

[1] Orissa: in this MS. it is clearly a *t*, but *t* and *r* are easily confounded in the handwriting of this period.

is another great kingdom, which is called Dely, of many provinces, and of large and rich cities of great trade. This kingdom is of the Moors, and has a Moorish king, a great lord; and in former times this kingdom was of the Gentiles, of whom there are still many who live amidst the Moors, with much vexation. And many of them nobles and respectable people, not to be subject to the Moors, go out of the kingdom and take the habit of poverty, wandering the world; and they never settle in any country until their death; nor will they possess any property, since they lost their lands and property, and for that go naked, barefooted, and bareheaded; they only cover their nakedness with coverings[1] of brass, in this manner: it must be said, that they wear belts of Moorish brass of pieces fitted together, of four fingers in breadth, carved with many images of men and women, sculptured and shining: and they wear it so tight that it makes their guts rise high up; and from the girdle below the hips there comes a bandage of the same brass, and in front it forms a sort of braguette, which comes and fastens in the girdle in front with its fastenings: all very tight. Besides this, they carry very heavy chains round their necks, and waists, and legs; and they smear all their bodies and faces with ashes. And they carry a small brown horn at their necks, after the fashion of a trumpet, with which they call and beg for food at the door of any house where they arrive: chiefly at the houses of kings and great lords and at the temples; and they go many together, like the gipsies.[2] They are accustomed to stop very few days in each country. These people are commonly called jogues, and in their own speech they are called zoame, which means servant of God. They are brown, very well made and proportioned, of handsome faces; they wear their hair without ever combing it, and made into many plaits, wound round the head. And I asked them many times why they went in

[1] Bragueros de laton.

[2] Eyicianos.

this fashion. And they answered me, that they wore those chains upon their bodies as penance for the sin which they committed for allowing themselves to be captured by such bad people as the Moors, and that they went naked as a sign of dishonour, because they had allowed their lands and houses to be lost, in which God brought them up; and that they did not want more property since they had lost their own, for which they ought to have died; and that they smeared themselves with ashes in order to remind themselves perpetually that they were born of earth and had to return again to the earth, and that all the rest[1] was falsehood. And each one of them carries his little bag of these ashes with him; and all the Gentiles of the country honour them greatly, and receive from them some of these ashes, and put it on their heads,[2] shoulders, and breasts, making a few lines with it. And throughout all the country the Gentiles are in the habit of doing this. And so also throughout all India among the Gentiles, many of them turn jogues; but most of them are from the kingdom of Dely. These jogues eat all meats and do not observe any idolatry, and they mingle with all kinds of people: neither do they wash like other Gentiles, except when the wish to do so comes to them.

In this kingdom of Dely there are many very good horses, which are born and bred there. The people of the kingdom, both Moors and Gentiles, are very good fighting men and good knights, armed with many kinds of weapons; they are great bowmen, and very strong men; they have very good lances, swords, daggers, steel maces, and battle-axes, with which they fight; and they have some steel wheels, which they call chacarani, two fingers broad, sharp outside like knives, and without edge inside; and the surface of these[3] is of the size of a small plate. And they carry seven or

[1] Lo al, old expression for Lo demas.

[2] The Chulias or people of Southern India do this always.

[3] Or—these on being opened.

eight of these each, put on the left arm; and they take one and put it on the finger of the right hand, and make it spin round many times, and so they hurl it at their enemies, and if they hit anyone on the arm or leg or neck, it cuts through all. And with these they carry on much fighting, and are very dexterous with them.

This king of Dely confines with Tatars, and has taken many lands from the King of Cambay; and from the King of Dacan, his servants and captains, with many of his people, took much, and afterwards in time they revolted and set themselves up as kings. In this kingdom of Dely there are some trees, the root of which is called Baxarague,[1] and it is so poisonous that any one who eats it dies at once; and its fruit is called Nirabixy,[2] and it is of such virtue that it extinguishes all poison, and gives life to any one poisoned with the said root or with other poisons. These jogues, who come from the kingdom of Dely, carry this root and fruit; some of them give it to some Indian kings; and so likewise they carry with them sometimes rhinoceros' horn and Pajar stone, which possess great virtue against all poisons. And this stone, Pajar, is grey and soft, of the size of an almond; and they say that it is found in the head of an animal: it is greatly esteemed amongst the Indians.[3]

COUNTRY OF MALABAR.

Having passed the province of Tulynate, which is of the kingdom of Narsinga, along the coast of the sea, which province begins from Cinbola near the mountain Dely, and ends at the Cape of Conmery, which is a distance of seventy leagues along the coast towards the south and south-east. And there begins the country of Malabar, which was

[1] Baxana in Ramusio, and Braechagua in the Lisbon edition.

[2] Nirabixi in Ramusio and Miralexy in Lisbon edition.

[3] People in the East carry stones of this description, which are said to draw out the venom from the bite of a serpent.

governed by a king who was called Sernaperimal,[1] who was a very great lord. And after that the Moors of Mekkah discovered India, and began to navigate near it, which was six hundred and ten years ago; they used to touch at this country of Malabar on account of the pepper which is found there. And they began to load their ships with it in a city and seaport, Coulom,[2] where the king used frequently to be. And so for some years these Moors continued their voyages to this country of Malabar, and began to spread themselves through it, and became so intimate and friendly with the said king, that they made him turn Moor, and he went away with them to die at the house of Mekkah, and he died on the road. And before he set out from his country, he divided the whole of his kingdom of Malabar amongst his relations; and it remained divided amongst them and their descendants as it now is. And when he distributed the lands, he abandoned those that he gave, never to return to them again; and at last, when he had given away all, and there did not remain anything more for him to give, except ten or twelve leagues of land all round the spot from which he embarked, which was an uninhabited beach, where now stands the city of Calicut. And at that moment he was accompanied by more Moors than Gentiles, on account of having given to the latter almost all that he possessed, and he had with him only one young nephew, who waited on him as a page, to whom he gave that piece of land; and he told him to get it peopled, especially that very spot whence he embarked. And he gave him his sword and a chandelier, which he carried with him for state. And he left an injunction to the other lords, his relations to whom he had made gránts of lands, that they should obey him, only leaving exempt the

[1] Camoens addresses the King of Malabar as: "O nobre successor de Perimal." Canto viii, stanza 82.

[2] This agrees with the account of the Arab travellers of the ninth century. Paris, Langlès.

King of Coulam and the King of Cavanor:[1] so that he instituted three kings in the country of Malabar, and commanded that no one should coin money except the King of Calicut. And so he embarked at the same place where the city of Calicut was founded; and the Moors held this time and place in much veneration, and would not after that go and load pepper any more in any other part since the said king embarked there after becoming a Moor and going to die at Mekkah. This city of Calicut is very large, and ennobled by many very rich merchants and great traffic in goods. This king became greater and more powerful than all the others: he took the name of Zomodri,[2] which is a point of honour above all other kings. So that this great King of Malabar did not leave more kings than these three: that is to say, the Zomodry, who was named Cunelava-dyri, and the King of Culaon, who was named Benate-diry, and the King of Cananor, who was named Coletry.[3] And there are many other lords in the country of Malabar, who wish to call themselves kings; and they are not so, because they are not able to coin money, nor cover houses with roofs under penalty of all the others rising up against whomsoever should do such a thing, or of having to destroy them. And these kings of Culam and Cananor afterwards struck money for a certain time in their countries without having the power of doing so. In all the country they use one language, which is called Maleama, and all the kings are of one sect, and almost of the same customs.

In these kingdoms of Malabar there are eighteen sects of Gentiles, each one of which is much distinguished from the others in so great a degree that the ones will not touch the others under pain of death or dishonour or loss of their

[1] Cananor.

[2] Called Zamorin in other works, and Samorim by Camoens.

[3] Ramusio calls them Cunelanadyri, Benatederi, and Coletri; the Lisbon edition, Maly Couadary, Benatady, Cobertorim.

property: and all of them have separate customs in their idol-worship, as will be set forth further on.

CUSTOMS OF THE SAID KINGDOMS AND COUNTRY OF MALABAR.

In the first place, the Kings of Malabar are, as has been said, Gentiles, and honour their idols: they are brown, almost white, others are darker; they go naked from the waist upwards, and from the waist downwards are covered with white cotton wraps and some of them of silk. Sometimes they clothe themselves with short jackets open in front, reaching halfway down the thigh, made of very fine cotton cloth, fine scarlet cloth, or of silk and brocade. They wear their hair tied upon the top of their heads, and sometimes long hoods like Galician casques, and they are barefooted. They shave their beards and leave the moustaches[1] very long, after the manner of the Turks. Their ears are bored, and they wear in them very precious jewels and pearls set in gold, and on their arms from the elbows upwards gold bracelets, with similar jewels and strings of very large pearls. At their wrists over their clothes they wear jewelled girdles three fingers in width, very well wrought and of great value.

And on their breasts, shoulders, and foreheads, they make marks by threes with ashes, which they wear in accordance with the custom of their sect, saying that they do it to remind themselves that they have to turn to ashes: for when they die they burn their bodies, and so this ceremony continues among them. And many use it mixed with sandal wood, saffron, aloes wood, and rose water, all this ground up. When they are in their houses they always sit on high benches, and in houses without stories; these benches are very smooth, and are slightly smeared once every day with cow dung. And they keep there a stand very white and four fingers high, and a cloth of brown wool undyed, after

[1] Mostasos: old word, before introduction of bigotes from the German soldiers, and still used in Majorca.

the manner of a carpet of the size of a horsecloth[1] folded in three folds; and upon this they sit, and they lean upon pillows, round and long, of cotton, silk, or fine cloth. And they also sit on carpets of cloth of gold and silk; but they always keep under them, or near them, that cloth of brown wool, on account of their sect, and for state. And frequently they happen to be lying on couches and cushions of silk and very fine white sheets, and when any one comes to see them, they bring him this brown woollen cloth and put it near him, and when he goes out, a page carries the cloth folded before him for state and ceremony. And likewise he always keeps a sword near him, and when he changes from one spot to another, he carries it in his hand naked, as they always keep it. These kings do not marry, nor have a marriage law, only each one has a mistress, a lady of great lineage and family, which is called nayre, and said to be very beautiful and graceful. Each one keeps such a one with him near the palaces in a separate house, and gives her a certain sum each month, or each year, for expenses, and leaves her whenever she causes him discontent, and takes another. And many of them for honour's sake do not change them, nor make exchanges with them; and they seek much to please their king, for that honour and favour which they receive. And the children that are born from these mistresses are not held to be sons, nor do they inherit the kingdom, nor anything else of the king's; they only inherit the property of the mother. And whilst they are children, they are favoured by the king like children of other people whom he might be bringing up; but not like his own, because since they are men, the children are not accounted for more than as children of their mothers.[2] The king sometimes makes grants of money to them, for them to maintain themselves better than

1 Repostero: a cloth marked with the arms of a grandee for putting over a beast of burden, or hanging in a doorway,—a portière.

2 No valen mas de que ser hijos de sus madres.

the other nobles. The heirs of these kings are their brothers, or nephews, sons of their sisters, because they hold those to be their true successors, and because they know that they were born from the body of their sisters. These do not marry, nor have fixed husbands, and are very free and at liberty in doing what they please with themselves.

In this wise the lineage of the kings of this country, and the true stock, is in the women: that is to say, if a woman[1] gives birth to three or four sons and two or three daughters, the first is king, and so on, all the other brothers inherit from one another; and when all these have died, the son of the eldest sister, who is niece of the king, inherits, and so also his other heirs after him; and when these have deceased, the children of the next sister. And the kingdom always goes in this way to brothers, and nephews sons of sisters, and if by good or evil fortune these women happen not to give birth to male children, they do not consider them as capable of inheriting the kingdom; and these ladies, in such a case, all unite in council and institute some relation of theirs as king, if they have one, and if there is none, they name any other person for this office. And on this account the kings of Malabar are old men when they succeed to reign, and the nieces or sisters from whom has to proceed the lineage of the kings are held in great honour, guarded and served, and they possess revenues for their maintenance. And when one of these is of age to bring forth, on arriving at from thirteen to fourteen years, they prepare to make festivity and entertainment for her, and to make her enceinte. And they summon some young man, a nobleman and honourable person, of whom there are many deputed for this. And they send to fetch him that he may come for this purpose. And he comes, and they give him a great entertainment, and perform some ceremonies, and he ties some gold jewel to the neck of the damsel, and she wears it all her life in sign of her

[1] Sister of the king, apparently, from what follows.

having performed those ceremonies, in order to be able to do with herself whatever she chooses; because, until the performance of this ceremony, she could not dispose of herself. And the before mentioned youth remains with her for some days, very well attended to, and then returns to his land. And she sometimes remains in the family way, and sometimes not, and from this time forth for her pleasure she takes some Braman, whomsoever she likes best, and these are priests among them, and of these she has as many as she likes.

This King of Calicut, and so also the other kings of Malabar, when they die, are burned in the country with much sandal and aloes wood; and at the burning all the nephews and brothers and nearest relations collect together, and all the grandees of the realm, and confidantes of the king, and they lament for him and burn him. And before burning him they keep him there when dead for three days, waiting for the assembling of the above mentioned persons, that they may see him if he died of a natural death, or avenge his death if any one killed him, as they are obliged to do in case of a violent death. And they observe this ceremony very rigidly. After having burned him, all shave themselves from head to foot, excepting the eyelashes, from the prince, the heir to the throne, to the smallest child of the kingdom: that is, those who are Gentiles, and they also clean their teeth, and universally leave off eating betel for thirteen days from that time; and if in this period they find any one who eats it, his lips are cut off by the executioner. During these thirteen days the prince does not rule, nor is he enthroned as king, in order to see if in this time any one will rise up to oppose him; and when this term is accomplished, all the grandees and former governors make him swear to maintain all the laws of the late king, and to pay the debts which he owed, and to labour to recover that which other former kings had lost. And he takes this oath, holding a drawn sword in his left hand, and his right hand placed upon a chain lit up with many oil wicks, in the midst of which is a gold ring, which he touches with his fingers, and there he swears to maintain everything with that sword. When he has taken the oath, they sprinkle rice over his head, with many ceremonies of prayer and adoration to the sun, and immediately after certain counts, whom they call caymal,[1] along with all the others of the royal lineage, and the grandees, swear to him in the same manner to serve him, and to be loyal and true to him. During these thirteen days one of the caymals governs and rules the State like the king himself: he is like an accountant-general of the king, and of all the affairs of the kingdom. This office and dignity is his by right and inheritance. This person is also the chief treasurer of the kingdom, without whom the king cannot open or see the treasury; neither can the king take anything out of the treasury without a great necessity, and by the counsel of this person and several others. And all the laws and ordinances of the kingdom are in the keeping of this man. No one eats meat or fish in these thirteen days, nor may any one fish under pain of death. During that period large alms are given from the king's property, of food to many poor people, and to Bramans; and when the thirteen days are ended, all eat what they please, except the new king, who observes the same abstinence for one year, neither does he shave his beard, nor cut a hair of his head nor of his body, nor his nails: and he says prayers for certain hours of the day, and does not eat more than once a day. And before he eats he has to wash himself, and after washing, he must not drink anything until he has eaten. This king is always in the city of Calicut, in some very large palaces which he possesses outside of the city, and when the year of this mourning is accomplished, the prince who is to succeed him, and all those of the royal family and all the other grandees and nobles of the country,

[1] Ramusio, Caimaes; Lisbon edition, Cahimal.

come to see him, and to perform a ceremony, which takes place at the end of the year, in honour of the death of his predecessor: at which great alms are given, and much money is spent in giving food to many Bramans and poor people, and to all those who come to visit him, and to their retinues, so that more than a hundred thousand people are assembled there. And on this occasion he confirms the prince as the heir, and likewise the others as his successors step by step. And he confirms to all the lords their estates, and he confirms or changes as he sees fit the governors and officers who were under the former king. And he then dismisses them, and sends each to his duties, and he sends the prince to the estates which are assigned to him. And he must not re-enter Calicut until the king dies; and all the other successors may go and come to the court, and reside with the king. When the before mentioned crown prince departs, after he has left Calicut, and on passing the bridge of a river, he takes a bow in his hand and shoots an arrow towards the residence of the king, and then says a prayer with uplifted hands in the manner of prayer, and then goes on.

This prince, when he comes to visit the king at the said feast and ceremony, brings all his nobles with him, and his instruments of music, which are kettle-drums,[1] drums of many shapes, trumpets, horns, flutes, small brass plates,[2] and lutes;[3] these come making a great harmony, and the nobles in front, all drawn up in order, as they regulate processions here. That is to say, the bowmen in the van, next the lancers, after them the bearers of sword and buckler. And the king issues from the palaces and places himself at a great door, on foot, and there he stands looking at all these people who come up to him with great reverence, and do as though they worshipped him. All retire after a while, and so he remains for the space of two hours, until all have done, and the prince appears at a considerable distance[4] with a drawn

[1] Atabal. [2] Cymbals. [3] Sistra. [4] Of a cross-bow shot.

sword in his hand, which he brandishes as he advances, with his face raised up, and eyes fixed upon the king. And on seeing him, he worships him and throws himself with his face upon the ground, and with outstretched arms; and he lies thus for a short time, then gets up again, and goes forward very slowly brandishing his drawn sword in his hand, and with his eyes still fixed upon the king, and at half way he does the same thing again, and the king looks at him fixedly, without making any movement, and the prince gets up again, and so arrives where the king stands: and there he again throws himself on the ground in front of him. The king then goes forward two steps and takes him by the hand, and raises him up, and so they enter both together into the palaces. The king then sits on his dais, and the prince with all the other heirs, stand in front with their drawn swords in their right hands, and their left hands placed upon their mouths out of respect, withdrawn a little from the king's dais. They speak there to the king with much reverence, without speaking to one another, and if it is necessary for one to say anything to another, they speak so softly that no one hears them: so much so, that there are two thousand men before the king in the palace, and no one hears them; and they may not spit or cough before the king.

This King of Calicut keeps many clerks constantly in his palace, they are all in one room, separate and far from the king, sitting on benches, and there they write all the affairs of the king's revenue, and his alms, and the pay which is given to all, and the complaints which are presented to the king, and, at the same time, the accounts of the collectors of taxes. All this is on broad stiff leaves of the palm tree, without ink, with pens of iron: they make lines with their letters, engraven like ours. Each of these clerks has great bundles of these leaves written on, and blank, and wherever they go they carry them under their arms and the iron pen in their hand: in this way they are known to all people as scribes of the palace. And among these there are seven or eight who are great confidants of the king, and the most honoured, and who always stand before him with their pens in their hand, and writings under their arm, ready for the king's orders to do anything, as he is in the habit of doing. These clerks always have several of these leaves subscribed[1] by the king in blank, and when he commands them to despatch any business, they write it on those leaves. These accountants are persons of great credit, and most of them are old and respectable: and when they get up in the morning and want to write anything, the first time that they take the pen and the leaf in their hand, they cut a small piece off it with the knife which is at the end of the pen, and they write the names of their gods upon it and worship them towards the sun with uplifted hands; and having finished their prayer, they tear the writing and throw it away, and after that begin writing whatever they require.

This king has a thousand waiting women, to whom he gives regular pay, and they are always at the court, to sweep the palaces and houses of the king: and this he does for state, because fifty would be enough to sweep. These women are of good family, they come into the palace to sweep and clean twice every day, and each one carries a broom and a brass dish with cow dung dissolved in water; and all that they sweep, after having swept it, they smear it with their right hand, giving a very thin coating, which dries immediately. And these women do not all serve, but take turns in the service; and when the king goes from one house to another, or to some temple, on foot, these women go before him with these dishes of the said cow dung, spilling it on the road by which he has to pass. And these thousand women give a great feast to the king when he newly comes to the throne, after he has finished his year of mourning and abstinence. It is fitting to know that all the thousand assemble

[1] Sygnadas.

together, both the old and the young ones, in the king's house, very much adorned with jewellery, gold belts, pearls, and many bracelets of gold, and many rings with precious stones, and ankle rings of gold on their legs, and dressed from the waist downwards with very rich silk stuffs, and others of very fine cotton, and from the waist upwards bare, and anointed with sandal and perfumes, and their hair wreathed with flowers, and rings of gold and precious stones in their ears, the feet bare, as they always are accustomed to be. And they have there all sorts of musical instruments, and many guns and other fireworks of various kinds. Many nobles who accompany them come there very smart and gay, and are their admirers: and seven or eight elephants covered with silk housings and small bells in great quantity hanging to them, and large chains of iron suspended from their backs. And the ladies take an idol for their protector,[1] and put it on the top of the biggest elephant, and a priest who carries it in his arms sits on the back of the elephant. So they set out in procession with their music and rejoicing, and much firing of guns, going along a very broad street to a house of prayer. There they lower the idol which is to be seen with another which is in that temple, and they perform to them great ceremonies, and many people assemble to see and adore those idols, and pay honour to their images. These thousand women have each got a brass dish full of rice, and on the top of the rice lamps full of oil, with many lighted wicks, and between the chandeliers are many flowers. And at nightfall they set out from the temple with their idol for the king's palace, where they have to place it; and all come in procession before the idol which is set upon the elephant, in bands of eight, with the before mentioned salvers, and many men accompany them with oil, with which they replenish the lamps. And the nobles, their admirers, go along with them, talking to them with much courtesy;

[1] Valedor.

and they remove the perspiration from the ladies' faces, and from time to time put into their mouths the betel, which both men and women are constantly eating; and they fan them with fans, because their hands are fully occupied with the salvers. And all the instruments are sounding, and there is a great firing of rockets, and they carry some burning shrubs, so that it is a very pretty sight. Also at night some gentlemen go in front of the idol inflicting wounds with their swords upon their own heads and shoulders, and shouting like madmen, and foaming at the mouth like persons possessed: and they say that the gods enter into them and make them do this. Many tumblers and buffoons also go along performing feats of agility, and the governors and chief men of the city go there to direct and arrange that procession, which is conducted with much order until it arrives at the king's palace, where it disperses.

This king is for the most part sitting on his dais, and sometimes his confidential advisers are there, rubbing his arms and legs, or his body, and a page with a napkin round his neck full of betel, which he gives him to chew, and sometimes it is kept in a gilt and coloured casket edged with silver, and at times in a gold plate, and the page gives it to him leaf by leaf, smeared with a little lime of sea shells diluted with rose water, like a sauce, which he keeps in a small box[1] of gold; and he also gives him areca, which is a small fruit, cut into pieces, and he chews it all together; and it colours his mouth, and what he spits is like blood. And another page holds in his hand a large gold cup, into which he spits the juice of that leaf which he does not swallow, and he washes his mouth from time to time, so that he is almost always munching these leaves.

His manner of eating is that no one sees him eat: only four or five servants wait upon him. First of all, when he

[1] Buxen, not in the dictionaries: buxeta, a small casket for perfumes to put in the pocket, so called because made of bux or box; Anglicè, box.

wishes to eat, he bathes in a pool of water which he has in his palaces, very clean and prettily kept; and there, when undressed, he performs his ceremonies and worships three times to the east, and walks three times round, and plunges three more times under the water, and after that dresses in clean clothes, each time fresh washed; and then he goes and sits in the place which he has appointed for eating, the ground having been swept, or on a very low, round stand. There they bring him a large silver tray, and upon it are many small silver saucers, all empty. And they are set before him on the ground upon another low stand: and the cook comes, who is a Braman, and brings a copper pot with cooked rice, which is very dry and entire, and with a spoon they take it out, and make a pile of it in the middle of the said large tray; afterwards they bring many other pans with divers viands, and put portions of them into the small saucers. He then begins to eat with the right hand, taking handfuls of the rice without a spoon, and with the same hand he takes some of all the dishes and mixes it with the rice; and with his left hand he must not touch anything of what he eats; and they set near him a silver pitcher of water; and when he wants to drink, he takes it with the left hand, and raises it in the air, and pours the water into his mouth in a small jet; thus he drinks without the pitcher touching his mouth;[1] and the viands which they give him, both of flesh and fish, or vegetables and herbs, are done with so much pepper, so that no one from our parts could endure them in his mouth. And he never cleans his right hand, nor uses a napkin or cloth for that, whilst eating, until he has done eating, when he washes his hand. And if, during his meals, there should be present with him any honourable Bramans, in his confidence, he bids them eat there apart

[1] If the writer had been a Spaniard, especially from Catalonia, he would have added here, "in our fashion." This way of drinking extends into Roussillon, and this custom was not introduced by the Arabs.

from himself on the ground; and they set before them leaves of the Indian fig-tree, which are very large and stiff, a leaf for each man, and upon these they set food before them, the same as for the king; and he who is not going to eat there goes away, because no one else may be where the king eats; and when he has ended his meal, the king returns to his dais, and is almost always chewing betel. Whenever the king goes out of the palace to amuse himself, or to pray to some idol, all his gentlemen are summoned who are in waiting, and also the minstrels, and they carry the king in a litter, which is borne by men, and is covered with silk stuffs and jewels. Many jugglers and tumblers go before the king, with whom he amuses himself, and he stops frequently to look at them, and praises the one who performs best. And one Braman carries a sword and shield, and another a long gold sword, and another a sword in his right hand, which the King of all Malabar, who went to die at Mekkah, left behind him; and in his left hand a weapon which is like a fleur-de-lis. And on each side go two men with two fans, very long and round, and two others with two fans made of white tails of animals, which are like horses, and which are much valued amongst them, set on gold spears; these men fan the king, and close to them is a page with a gold pitcher full of water, and on the left side another with a silver one; and a page with a napkin, for when the king wishes to clean his nose, or if he touch his eyes or mouth, they pour water and wash his fingers, and the other gives him the napkin to dry them; they also carry vases, in which the king spits the betel. His nephews, governors, and other lords go along with him, and all accompany him with their swords drawn and shields. And a great quantity of buffoons, musicians, tumblers, and musqueteers firing guns accompany the king; and if he goes by night, they carry four large chandeliers of iron full of oil with many lighted wicks.

ON THE FASHION OF JUSTICE IN THE KINGDOM OF MALABAR.

In the said city of Calicut there is a governor, whom they call Talaxe, a gentleman appointed by the king,[1] who has under him five thousand gentlemen, to whom he pays their salaries from the revenue, which is assigned for that purpose. This person administers justice in the city of Calicut, and gives an account of everything to the king. And justice is administered according to the qualities of the persons, because there are divers sects and laws amongst them; that is to say, of gentlemen, Chetres, Guzurates, Brabares, who are very honourable people; and thence downwards there are also divers sects of low and base people who are all serfs of the king, or of the other lords and governors of the country. And if any of these low people commits a robbery, concerning which a complaint has been made to the king or to the governor, they send to take the robber, and if they find the thing stolen in his hands, or if he confess that he did it, if he is a Gentile, they take him to a place where they carry out executions, and there they set some high posts with sharp points and a small stand, through which passes one of those points; and there they cut off his head with a sword, and spit him through the back and the pit of the stomach, and that point comes out about a cubit, and on it they also spit his head. And they tie ropes to his legs and arms, and fasten them to four posts, so that the limbs are stretched out and the body on its back upon the stand. And if the malefactor is a Moor, they take him to a field, and there kill him by stabbing him; and the stolen property is appropriated to the governor without its owner recovering anything, because their law so disposes, doing justice on the

[1] Hidalgo por el Rey: an expression meaning a modern noble, not one whose origin is anterior to the Spanish monarchy: here it may imply official position only. Ramusio, Talassen; Lisbon edition, Talixe.

thief. And if the stolen property is found and the thief escapes, it is for a certain number of days in the charge of the governor; and if during that time they do not catch the thief, they return the stolen goods to its owner, a fourth part of it, however, remaining for the governor; and if the thief denies the robbery, they keep him eight days in prison, making his life uncomfortable, to see if he will confess, and throwing him his food; and when the eight days are passed without his confessing, they call the accuser, and he is told that the accused does not confess, and they ask him if he requires them to take his oath or let him go. If the accuser then requires the accused to swear, they make him wash and commend himself to his gods, and eat no betel, and cleanse his teeth from the blackness caused by the betel, in order that he may swear next day, and that he may prepare himself for it. Next day they take him out of prison, and take him to a pool of water where he washes, performing his ceremony, and from there they take him to a house of prayer where his idols are kept, before which he takes his oath in this manner. It must be known that, if he is a Gentile, they heat a copper-pot full of oil until it boils, and they throw in a few leaves of trees, and with the great heat of the pot the leaves fly out, and this is in order that the parties may see that the oil is hot and boiling; and then two scribes come near, and take the right hand of the accused and look if he has any wound of itch or other disease, and write down in what condition his hand is, in the presence of the party. Then they bid him look at the idol, and say three times "I did not commit this theft of which I am accused, nor do I know who did it," and then put his two fingers up to the middle joints in the oil which is boiling upon the fire; and he does so; and they say that if he did not commit the theft, that he does not burn himself, and that if he did it, he burns his fingers.

[And then the scribes, and governor and party, look at

him again, and the scribes write down the condition in which his hand is, and they tie it up with a cloth whether it is burned or not, and put seals on the fastenings of the cloth, and send him back to prison. And three days later, all return to the same place where the oath was taken, and they untie his hand before the governor and party, and if they find it burned they kill him, but first give him so many torments that they make him confess where he has got the stolen property, or that he did it. And even if he does not confess, all the same he suffers the penalty because his hand was burned; and if they find his hand not burned, then they let him go, and he who accused him pays a certain sum as a fine to the governor. And they have the same method for him who kills another, or for him who kills a cow, or raises his hand in anger against Bramans or noblemen. And this is to be understood as amongst the Gentile peasants and low people. And if it is a Moor who does such things, he passes through the same examinations, only that instead of putting his fingers in oil, they make him lick with his tongue a red-hot axe, and if he does not burn himself he remains free, and if he burns his tongue he suffers death.

And if any of the common people, whether Gentiles or Moors, commit other offences for which they do not deserve death, they punish them with a pecuniary penalty for the governor, and this produces much revenue to him; and he lays hold of vagabonds as slaves, and he has the power of selling them, and sells them without any opposition whatever, at a price of from four to five ducats.

The nobles enjoy exemption and the privilege, that they cannot be taken and put in irons for anything which they do. And if a noble were to rob or kill any one, or kill a cow, or were to sleep with a woman of low caste, or of the Bramans, or if he eat or drank in the house of a low caste man, or spoke ill of his king—this being established by his own words—they call three or four honourable gentlemen in whom the king places confidence, and he bids them go and kill this noble wherever they may meet with him, and they give them a warrant[1] signed by the king for them to kill him without penalty. They then kill him with daggers or spears, or shoot him with arrows, because at times these men who are accused are such that before being put to death, they wound two or three of the slaughterers, if they have been forewarned. And after he is dead they lay him on his back and place that king's warrant upon his breast. And if they kill him in the country they leave him there, and no one comes near him, so that the fowls and dogs devour him. And if they kill him in the city, the people of the street where he lies dead go and beg the king to order his removal; and the king gives the orders, sometimes as a favour, sometimes with a fine.[2]]

And if any noble comes to the king or to the governor, and complains to him of any other noble who has robbed or murdered or done any other evil deed, the governor reports it to the king, and the king gives orders to summon the accused, and if he absents himself they hold him guilty, and he is ordered to be executed in the same manner without further investigation. And if he presents himself, they summon the accuser, and examine both of them together. And the accuser takes a small branch of a tree or green herbs in his hand, and says, such a one did such a thing; the other one takes another branch, and denies it. The king then bids them return eight days thenceforward to the house of the governor to take oath and prove that which each one asserts; and so they depart, and return on the day

[1] Albalá, from Alberat, Letters Patent, Brevet, Warrant, Letter for drawing Pay. This word is in little use in Castile, but is common in Valencia and Aragon. Spanish, Latin, and Arabic Dict., Fr. Francisco Cañes. Madrid, 1787.

[2] This part is wanting in Ramusio, who says a little lower down, "Here several lines are wanting."

fixed to the house of the governor, where the accused swears in the manner already described with boiling butter, and having concluded taking the oath, they tie up his fingers as has been said, and both of them are detained in a house under a guard, so that neither of them can run away. And on the third day they untie his fingers, and clear up the truth, and if they find the fingers burned, they kill the accused; and not finding them injured, they kill the accuser. And if the accused is not of as great value, they do not kill the accuser, on whom in such case they inflict a pecuniary penalty and that of banishment. And if such a noble was accused of a great robbery of the king's property, they have him imprisoned in a close room and well guarded, and conduct him thence to take the oath.

In this kingdom of Calicut there is another governor, who is like the chief justice of all the kingdom, with the exception of the city of Calicut. This chief justice is called Coytoro tical carnaver; he has his lieutenants in all the villages, to whom he farms the administration of justice: that is to say, the fines, not capital penalties. And people come to this chief justice for any injury, and he gives an account of it and reports to the king, and renders justice in the manner followed at Calicut.

In this kingdom of Calicut no women ever die by sentence of law for any offence whatever; they are only subject to pecuniary penalties. And if any woman of Nayr family should offend against the law of her sect, and the king know of it before her relations and brothers, he commands her to be taken and sold out of the kingdom to Moors or Christians. And if her male relations or sons know of it first, they shut her up and kill her with dagger or spear wounds, saying that if they did not do so they would remain greatly dishonoured. And the king holds this to be well done.

SECTION OF THE BRAMANS AND THEIR CUSTOMS.

The Gentile Bramans are priests all of one lineage, and others cannot be priests, but only their own sons. And when these are seven years old, they put round their necks a strap two fingers in width of an animal which they call Cressua mergan,[1] with its hair, which is like a wild ass; and they command him not to eat betel for seven years, and all this time he wears that strap round the neck, passing under the arm, and when he reaches fourteen years of age they make him a Braman, removing from him the leather strap round his neck, and putting on another of three threads, which he wears all his life as a mark of being a Braman. And they do this with much ceremony and festivity, just as here at the first mass,[2] and from this time forward he may eat betel. They do not eat flesh nor fish, they are much reverenced and honoured by the Indians, and they are not executed for any offence which they may commit: but their chief, who is like a bishop, chastises them in moderation. They marry only once, and only the eldest brother has to be married, and of him is made a head of the family like a sole heir by entail,[3] and all the others remain bachelors, and never marry. The eldest is the heir of all the property. These Bramans, the elder brothers, keep their wives very well guarded, and in great esteem, and no other man can approach them; and if any of the married ones die, the person who becomes widowed does not marry again. And if the wife commits adultery, the husband kills her with poison. These young men who do not marry, nor can marry, sleep with the wives of the nobles, and these women hold it as a great honour because they are Bramans, and no woman refuses

[1] Or it may be read Ciessua; Ramusio, Cressuamengan; Lisbon edition, Cryuamergam.

[2] That is, the first mass said by a new priest.

[3] Como mayorazgo.

them. And they must not sleep with any woman older thân themselves. And these live in their houses and estates, and they have great houses of prayer, in which they do service as abbots, and whither they go to rècite their prayers at fixed times of the day, and worship their idols and perform their ceremonies. And these temples have their principal doors to the west, and each temple has three doors, and in front of the principal gate, outside of it, is a stone of the height of a man, with three steps all round it, and in front of that stone inside the church is a small chapel, very dark, inside of which they keep their idol, of gold, silver, or metal, and three lamps burning. And no one may enter there except the minister of that church, who goes in to set before the idol flowers and scented herbs, and they anoint it with sandal and rose water, and take it out once in the morning, and another time in the evening with sound of trumpets and drums, and horns. And he who takes it out first washes thoroughly, and carries it on his head with the face looking backwards, and they walk with it three times in procession round the church, and certain wives of the Bramans carry lighted lamps in front, and each time that they reach the principal door, they set the idol on that stone and there worship it, and perform certain ceremonies; and having ended the three turns with music and rejoicing, they again place it in the chapel, and each day they do this twice, by day and at night. And around this church there is a stone wall, between which and the church they walk in the before mentioned procession, and they carry over the idol a very lofty canopy upon a very long bamboo for state as for kings. They place all the offerings upon the stone before the principal gate of the temple, and twice a day it is washed, and they set cooked rice upon it to feed the crows twice a day with great ceremony. These Bramans greatly honour the number trine: they hold that there is a God in three persons, and who is not more than one. All their prayers and ceremonies are in honour of the trinity, and they, so to say, figure it in their rites, and the name by which they call it is this, Berma Besnu Maycereni, who are three persons and one sole god.[1] Thus they confess him to be from the beginning of the world. They have no knowledge or information of the coming of Jesus Christ. They believe many more vain things, which they speak of. These people each time that they wash put some ashes upon their heads, foreheads and breasts, in token that they have to turn again into ashes; and when they die they have their bodies burned. When the wife of a Braman is in the family way, as soon as the husband knows it he cleans his teeth, and eats no more betel nor trims his beard, and fasts until his wife gives birth to her child. The kings make great use of these Bramans for many things, except in deeds of arms. Only Bramans can cook the king's food, or else men of the king's own family, and so all the king's relations have this same custom of having their food cooked by Bramans. These are the messengers who go on the road from one kingdom to another, with letters and money and merchandise, because they pass in safety in all parts, without any one molesting them, even though the kings may be at war. These Bramans are well read in the law of their idolatry, and possess many books, and are learned and masters of many arts: and so the kings honour them as such.

[1] See Cardinal Wiseman's Lectures with regard to this subject, also the work of another Catholic author, where this Hindu doctrine is termed an *adumbration.* The Abbé Huc is opposed to the above-mentioned divines, and calls this a *counterfeit of Satan.* Unless his theory, or another alternative, be adopted, it must be assumed, since the Brahminical books were contemporary with David, perhaps with Moses, that the Hindus were more favoured than the Chosen People of Israel: which is impossible.

"Il faut ajouter que la science brâhmanique n'a pas été étrangère au développement du génie grec, l'une des sources de notre civilisation, ni à la formation du christianisme, religion de tout l'Occident." M. Emile Burnouf, La Civilisation Chrétienne en Orient, Revue des deux Mondes, 1er Juin, 1865, pp. 632, 633; see also pp. 638, 639.

SECTION OF THE NAIRS OF MALABAR, WHO ARE THE GENTRY, AND THEIR CUSTOMS.

In these kingdoms of Malabar there is another sect of people called nairs, who are the gentry, and have no other duty than to carry on war, and they continually carry their arms with them, which are swords, bows, arrows, bucklers, and lances. They all live with the kings, and some of them with other lords, relations of the king, and lords of the country, and with the salaried governors; and with one another. And no one can be a nair if he is not of good lineage. They are very smart men, and much taken up with their nobility. They do not associate with any peasant, and neither eat nor drink except in the houses of other nairs. These people accompany their lords day and night; little is given them for eating and sleeping, and for serving and doing their duty; and frequently they sleep upon a bare bench to wait for the person whom they serve, and sometimes they do not eat more than once a day; and they have small expenses for they have little pay. Many of them content themselves with about two hundred maravedis[1] each month for themselves and the servant that attends to them. These are not married nor maintain women or children; their nephews the sons of their sisters are their heirs. The nair women are all accustomed to do with themselves what they please with bramans or nairs, but not with other people of lower class under pain of death. After they are ten or twelve years old or more, their mothers perform a marriage ceremony for them in this manner. They advise the relations and friends that they may come to do honour to their daughters, and they beg some of their relations and friends to marry these daughters, and they do so. It must be said they have a small gold jewel made, which will contain half a ducat of

[1] This may be estimated from the value of rice, 150 to 200 maravedis the 4 bushels or 90 lbs. See above.

gold, a little shorter than the tag of a lace, with a hole in the middle passing through it, and they string it on a thread of white silk; and the mother of the girl stands with her daughter very much dressed out, entertaining her with music and singing, and a number of people. And this relation or friend of hers comes with much earnestness, and there performs the ceremony of marriage, as though he married with her, and they throw a gold chain round the necks of both of them together, and he puts the above mentioned jewel round her neck, which she always has to wear as a sign that she may now do what she pleases. [1] And the bridegroom leaves her, and goes away without touching her nor having

[1] The explanation of this ceremony is to be found in Plato :—

"We said, you remember, that the children ought to be the issue of parents who are still in their prime." "True." "And do you agree with me that the prime of life may be reasonably reckoned at a period of twenty years for a woman, and thirty for a man ?" "Where do you place these years ?" "I should make it the rule for a woman to bear children to the state from her twentieth to her fortieth year : and for a man, after getting over the sharpest burst in the race of life, thenceforward to beget children to the state until he is fifty-five years old." "Doubtless," he said, "in both sexes, this is the period of their prime both of body and mind." "If, then, a man who is either above or under this age shall meddle with the business of begetting children for the commonwealth, we shall declare his act to be an offence against religion and justice ; inasmuch as he is raising up a child for the state, who, should detection be avoided, instead of having been begotten under the sanction of those sacrifices and prayers, which are to be offered up at every marriage ceremonial by priests and priestesses, and by the whole city, to the effect that the children to be born may ever be more virtuous and more useful than their virtuous and useful parents, will have been conceived under cover of darkness by aid of dire incontinence." "You are right." "The same law will hold should a man, who is still of an age to be a father, meddle with a woman, who is also of the proper age, *without the introduction of a magistrate ; for we shall accuse him of raising up to the state an illegitimate, unsponsored, and unhallowed child.*" "You are perfectly right." "But as soon as the women and the men are past the prescribed age, we shall allow the latter I imagine to associate freely with whomsoever they please, so that it be not a daughter, or mother, or daughter's child, or grandmother ; and in like manner we

more to say to her, on account of being her relation; and if he is not so, he may remain with her if he wish it, but he is not bound to do so if he do not desire it. And from that time forward the mother goes begging some young men, "que le desvirguen aquella hija, porque lo an entre sy por cosa sucia y casi vileza a desvirgar mugeres." And after she is already a woman the mother goes about seeking who will take her daughter to live with him. But when she is very pretty three or four nairs join together and agree to maintain her, and to live all of them with her; and the more she has the more highly is she esteemed, and each man has his ap-

shall permit the women to associate with any man, except a son or a father." Republic, book v, sect. 461. Davis and Vaughan's Translation, p. 190.

"Explicemus jam tandem, quam nam florentem ætatem in utroque sexu existimemus, mulierem porro florenti esse ætate arbitramur, si a vigesimo ætatis suæ anno usque ad quadragesimum generationi incumbat, virum autem a trigesimo usque ad quinquagesimum quintum operam suam in gignendo civitati præbere præcipimus, in hoc enim annorum cursu et robur corporis, et prudentiæ vim sexus utriusque consistere certum est. Si quis igitur vel senior vel junior his generationes eas, quæ ad publicum civitatis commodum ordinatæ sunt, attigerit profanum et illegitimum hoc esse censebimus, quasi civitati fœtum largiatur, qui si latuerit non sacrificiorum vel præcationum fiat inauguratione, quas tamen in singulis nuptiis cum universâ civitate peragent sacerdotes, ut ex bonis meliores et ex utilibus utiliores semper enascantur vota concipientes; sed id fiat sub tenebris ex vehementis cujusdam incontinentiæ libidine, eadem autem lex etiam erit servanda, si quis eorum qui et in ætate sunt apta ad matrimonium contrahendum, non assentiente tamen magistratu ad mulieres ætate nubiles accesserit, hunc enim statuemus edere civitati spurium profanum, et illegitimum partum; ubi vero et mulieres, et viri statutum generationi tempus pertransierint, *immunes a lege faciemus ut possint cum quacumque libuerit commisceri;* præter quam cum filia et matre et filiis filiarum ac matris ascendentibus; *et parem concedemus quoque libertatem mulieribus, ut possint cum quovis conjungi,* præter quam cum filio, vel patre, et ascendentibus, vel descendentibus ex his, quæ omnia, ubi mandaverimus curabimus, ne partus ullus omnino ex hujusmodi coitibus ortus in lucem proferatur, quod si proferetur sic expositus sit perinde ac quasi nulla ei adsint alimenta." Plato's Republic, book v. Translation of John Sozomenus, Venice, 1626.

pointed day from mid-day till next day at the same hour, when the other comes; and so she passes her life without anyone thinking ill of it. And he who wishes to leave her, does so whenever he pleases, and goes to take another. And if she takes a dislike to any of them she dismisses him. The children which she has remain at the expense of the mother and of the brothers of the mother, who bring them up, because they do not know the fathers, and even if they should appear to belong to any persons in particular, they are not recognised by them as sons, nor do they give anything for them. And it is said that the kings made this law in order that the nairs should not be covetous, and should not abandon the king's service.[1]

[1] Plato perhaps got this idea as well as others from India:

"Consider, then, I continued, whether the following plan is the right one for their lives and their dwellings, if they are to be of the character I have described. In the first place no one should *possess any private property*, if it can possibly be avoided: secondly, *no one should have a dwelling or storehouse into which all who please may not enter*; whatever necessaries are required by temperate and courageous men who are trained to war, they should receive by regular appointment from their fellow-citizens, as wages for their services, and the amount should be such as to leave neither a surplus on the year's consumption nor a deficit...; but whenever they come to possess lands and houses and money of their own, they will be householders and cultivators instead of guardians, and will become hostile masters of their fellow-citizens rather than their allies." Republic, book iii, sect. 417. Davis and Vaughan's Translation, pp. 129, 130.

"Itaque Adiutores communes habere filios et uxores summopere expedit, quæ et consentiunt omnino iis quæ superius a nobis dicta sunt, diximus enim *hos neque domos proprias habere debere; neque terram possidere, vel aliud quidpiam in bonis adnumerare*: sed a cæteris enutritos hanc quasi custodiæ mercedem accipere, quam et in communi positam consumant, si re vera custodes futuri sunt; ut et quæ prius a nobis dicta sunt, et quæ nunc etiam dicuntur efficiant ipsos veros custodes, et ne Rempublicam in partes dividant; sed ut uno potius animo de propriis judicantes, et ad id tendantes omnes, uno eodemque et doloris et voluptatis sensu afficiantur." Platonis de Rebuspublicis, liber quintus. A Joanne Sozomeno, Venetiis, 1626.

"Etenim Plato cum multas Regiones lustrasset, et mores hominum varios inspexisset, ac sui temporis Respublicas contemplatus abundé

These nairs, besides being all of noble descent, have to be armed as knights by the hand of the king or lord with whom they live, and until they have been so equipped they cannot bear arms nor call themselves nairs, but they enjoy the freedom and exemption and advantages of the nairs in many things. In general when these nairs are seven years of age they are immediately sent to school to learn all manner of feats of agility and gymnastics for the use of their weapons. First they learn to dance, and then to tumble, and for that purpose they render supple all their limbs from their childhood, so that they can bend them in any direction. And after they have exercised in this, they teach them to manage the weapons which suit each one most. That is to say bows, clubs, or lances; and most of them are taught to use the sword and buckler, which is of more common use among them. In this fencing there is much agility and science. And there are very skilful men who teach this art, and they are called Panicars;[1] these are captains in war. These nairs when they enlist to live with the king, bind themselves and promise to die for him; and they do likewise with any other lord from whom they receive pay. This law is observed by some and not by others; but their obligation constrains them to die at the hands of anyone who should kill the king or their lord: and some of them so observe it; so that if in any battle their lord should be killed, they go and put themselves in the midst of the enemies who killed him, even should those be numerous, and he alone by himself dies there: but before falling he does what he can against them; and after that one is dead another goes to take his place, and then another: so that sometimes ten or twelve nayrs die for their lord. And

fuisset, nec non antiquorum philosophorum ac legumlatorum monumenta studiosissime perquisivisset, senior tandem factus, politias quidem omnes nihil aliud esse intelligens, nisi concordem quandam in societate civili Regulam, ac ordinem quo eædem continerentur." Joannes Sozomenus Lectoribus.

[1] Or it might be Pasicars.

even if they were not present with him when he was killed, they go and seek him who killed him, or the king who ordered him to be killed: and so one by one they all die. And if anyone is in apprehension of another man, he takes some of these nairs, as many as he pleases, into his pay; and they accompany and guard him; and on their account he goes securely, since no one dares to molest him; because if he were molested they and all their lineage would take vengeance on him who should cause this molestation. These guards are called Janguada:[1] and there are some people who sometimes take so many of these nairs, and of such quality, that on their account they no longer fear the king, who would not venture to command the execution of a man who was guarded by these, in order not to expose many nairs to danger for it. And even if the nairs were not in his company when the man they guard was killed, they would not any the less revenge his death.

These nayrs live outside the towns, separate from other people, on their estates which are fenced in. They have there all that they require; they do not drink wine. When they go anywhere they shout to the peasants that they may get out of the way where they have to pass; and the peasants do so, and if they did not do it the nayrs might kill them without penalty. If a young man of family who is very poor meets a rich and respectable peasant, one favoured by the king, he makes him get out of the road in the same manner, as if he were a king. These nayrs have great privileges in this matter, and the nayr women even greater with the peasants, and the nairs with the peasant women. This, they say, is done to avoid all opportunity of mixing their blood with that of peasants. And if a peasant were by misfortune to touch a nayr lady, her relations would immediately kill her and likewise the man that touched her, and all his relations, When these nayrs order any work to

[1] Ramusio, *Sanguada*. Not in Lisbon edition.

be done by the peasants, or buy anything of them which they take, being between man and man, they are not exposed to any other penalty on touching one another than the not being able to enter their houses without first washing themselves and changing their clothes for others that are clean. And likewise as regards the nair women and the peasant women: these practices are more observed in the country.

No nair woman ever enters the towns under pain of death except once a year, when they may go for one night with their nayrs wherever they like. On that night more than twenty thousand nair women enter Calicut to see the town, which is full of lamps in all the streets, which the inhabitants set there to do honour to the nairs, and all the streets are hung with cloth. And the nair women come in to see the houses of their friends and of their husbands, and there they receive presents and entertainment, and are invited to eat betel: and it is held to be a great politeness to receive it from friends. Some of them come wrapped up,[1] and others uncovered; and the women relations of the kings and great lords come also to see the city on this night, and to walk about it, looking at the property of the great merchants, from whom they receive presents, in order that they may favour them with the king.

Those nayrs whom the king has received as his, he never dismisses however old they may be; on the contrary, they always receive their pay and rations, and he grants favours to whoever has served well. And if some years should pass without their being paid, some four or five hundred of the aggrieved rise up, and go in a body to the palace, and send word to the king that they are going away dismissed, to take service with another king, because he does not give them food. Then the king sends to beg them to have patience, and that he will send and pay them immediately. And if he does not immediately give them a third part of what is

[1] Enbarbatadas.

due, and an order for the payment of the rest, they go away to another king, wherever it appears to them that they can best suit themselves; and they engage with him, and he receives them willingly, and gives them food for thirteen days before he has them enrolled for pay. And during this time this king sends to inquire of their king if he intends to send and pay them; and if he does not pay them, then he receives them in his pay, and gives them the same allowances which they had in their own country, from which and from their king in such a case they remain disnaturalized. And many undertake, but few perform this, because their king grants them a remedy, and holds it to be a great disgrace should they go away.

When these nayrs go to the wars their pay is served out to them every day as long as the war lasts; it is four taras per day each man, which are worth five maravedis each,[1] with which they provide for themselves. And during the time that they are at war, they may touch any peasant, and eat and drink with them in their houses, without any penalty. And the king is obliged to maintain the mother and family of any nayr who may die in the war, and those persons are at once written down for their maintenance. And if these nayrs are wounded, the king has them cured at his expense, besides their pay, and has food given them all their lives, or until they are cured of their wounds.

These nayrs show much respect to their mothers,[2] and

[1] That is 20 maravedis a day, about three times the peace allowance. See p. 124. Ramusio says 40 cas a day, which are 40 maravedis; the Lisbon edition has 4 taras a day.

[2] Though the nairs were deprived of their fathers, it appears that they retained their own family relations: the "divine Plato!" however, goes beyond his Hindu teachers, and would have reduced men altogether to the condition of brutes. He says:

"But how are they to distinguish fathers and daughters, and the relations you described just now?" "Not at all, I replied; only all the children that are born between the seventh and tenth month from the day on

support them with what they gain, because besides their allowances, most of them possess houses and palm trees and estates, and some houses let to peasants, which have been granted by the king to them or to their uncles, and which remain their property. They also have much respect for their elder sisters, whom they treat as mothers. And they do not enter into a room with those that are young girls, nor touch them nor speak to them, saying that it would give occasion to sin with them, because they are younger and have less understanding, which could not happen with the elder ones, on account of the respect they have for them. These nair women every month set themselves apart in their houses for three days without approaching anyone; at which time a

which one of their number was married, are to be called by him, if male, his sons, if female, his daughters; and they shall call him father, and their children he shall call his grandchildren; these again shall call him and his fellow-bridegrooms and brides, grandfathers and grandmothers; likewise all shall regard as brothers and sisters those that were born in the period during which their own fathers and mothers were bringing them into the world; and as we said just now, all these shall refrain from touching one another. But the law will allow intercourse between brothers and sisters, if the lot chances to fall that way, and if the Delphian priestess also gives it her sanction." Republic, book v, §461. Davies and Vaughan's Translation, p. 190.

"At dices quomodo patres, et filiæ, ac cæteræ hujusmodi personæ, inter quas interdicta est conjunctio, cognoscent se invicem; siquidem, ut dictum superius est *post editos partus permiscendi sunt in ovili fœtus omnes, ut neque mater, quæ genuit, vel proprium filium a ceteris dignoscat?* Verum tamen non est difficile hanc solvere difficultatem, etenim quicumque nascentur partus, a quo primum die quis sponsus factus fuerit post decimum mensem vel post septimum, hos omnes filios suos nominabit, et fœminas pari modo filias, et illi vice versa ipsum patrem appellabunt, eosque qui ex his nascentur filios filiorum vocabit; illi è contra hos et avos, et avias, eos verò omnes, qui eodem tempore nati fuerint, quo matres ipsorum generabant, sorores, ac fratres nuncupabunt; quæ servata regula quod modò dicebamus a mutuo hi concubitu abstinebunt; fratres autem ac sorores, si sors ita tulerit, et annuerit Pithiæ oraculum, lex cohabitare permittet: talis erit itaque nobis constituenda, inter custodes nostros communitas mulierum et filiorum." De Rebuspubl., liber quintus.

woman has to prepare her food in separate pots and pans. And when the three days are ended, she bathes with hot water which is brought there, and after bathing dresses in clean clothes, and so goes out of the house to a pool of water and bathes again, and again leaves those clean clothes, and takes other fresh ones, and so returns home, and talks with her mother and sisters and the other people. And the room where she was for those three days is well swept and wetted, and plastered with cow dung, because otherwise no one would dwell there. These women when they are confined, three days afterwards are washed with hot water, and after getting up from their confinement they bathe many times each day from head to foot. They do no business, eat the bread of idleness, and only get their food to eat by means of their bodies : because besides each one having three or four men who provide for them, they do not refuse themselves to any braman or nayr who pays them. They are very clean and well dressed women, and they hold it in great honour to know how to please men. They have a belief amongst them that the woman who dies a virgin does not go to paradise.[1]

SECTION OF THE BRABARES WHO ARE MERCHANTS OF THE KINGDOM OF MALABAR, OF THEIR CUSTOMS AND SECT.

In this kingdom of Calicut, and in all the other Malabar kingdoms, there is a sect of gentile merchants who are called amongst them brabares, who trafficked also before foreign persons came to port or navigated in these seas. These still deal, especially in the interior, in all sorts of goods, and col-

[1] This legalised disorder appears to be exaggerated, but it is the natural consequence and result of the carrying out of Plato's theories with regard to the destruction of family among the nairs or military caste. It is singular that the author of such extravagant abominations should have found acceptance because he wrote in the Hellenic language.

"Such are the main features of Plato's Republic, in reference to his Guardians. They afford a memorable example of that philosophical analysis, applied to the circumstances of man and society, which the

lect all the pepper and ginger from the nayrs and cultivators, and frequently buy them in advance in exchange for cotton stuffs, and other goods which come from beyond the sea. These people are also great changers, and gain much upon coin. They enjoy such freedom in this country that the kings cannot sentence them to death, but the chief men of these brabares assemble together in council, and having arrived at the knowledge that the offender deserves death, they kill him, the king having information thereof: and if the king knows first of the offence before them, he informs them of it, and they kill him with dagger or lance thrusts. For the most part they are very rich people, and possess in the country many estates inherited from old times. They marry only one wife in our fashion, and their sons are their immediate heirs; and when they die their bodies are burned, and their wives accompany the body weeping for him: and she takes from her neck a small gold jewel which he gave her when he married her, and she throws it into the fire upon him, and then returns to her house, and never more can be married, however young she may be. And if she were to die before her husband he has her burned, and may marry again.

These people are of as pure lineage as the nairs, men and women, and they may touch one another.

SECTION OF THE CUJAVEN, WHO ARE POTTERS AND WORKERS OF CLAY.

There is another sect of people among the Indians of Malabar, which is called Cujaven, and which is only separated from the nayrs on account of a fault which they committed.[1] For this reason they remained as a separate

Greek mind was the first to conceive and follow. Plato lays down his ends with great distinctness as well as the means whereby he proposes to attain them. Granting his ends, the means proposed are almost always suitable and appropriate, whether practicable or otherwise." Grote's Plato, vol. iii, p. 207.

[1] "If one of the soldiers deserts his rank or throw away his arms,

sect. Their business is to work at baked clay, and tiles for covering houses, with which the temples and Royal buildings are roofed; and by law no other persons may roof their houses except with palm branches. Their idolatry and their idols are different from those of the others; and in their houses of prayer they perform a thousand acts of witchcraft and necromancy; they call their temples pagodes, and they are separate from the others. Their descendants cannot take any other sect nor any other occupation. In their marriages they follow the law of the nayrs. The nayrs may cohabit with their women, provided that they do not re-enter their houses without washing themselves from that sin, and putting on a change of clean garments.

SECTION OF THE WASHERMEN.

In this country there is another sect of gentiles whom they call manatamar,[1] and their business is only to wash the clothes of the bramans, kings, and nayrs; and they live by this business, and they cannot adopt other employments, nor can their descendants. The men are those that wash, and they wash in their houses in large tanks and reservoirs which they have got for this purpose. They have constantly in their houses such a large quantity of clothes to wash, both of their own and of strangers, that they hire out many of them day by day to the nayrs who have not got their own, and they pay so much a day for them when clean; and so each day they return them the dirty ones, and fetch away clean clothes. And the clothes have to be suitable to each person. They

or is guilty of any such act of cowardice, must we not degrade him to the rank of an artisan, or an agricultural labourer?" "Decidedly." Republic, book v, sect. 468. Davis and Vaughan's Translation, p. 200.

"Existimo autem imprimis ego eum, qui ordinem deseruevit, vel arma abjecerit, vel tale quid ex ignavia commiserit, in Opificum aut Agricolarum ordinem amandandum esse." Platonis de Rebuspubl., liber quintus.

[1] Ramusio, Manantamar; Lisbon edition, Mainatos.

wash for a great many people for money, so that they serve all with cleanliness, and they all gain their livelihoods very sufficiently. Their lineage does not mix with any other, neither can any other with theirs ; only the nayrs can have mistresses from amongst the women of this lineage, with the condition that each time that they approach them, they have to bathe themselves and change their garments before entering their houses. These washermen have got idolatries of their own, and their houses of prayer are separate, and they believe in many extravagant things. They marry like the nairs, their brothers and nephews inherit their property, and they do not recognise their sons.

SECTION OF THE WEAVERS OF THE MALABAR COUNTRY.

There is another set of gentiles, still lower, whom they call chalien, who are weavers and have no other business except to weave cloths of cotton, and some of silk, which are of little value, and are used by the common people. And these also have a sect and form of idolatry apart. Their lineage does not mix with any others ; only the nairs may have mistresses amongst the women of these people, so that they do not enter their houses without bathing and changing their clothes, whenever they have visited them. Many of these are sons of nairs, and so they are very fine men in their figures ; and they bear arms like the nayrs and go to the wars, and fight very well. In marriages they have the law of the nairs, and their sons do not inherit. Their wives have the power of doing what they please with themselves with the nairs, or with other weavers : and they cannot mix with any other lineage under pain of death.[1]

[1] Plato explains the object of this regulation :

"Itaque sacra deinceps connubia quam maxime fieri poterit efficiemus : erunt autem sacra constituenda, quæ utilissima fuerint, utilissima verò erunt, si lege marium cum feminis conjunctiones præscribantur, et tale quid in his conjunctionibus observetur, quale in propagatione cete-

SECTION OF LOW PEOPLE: ZIVIL TIVER.

Of low people zevil tiver,[1] there are eleven sects, which no respectable people touch under pain of death: and between each other there is a great difference and separation, and one family does not mix with another. The best of these are labourers, whom they call tiver. Their principal employment is to till the palm trees, and gather their fruits; and to carry everything for hire from one point to another, because they are not in the habit of transporting them with beasts of burden, as there are none: and they hew stone, and gain their livelihood by all kinds of labour. Some of them learn the use of arms, and fight in the wars when it is necessary. They all carry a staff in their hand of a fathom's length as a sign of their lineage. Most of them are serfs of the nayrs, to whom the king of the country gives them, in order that their masters may be supported by their labour,

rorum animalium ab iis observatum videmus, quibus id est propositum, ut quam generosi partus edantur, etenim licet sæpe sæpius animadvertere eos qui vel canes venatorios alunt, vel generosas aves enutriunt, et si generosas omnes existiment, eximias tamen ac præstantissimas quasdam e reliquarum numero eligere, ex quibus præcipue progenies suscipiatur." De Rebuspubl., liber quintus.

. . . .

"Oportet enim ut ex hactenus dictis constitit optimos viros cum optimis mulieribus sæpissime congredi, deteriores verò cum deterioribus per raro, et illorum quidem editos partus nutrire, horum verò nequaquam: si modo præstantissimum sit futurum ovile." De Rebuspubl., liber quintus.

"It follows from what has been already granted, that the best of both sexes ought to be brought together as often as possible, and the worst as seldom as possible, and that the issue of the former unions ought to be reared, and that of the latter abandoned, if the flock is to attain to first-rate excellence." Republic, bk. v, sect. 459. Davis and Vaughan's Translation, p. 187.

[1] As no explanation of Zevil is given, it is possible that it is a slip of the pen for *e vil* and vile. Ramusio, Tiberi; Lisbon edition calls them Tuias; in the Portuguese this caste is called tiar and *civel* or rustic by antiphrasis, which has been mistaken by the translators for an Indian word.

and these protect and shew favour to these slaves. These people have an idolatry of their own, and believe in their idols. Their nephews are their heirs, and their sons do not inherit, because the wives whom they marry get their livelihood with their bodies, and give themselves to the Moors, natives of the country, and also to foreigners of all kinds; and this very publicly, and with the knowledge of their husbands who give them opportunities for so doing. They make wines in the country, and they alone can sell it. They take much care not to touch other people lower than themselves; and live separate from other people. Of this sect sometimes two brothers have one wife only and both of them live with her.

MOGUER.

I find another sect of people still lower, moguer, which they call moguer,[1] who are almost like the tivers, but they do not touch one another. These are the people who transport the king's property from one place to another when he moves. There are very few of these in the country, they have a sect of their own, and have no law of marriage; their wives are public for all, and for strangers. These people for the most part get their living at sea, they are mariners and fishermen. They have a separate idolatry: they are slaves of the kings and nayrs and bramans. There are some of them very rich men who have got ships with which they navigate, for they gain much money with the Moors. Their nephews are their heirs, and not their sons, because they do not marry. They take care not to touch other people lower than themselves. These people live in separate villages: their women are very pretty, and whiter than others of this country, because they are for the most part daughters of foreigners who are white: they are very smartly dressed and adorned with gold.

[1] Repeated thus in the manuscript.

CANION.

There is another lower set of gentiles called canion. Their business is to make shields and shades[1]: they learn letters and astronomy, and some of them are great astrologers, and they foretell many future things, and form very accurate judgments upon the births of men. Kings and great persons send to call them, and come out of their palaces to the gardens and pleasure grounds to see them and ask them what they desire to know: and these people form judgments upon these things in a few days, and return to those that asked of them, but they may not enter the palaces, nor may they approach the king's person on account of being low people. And the king is then alone with them. They are great diviners, and pay great attention to times and places of good and bad luck, which they cause to be observed by these kings and great men, and by the merchants also: and they take care to do their business at the times which these astrologers advise them, and they do the same in their voyages and marriages. And by this means these men gain a great deal. They reckon the months, seasons, signs and planets as we do, except that they have months of twenty-nine, thirty, thirty-one and thirty-two days: and their first month of the year is April. From May till the middle of October they have their winter, and during this time it rains much in that country, and there are frequent storms, without any cold: and from the middle of October till the end of April is the summer, of great heat and little wind. And on the coast there are many land breezes, and frequent changes in the sea breezes. They navigate their ships in the summer, and in the winter they draw them up on shore, and cover them up on account of the heavy falls of rain.

[1] Or hats.

AJARE.

Another lower lineage amongst these gentiles is called ajare. Their business is that of quarrymen and carpenters, and others are blacksmiths, carvers of metals, and silversmiths. These are all of a sect different from the idolatry of the other people. These people marry and their sons inherit their property and employments which they teach them from their childhood. They are slaves of the king and the nairs, and very skilful in their business.

MUCOA.

There is another lower sect of gentiles called mucoa, who are fishermen and mariners, without other business. They sail in ships of moors and gentiles, and are quite at home on the sea: they also live in separate villages. They are great thieves, and shameless: they marry and their children inherit, and their wives sleep with whom they like without their thinking ill of it. They have a separate sect and form of idolatry, and are also slaves of the king and the nayrs of the country. They do not pay any duty on the fresh fish which they sell, and if they dry it they pay four per cent. duty: and the fresh fish is very cheap. This is the chief food in use amongst the Indians, for they are people who eat very little meat on account of the country being very populous[1] and of few flocks. There are some of these fishermen who are very rich and well supplied, they have large houses and property. The king takes them when he pleases, and puts much pressure on them because they are slaves.

BETUA.

There is another lower sect of gentiles called betua. Their business is to make salt, to plough and sow rice, and they do not live by anything else: they have houses in the

[1] Apretada or hard pressed.

country apart from the roads where respectable people pass. These people have a form of idolatry of their own: they also are slaves of the king and of the nayrs. They live very miserably: the nayrs make them keep far aloof from them, and speak to them from a great distance: they have no intercourse with other people. They are married and their children inherit.

PANEU.

There is another sect even lower of these people, called paneu,[1] who are great practisers of witchcraft, and they do not gain their living by anything else than charms. They visibly speak with devils who put themselves within them, and make them do awful things. When any king falls ill of fevers or any other illness, he immediately sends to call these men and women; of whom the most accomplished charmers come with their wives and children. Twenty-two families establish their dwellings at the gate of the palace of the king, or house of the person who is suffering, and has sent to call them: and there they set up a tent of coloured cloth in which they all place themselves. And there they paint their bodies with colours, and make crowns of painted paper and cloth, and other inventions of many sorts, with plenty of flowers and herbs, and great bonfires, and lighted lamps, and kettle-drums, trumpets, horns, and lutes, which they sound; and in this manner they come out of the tent two and two, with their swords in their hands, shouting and jumping, and running about the place or the court of the palace, and they jump upon one another's backs, and go on this way for some time, sticking one another with knives, and pushing one another naked and barefooted into the fire, until they are tired; and so they come out both men and boys two and two together to do the same thing again: and the women shout and sing with a great noise. And they go on this way for

[1] Ramusio, Paneru; Lisbon edition, Panceni.

two or three days, night and day, always performing together, and they make rings of earth, and lines of red ochre and white clay, and spread upon them rice and flowers of various colours, and put lights all round, and go on this way until the devil, for whose service they do all this, enters into one of them, and makes him say what the king is suffering from, and what must be done to cure him. And then they tell it to the king, and he remains satisfied and gives them many presents, and does what they tell him, either as to making offerings to their idols, or any other matter which they enjoin him to do. And so he gets well by the work of the devil, to whom they all belong. These also live separated from intercourse with the nayrs and respectable people, and do not touch any other sect. They are great hunters and archers: they kill many boars and stags upon which they maintain themselves. They are married and their children inherit.

RENOLENI.

There is another sect of people still lower, who are called renoleni,[1] who live in the mountains very poorly and miserably. And they have no other occupation than bringing wood and grass to the city for sale, to support themselves. And these people have no intercourse with any others, nor others with them, under pain of death; and they go naked, covering only their middles, many of them do so with only leaves of trees, and some with small and very dirty cloths. They marry and their children are their heirs. The women wear much brass on their ears, necks, arms, and legs, in bracelets, rings, and beads.

PULER.

There is another lower sect of gentiles called puler.[2] These are held as excommunicated and accursed; they live in

[1] Ramusio, Revoler; Lisbon ed., Revoleens.

[2] Ramusio, Puler; Lisbon, Poleas.

swampy fields and places where respectable people cannot go: they have very small and abject huts, and plough and sow the fields with rice, they use buffaloes and oxen. They do not speak to the nairs, except from a long way off, as far as they can be heard speaking with a loud voice. When they go along the road they shout, so that whoever comes may speak to them, and that they may withdraw from the roads, and put themselves on the mountains. And whatever woman or man should touch these, their relations immediately kill them like a contaminated thing: and they kill so many of these pulers until they are weary of it, without any penalty. These low people during certain months of the year try as hard as they can to touch some of the nair women, as best they may be able to manage it, and secretly by night, to do harm. So they go by night amongst the houses of the nayrs to touch women, and these take many precautions against this injury during this season. And if they touch any woman, even though no one see it, and though there should be no witnesses, she, the nair woman herself, publishes it immediately, crying out, and leaves her house without choosing to enter it again to damage her lineage. And what she most thinks of doing is to run to the house of some low people, to hide herself, that her relations may not kill her as a remedy for what has happened, or sell her to some strangers as they are accustomed to do. And touching is in this manner, that even if there is no contact from one person to another, yet by throwing anything, such as a stone or a stick, if the person is hit by it, he remains touched and lost. These people are great charmers, thieves, and very vile people.

PARENI.[1]

There is yet another sect of people among them still lower, who live in desert places, called pareni. These like-

[1] Ramusio, Pareas; Lisbon, Parcens.

wise do not converse with any one. They are looked upon as worse than the devil, and as altogether condemned:[1] so that by looking at them only they consider themselves as defiled and excommunicated, which they call contaminated. They support themselves on yname, which is like the root of the maize which is found in the island of Antilla, and on other roots and wild fruits, and they cover themselves with leaves and eat the flesh of wild animals. And with these ends the diversity of the sects of the gentiles, which are in all eighteen, each one by itself: they live without intercourse or intermarriage of one with another.

OTHER KINDS OF PEOPLE.

In these kingdoms of Malabar, besides the races of the kings and gentiles and natives of the country, there are other foreign people who are merchants and traders in this country, in which they possess houses and estates; and they live like natives of the country, and observe their own sect and customs, which are the following.

CHETIS.

Some of these are called Chetis,[2] who are gentiles, natives of the province of Cholmender, which will be mentioned further on. For the most part they are brown men, and some of them are almost white; they are tall and stout. These people are considerable merchants and changers, they deal in precious stones of all sorts, and in seed pearl, coral, and other valuable merchandise; and in gold, silver, either bullion or coined, which is a great article of trade amongst them, because they rise and fall many times. They are rich and respected, and live very decently; they have very good

[1] Dañados de todo, this might be intended for dañosos, hurtful in every way; the word occurs before and is translated contaminated, but hurtful or noxious would make a better reading.

[2] Ramusio, Cheliis; Lisbon, Chatis.

houses in streets set apart for themselves; and also their temples and idols are different from those of the country. They go bare from the waist upwards, and have cotton cloths many cubits in length wrapped round them; on their heads they wear small caps, and very long hair gathered up inside the caps; their beards shaved, and a few pinches of ashes with sandal and saffron, on their heads, breasts, and arms. They have holes in their ears, so large that they would almost hold an egg, full of rings of gold and jewelry, and many gold rings with jewels on their fingers, and round their waists gold belts, some of them studded with precious stones. They also carry with them continually large bags in which their scales and weights are kept, and their money, and jewels and pearls. And their sons as soon as they have passed the age of ten do the same, and go about changing small coin. They are great clerks and accountants, and make out all their accounts on their fingers: they are great usurers, so much so that from one brother to another they do not lend a real without gain. They are very orderly people in their food and expenditure; they keep account of everything, and are very subtle in their dealings. Their language differs from that of the Malabars, like that of Castilians and Portuguese. They marry in our fashion, and their children are their heirs: and if their wives become widows, they never marry again, however young they may be; but if the husband becomes a widower he may marry again. Should the wife commit adultery the husband may kill her with poison. And these people have their own jurisdiction, and the king cannot have anything to say in their deeds and faults; they do justice amongst one another, with which the king is well-satisfied. When they die their bodies are burned. They eat all flesh except cow.

GUZURATES.

There is another sect of gentile merchants in the city of Calicut, which they call Guzarates, who are natives of the

Kingdom of Cambay, whose customs have already been related; and they observe them in this city as in their own country. They are men who possess ships, and trade in spices, drugs, cloth, copper, and other kinds of merchandise from this place to the kingdom of Cambay, and that of Decan, where they have other correspondents; and they at the same time are correspondents of others. They have very good houses in separate streets, and their temples and idols different from the others, and many large and small bells in our fashion. The king shows them great honour and favour, and is much pleased with them because they give him much revenue from their trade. Some of them also live in the city of Cananor, and others in Cochin; and so also in other ports of Malabar. But in general most of them reside in Calicut.

MAPULER.

In all this said country of Malabar there are a great quantity of Moors, who are of the same language and colour as the gentiles of the country. They go bare like the nairs, only they wear, to distinguish themselves from the gentiles, small round caps on their heads and their beards fully grown. So that it appears to me that these people are a fifth part of all the inhabitants that there are in this country. They call these Moors Mapulers, they carry on nearly all the trade of the seaports: and in the interior of the country they are very well provided with estates and farms. So that if the King of Portugal had not discovered India this country would have had a Moorish king: because many of the gentiles turned Moors for any offence which they received amongst one another: and the Moors did them great honour, and if they were women they immediately married them. These people have many mosques in the country in which they also unite in council.

PARDESY.

There were other foreign Moors in Calicut, whom they

call Pardesy. These are Arabs, Persians, Guzarates, Khorasanys, and Decanys: they are great merchants, and possess in this place wives and children, and ships for sailing to all parts with all kinds of goods. They have among them a Moorish governor who rules over and chastises them, without the king meddling with them. And before the King of Portugal discovered the country they were so numerous and powerful in the city of Calicut, that the gentiles did not venture to dispute with them. And after that the King of Portugal made himself master there, and these Moors saw that they could not defend it, they began to leave the country, and little by little they went away from it, so that very few of them remain. And at the time that they prospered in their trade, without any exaggeration, they made ships in this city of a thousand and of eleven hundred bahars bulk, which make four quintals each.[1] These ships are with keels like ours and without any nails, because they sew the planks with mat cords, very well pitched, and the timber very good. The upper works are of different patterns from ours, and without decks,[2] with divisions in which they used to stow much pepper, ginger, cloves, cinnamon, mace, nutmeg, long pepper, sandal and brazil wood, lac, cardamoms, myrabolans, tamarinds, bamboos,[3] and all sorts of jewels and pearls, musk, amber, rhubarb, aloes-wood, many fine cotton stuffs, and much porcelain. And in this manner ten or twelve ships laden with these goods sailed every year in the month of February, and made their voyage to the Red Sea: and some of them were for the city of Aden, and some for Jiddah the port of Mekkah, where they sold their merchandise to others, who transported them thence in other smaller vessels to Turkey and to Suez, and thence by land to Cairo, and from Cairo to Alexandria. And these ships returned laden with copper, quicksilver, vermilion, coral, saffron,

[1] About two hundred tons.

[2] Cubiertas.

[3] Caña fistola.

coloured velvets, rose-water, knives, coloured camlets, scarlet and other coloured cloths, gold and silver, and other things, and they returned to Calicut from August to the middle of October of the same year that they sailed. These Moors were very well dressed and fitted out, and were luxurious in eating and sleeping. The king gave to each one a nair to guard and serve him, a Chety scribe for his accounts, and to take care of his property, and a broker for his trade. To these three persons such a merchant would pay something for their maintenance, and all of them served very well, and when the merchant bought spices the sellers gave him for each farazola of ginger, which is of twenty-five pounds, three or four pounds of it for them; and so of some other goods, which duties the merchant collects to pay these officials of his. [*Here follow eleven lines in the Lisbon edition, saying:* —These are white men and very gentlemanlike and of good appearance, they go well dressed, and adorned with silk stuffs, scarlet cloth, camlets and cottons: their head-dress wrapped round their heads. They have large houses and many servants: they are very luxurious in eating, drinking, and sleeping; and in this manner they prospered until the Portuguese came to India: now there are hardly any of them, and those that there are do not live at liberty. Hitherto I have spoken at length of all the sects, and different kinds of people of Malabar, and of some set apart in Calicut: now I will relate the position of each kingdom by itself, and how the said country of Malabar is divided.]

[*Here follows in the MS. No.* 570 *of the Munich Royal Library.* . . .

SECTION OF THE MANNER IN WHICH THE COUNTRY OF MALABAR IS DIVIDED, AND OF THAT WHICH GROWS IN IT.

You must know that from Cunbala, country of the King of Narsynga, towards the south and along the coast to the kingdom of Cananor, and within it there is a town called Cotcoulam, and on the seashore a fortress in which is a nephew of the King of Cananor, as guardian of the frontier. And further on there is a river called Nira-pura, in which is a good town, and seaport, of Moors and Gentiles, and of trade and navigation: in this town resides the said nephew, who at times rises up in rebellion: and the king goes to overthrow him with large forces, and puts him down under his authority. After passing this place along the coast is the mountain Dely, on the edge of the sea; it is a round mountain, very lofty, in the midst of low land: all the ships of the Moors and Gentiles that navigate in this sea of India, sight this mountain when coming from without, and make their reckoning by it. When they are going away the ships take in much good water and wood.... After this at the foot of the mountain to the south is a town called Marave, very ancient and well off, in which live Moors and Gentiles and Jews: these Jews are of the language of the country, it is a long time since they have dwelt in this place. There is much fishery in the neighbourhood of this mountain of Dely: which at sea is seen at a great distance by the ships that are trying to make it.

Further on along the coast is a river in which is a handsome town entirely of Moors, and all round many Gentiles, and at the entrance is a small hill on which is a fortress in which the King of Cananor constantly resides. It contains very good wells and which are very capacious. This city is called Balapatan, at four leagues from it is a city of Moors and Gentiles, very large, and of much trade with the merchants of the Kingdom of Narsynga; this town is called eah paranco, in which much copper is expended.

CANANOR.

Coming to the sea, and passing this town of Balapatan, in which the king lives, towards the south is a very good town called Cananor.]

CANANOR.

On the sea coast near the kingdom of Calicut towards the south is a city called Cananor, in which there are many Moors and Gentiles of many kinds, who are all merchants, and possess many large and small ships. They trade in all sorts of goods, principally with the kingdom of Cambay and Ormuz, Colan, Dabul Banda, Goa, Ceylon, and the Maldiu Islands. In this city of Cananor the King of Portugal has a fortress and a factory and very peaceable trade, and all round the fortress a town of Christians of the country, married with their wives, who were baptized after the fortress was made, and each day some are baptized.

CIECATE.

Having passed the said city along the coast towards the south, there is a town of Moors, natives of the country, which also possesses much shipping, named Ciecate.[1] [*Here Ramusio says :* Some lines are wanting here.]

TARMAPATAN.

Having passed beyond this place, there is a river which makes two arms, and near it a large town of Moors, natives of the country, and very rich, great merchants who likewise possess much shipping. It is called Tarmapatam, and has many and very large mosques; it is the last town of the kingdom of Cananor on the side of Calicut. These Moors when they receive any injury from the king of Cananor, immediately rise up, and withdraw their obedience until the king goes in person to remove the injury, and to cajole them. [*Here the Lisbon edition adds :* and if the Portuguese had not discovered India, this town would already have a Moorish king of its own, and would convert all Malabar to the sect of Mahomed.]

[1] Ramusio, Crecati; Munich MS. 571, Crecate.

COTAOGATO.

At four leagues higher up the said river there is another city of Moors, very large, rich, and of much trade, which deals with the people of Narsinga by land, and is called Cotaogato.[1]

DESCRIPTION OF WHAT GROWS IN THIS KINGDOM OF CANANOR.

Very good pepper grows in this kingdom of Cananor, but there is not much of it; much ginger is also produced in it, which is not of a very good quality, called *Hely* because it is near the mountain Dely. There grow also much cardamoms, myrobolans, bamboos, zerubs,[2] and zedoary.[3] There are in this country, especially in the rivers, very large lizards which eat men, and their scent when they are alive smells like civet. And throughout the country in the brushwood there are two kinds of venomous serpents, some which the Indians call murcas, and we call hooded snakes,[4] because there is something like an hood on their heads. These kill with their bite, and the person bitten dies in two hours, though he sometimes lasts two or three days. Many mountebanks carry some of these alive in earthen jars, and charmed so that they do not bite, and with them they gain money, putting them round their necks, and exhibiting them. There is another kind of more venomous serpents, which the Indians call mandal, and these kill suddenly by their bite, without the persons bitten being able to speak any more, nor even make any movement.

1 Ramusio, Capogato ; Lisbon ed., Quategatam.

2 Or ezerubs.

3 Root of ginger and other plants used in medicine.

4 Culebras de sombrero, a shade, canopy, hood, hat.

OF MANY TOWNS AND CITIES OF THE KINGDOM OF CALICUT WHICH POSSESS SHIPPING.

Leaving the kingdom of Cananor towards the south, on the further side of the river of Tarmapatam, there is a town of Moors of the country, called Terivangaty, which has shipping; and beyond that there is another river on which there is another large place, also belonging to Moors, great merchants and shippers, which is called Mazery; and beyond Mazery there is another town also of the Moors, which is called Chemonbay, which also possesses shipping. And the country inland of these three places is thickly peopled by Nairs, good men who do not obey any king, and they have got two Nair lords who govern them, the before-mentioned Moors are under their rule.

PUDOPATANI, FIRST TOWN OF THE KINGDOM OF CALICUT.

Having passed these places there is a river called Pudopotani on which is a good town of many Moorish merchants, who own many ships; here begins the kingdom of Calicut.

TIRCORE.

Further along the coast to the south south-east, is another village of the Moors called Tircore.

PANDARENI.

Further on south south-east is another Moorish place, which is called Pandarani, in which also there are many ships.

CAPUCAD.

Further on to south south-east is another town, at which there is a small river, which is called Capucad, where there are many country-born Moors, and much shipping and a great trade of exporting the goods of the country. In this place many soft sapphires are found on the sea beach.

CALICUT.

Having passed the said place at two leagues further to

the south and south-east, is the city of Calicut, where the King of Portugal has a very good fortress, made with the good will of the King of Calicut, after that the Portuguese had routed him; and they have there their principal fortress.

CHALYANI.

Beyond this city, towards the south is another city, which is called Chaliani, where there are numerous Moors natives of the country and much shipping.

PURPURANGARI.

Further on there is another city of the King of Calicut, called Purpurangari, inhabited by Moors and Gentiles who deal much in merchandise.

PARAVANOR AND TANOR.

Further on in the same direction are two places of Moors five leagues from one another. One is called Paravanor and the other Tanor, and inland from these towns is a lord to whom they belong; and he has many nairs, and sometimes he rebels against the King of Calicut. In these towns there is much shipping and trade, for these Moors are great merchants.

PANANX.

Having passed these towns along the coast to the south there is a river on which is another city of Moors, amongst whom a few Gentiles live, and it is called Pananx.[1] The Moors are very rich merchants and own much shipping. The King of Calicut collects much revenue from this city.

CHATNA.

There is another river further on called Chatna,[2] and higher up the stream there are many Gentile villages, and much pepper comes out by this river.

[1] Ramusio, Pananie; Lisbon edit., Pananee; Munich MS. 570, Panane, 571, Pananx.

[2] Ramusio, Catua; Lisbon, Chatua; Munich, 570 and 571, Chatua.

CRANGOLOR.

Further on there is another river which divides the kingdom of Calicut from the country of Cochin, and on this side of the river is a place called Crongolor,[1] belonging to the King of Calicut. The King of Cochin has some rights in this place. There live in it Gentiles, Moors, Indians, and Jews, and Christians of the doctrine of Saint Thomas; they have there a church of Saint Thomas and another of our Lady, and are very devout Christians, only they are deficient in doctrine, of which more will be said hereafter, because from this place further on as far as Cholmender there dwell many of these Christians.

OF WHAT IS GATHERED IN THIS KINGDOM OF CALICUT.

In the kingdom of Calicut, as has been said, there grows much pepper on trees like ivy, which climbs up the palms and other trees, and poles, and makes clusters; and much very good ginger of the country,[2] cardamoms, myrobolans of all kinds, bamboo canes, zerumba, zedoary, wild cinnamon; and the country produces this though covered with palm trees higher than the highest cypresses: these trees have clean smooth stems without any branch, only a tuft of leaves at the top amongst which grows a large fruit which they call tenga: by this they make profit, and it is a great article of trade, for each year more than four hundred ships are laden with it for many parts. We call these fruits cocoas: these trees give their fruits the whole year without any intermission; and there are others which support the people of Malabar, so that they cannot suffer famine even though all other provisions should fail them: because these cocoas, both green and dry, are very sweet and agreeable, and they give milk, like that of almonds. Now each of

[1] Caranganor, Ortelius: Cranganor, Homannus: it was taken by the Portuguese in 1505.

[2] Beledy: Arabic word no longer in use.

these cocoas when green has inside it a quart[1] of water very fresh, savoury, and cordial; it is very nourishing, and when they are dried that water congeals inside in a white fruit the size of an apple, which is very sweet and delicious: they eat the cocoa also when dry. They make much oil of these cocoas in presses as we do, and with the rind which these cocoanuts have close to the marrow, they make charcoal for the silversmiths, who do not work with any other charcoal. And with another husk which it has outside the first, which makes many threads, they weave cordage, which is a great article of trade; and from these trees they make wine with the sap, which is like spirits, and in such great quantities, that many ships are laden with it. With the same wine they make very good vinegar, and they also make very sweet sugar, which is yellow like honey, and is a great article of trade in India. With the leaves of the tree they make mats of the size of the leaf, with which they cover all their houses instead of with tiles: and with the tree they also make wood for their houses and for other services, and firewood.[2] And of all these things there is so great abundance that ships are laden with them. There are other palm trees of other kinds, and shorter, from which the leaves are gathered upon which the Gentiles write. There are other palms, slender and very lofty, and of very clean stems, upon which grow clusters of fruit the size of walnuts (which the Indians eat with the betel, which we call Folio Indio), and they call Areca. It is much esteemed among them and is very acid: there is such a quantity of it that they fill many ships with it for Cambay and the kingdom of Decan, and many other parts, after drying and packing it.

[1] Cuartillo, fourth part of an azumbre, equal to 2 litres and 0.16.618.

[2] Notwithstanding the extreme value and utility of these trees, as here described, some thousands of them were lately cut down to make way for sugar canes, and in spite of the remonstrances of the inhabitants, by a European who had got the loan of some land for a term of years, in one of the Comoro Islands. The loss to the islands was still greater from the fact that they depend chiefly on their own resources, being out of the regular track of trading vessels.

KINGDOM OF COCHIN.

Having passed the town of Crongolor, the extremity of the kingdom of Calicut, towards the south extends the kingdom of Cochin, in which also there is much pepper. It possesses a very fine large river where many and great ships enter, both Portuguese and Moorish. And within it is a large city inhabited by Moors and Gentiles, who are Chetis and Guzaratys, and Jews natives of the country. The Moors and Chetis are great merchants and own many ships, and trade much with Chormandel, Cambay, Cheul, and Dabul, with areca, cocoas, pepper, and jagara, which is sugar of palm trees. The King of Portugal has a very good fortress at the mouth of this river, all round which is a large village of Portuguese and Christians, natives of the country, who were baptised since the Portuguese have inhabited the country; and every day many more are converted. And there are likewise many of the above-named Christians of the doctrine of Saint Thomas, who come there from Culan and other Gentile places, where they are accustomed to live. In this fortress and town of Cochin there is much machinery and apparatus for caulking and refitting ships, and also galleys and caravels, with as much perfection as in our parts. And much pepper is put on board at this place, and spices and drugs which come from Malacca and which are transported every year to Portugal.

This King of Cochin has but a small country, and he was not a king before the Portuguese went there, because all the kings of Calicut when newly come into power, had the custom of entering Cochin and depriving the king of his state and taking possession of it, and afterwards they restored it to him again for life. The King of Calicut observed this as a law, and the King of Cochin used to give him a tribute of elephants, and so he returned to Calicut. And the King of Cochin could not coin money, nor roof his houses with tiles, under pain of losing his state. And now since the Portuguese went there, the King of Portugal made him exempt from all this; so that he lords it absolutely and coins money according to his custom.

PORCA.

Beyond this kingdom of Cochin towards the south, the kingdom of Coulam is entered; between these kingdoms there is a place which is called Porca, it belongs to a lord. In this place dwell many Gentile fishermen who have no other business than to fish in the winter, and in summer to plunder at sea the property of whoever is weaker than themselves: they have small vessels like brigantines, good rowers, and they assemble in numbers with bows and arrows, and go in such a crowd all round any ship that they find becalmed, that they make it surrender by discharging arrows, and take the vessels or ships and put the people safe on shore; and what they steal they divide with the lord of the country, and so they maintain themselves. They call these vessels catur.

KINGDOM OF COULAM.

Having passed this place the kingdom of Coulam commences, and the first town is called Caymcolan in which dwell many Gentiles, Moors, and Indian Christians of the before-mentioned doctrine of Saint Thomas. And many of these Christians live inland amongst the Gentiles. There is much pepper in this place, of which there is much exportation.

THE CITY OF COULAM.

Further on along the same coast towards the south is a great city and good sea-port, which is named Coulam, in which dwell many Moors and Gentiles, and Christians. They are great merchants and very rich, and own many ships, with which they trade to Cholmendel, the Island of Ceylon, Bengal, Malaca, Samatara, and Pegu: these do not trade with Cambay. There is also in this city much pepper. They have a Gentile king, a great lord of much territory and wealth, and of numerous men at arms, who for the most part are great archers. At this city, withdrawn a little from it, there is a promontory in the sea where stands a very great church which the apostle St. Thomas built miraculously before he departed this life.[1] It must be known that on arriving

[1] Here Ramusio adds: "which the Christians of the country affirmed to me was described in their books, which they preserve with great veneration."

Camoens puts this event, as well as the tomb of St. Thomas at Mailapur. Canto x, stanza

108.

Olha que de Narsinga o senhorio
Tem as reliquias santas, e bemditas
Do corpo de Thomé, varão sagrado
Que a Jesu Christo teve a mão no lado.

109.

Aqui a cidade foy, que se chamava
Meliapor, formosa, grande e rica:
Os idolos antiguos adorava,
Como inda agora faz a gente inica:
Longe do mar naquelle tempo estava
Quando a Fé, que no mundo se publica,
Thomé vinha pregando, e ja passara
Provincias mil do mundo, que ensinara.

110.

Chegado aqui pregando, e junto dando
A doentes saude, a mortos vida,
A caso traz hum dia o mar vagando
Hum lenho de grandeza desmedida:
Deseja o Rei, que andava edificando,
Fazer delle madeira, e não duvida
Poder tira-lo a terra com possantes
Forças d'homens, de engenhos, de elefantes.

111.

Era tão grande o pezo do madeiro,
Que, só para abalar-se, nada abasta;
Mas o nuncio de Cristo verdadeiro
Menos trabalho em tal négocio gasta:
Ata o cordão, que traz por derradeiro
No tronco, e facilmente o leva, e arrasta
Para onde faça hum sumptuoso templo,
Que ficasse aos futuros por exemplo.

112.

Sabia bem que se com fé formada
Mandar a hum monte surdo, que se mova,

at this city of Coulan where all were Gentiles, in a poor habit, and going along converting some poor people to our

Que obedecerá logo á voz sagrada ;
Que assi lho ensinou Christo, e elle o prova :
A gente ficou disto alvoroçada,
Os Brāhmenes o tem por cousa nova :
Vendo os milagres, vendo a sanctidade,
Hão medo de perder antoridade.

113.
São estes sacerdotes dos gentios,
Em quem mais penetrado tinha inveja,
Buscam maneiras mil, buscam desvios,
Com que Thomé, não se ouça, ou morto seja.
O principal, que ao peito traz os fios,
Hum caso horrendo faz, que o mundo veja,
Que inimiga não ha tão dura, e fera,
Como a virtude falsa da sincera.

114.
Hum filho proprio mata, logo accusa
De homicidio Thomé, que era innocente :
Dá falsas testemunhas, como se usa,
Condemnaram-no á morte brevemente :
O Sancto, que não vê melhor escusa,
Que appellar para o Padre Omnipotente,
Quer diante do Rei, e dos senhores,
Que se faça hum milagre dos maiores.

115.
O corpo morto manda ser trazido,
Que resuscite, e seja perguntado
Quem foi seu matador, e será crido
Por testemunho o seu mais approvado :
Viram todos o moço vivo erguido
Em nome de Jesu crucificado :
Da graças a Thomé, que lho deo vida,
E descobre seu pai ser homicida.

116.
Este milagre fez tamanho espanto,
Que o Rei se banha logo na agua santa,
E muitos após elle : hum beija o manto,
Outro louvor do Deos de Thomé canta.
Os Brahmenes se encheran de odio tanto,
Com seu veneno os morde inveja tanta,
Que, persuadindo a isso o povo rudo,
Determinam mata-lo em fin de tudo.

117.
Hum dia, que pregando ao povo estava,
Fingiram entre a gente hum arruido :
Ja Christo neste tempo lhe ordenava
Que, padecendo, fosse ao ceo subido.

holy faith he brought with him a few companions natives of the country, although they were very few: and while he was in this city, one morning there was found in this port of Coulam a very large piece of timber which had been stranded on the sea-beach, and news of it was immediately brought to the king. He sent many people and elephants to draw it out upon dry land, but they could never move it; and the king himself went in person to it later, and they were unable to draw it out. And as soon as St. Thomas saw them despair of the timber, he went to the king, and said to him: "If I were to draw out this timber would you give me a piece of land upon which to build a church with it, to the praise of our Lord God, Who sent me here." And the king laughed at him, and said to him: "If you see that with all my power it cannot be dragged out, how do you hope to draw it out." And Saint Thomas answered him: "To draw it out by the power of God, which is greater." The king immediately ordered all the land which he asked for this purpose to be given to him. And when it was granted to him, by the grace of the Lord, he went alone to the timber, and tied a cord to it, with which he began to draw it on shore without anyone assisting him. And the timber followed behind him as far as the place where he wished to build the church. The king seeing such a miracle commanded that they should let him do what he pleased with the timber and the land which had been given him; and that he should be shewn favour, because he held him to be a holy man. But he did not choose to turn Christian, and many people became con-

A multidão das pedras, que voava,
No Sancto dá já a tudo offerecido:
Hum dos maos, por fartarse mais depressa,
Com crua lança o peito lhe atravessa.

118.

Choraram-te, Thomé, o Gange e o Indo;
Chorou-te toda a terra, que pizaste;
Mais te choram as almas, que vestindo
Se hiam da sancta Fé que lhe ensinaste.

verted to our holy faith. And the said Apostle whom they call Martoma,[1] called many carpenters and sawyers of the country, and began to have the timber worked, and it was so large that it was sufficient by itself for the building of the whole church. And it is a custom amongst the Indians that when the workmen or any persons are going to set to work, the master of the work gives them at midday a certain quantity of rice to eat, and at night he gives to each man a small coin of inferior gold called fanam.[2] And St. Thomas at midday took a measure full of sand, and gave to each of these workmen his measure, which turned into very good rice, and at night he gave to each one a little bit of the wood which he was hewing, and they turned into fanams; so that they went away well satisfied, and so the said Apostle finished the church of Coulam. And when those people saw these miracles and many others which our Lord did by this glorious saint, many Indians turned to the Christian faith, through the whole kingdom of Coulam, which reaches to the frontier of Ceylon, so that there are more than two thousand houses of Christians scattered throughout the country among the Gentiles; and they have a few churches, but most of them are deficient in teaching and some of them wanting in baptism. And when the King of the Indians saw so great a change he feared that if he gave more opportunity for it, the said Christians would multiply so much that they would be able to rise and possess the country. And so he began to persecute the said St. Thomas, who withdrew himself to Cholmendel, and then to a city which was called Muylepur,[3] where he received martyrdom, and

[1] Mar Thomas is Syriac for St. Thomas; this word must have been introduced by the Nestorians or Armenians, as they are called here, though St. Thomas may have carried the word there himself in speaking of others, as of Mar Elias.

[2] Ancient coin equal to two reals vellon or sixpence.

[3] Mailapur, a league and two-thirds south of Madras, seat of a catholic bishop and two churches, was taken by the Portuguese in 1545 and by the French in 1672.

there he is buried, as will be mentioned hereafter. And so the Christians remained in the kingdom of Coulam with the before mentioned church which St. Thomas built, and with others about the country. This church was endowed by the King of Coulam with the revenue from the pepper, which remains to it to this day. These Christians had not any Christian doctrine amongst them, nor were they baptized, only they held and believed the faith of Christ in a gross manner. And at a certain period they held a council amongst them and sent men about the world to study the Christian doctrine, and manner of baptism; these men reached Armenia, where they found many Greek Christians and a patriarch who governed them, who seeing their good intention sent with them a bishop and six priests to baptize them and administer the sacraments and perform divine service, and indoctrinate them in the Christian faith. And these remain there for five or six years and then are relieved for an equal period of time, and so on. And in this manner they improved themselves somewhat. These Armenians[1] are white men; they speak Arabic, and have the sacred scriptures in Chaldean, and recite the offices in that language in our fashion. They wear tonsures on their heads the opposite of ours; that is to say, that, where ours shave they wear hair, and where we have the hair they shave it. They go dressed in white shirts and caps on their heads, barefooted, and with long beards; they are very devout people, and say mass on altars like ours with a cross (+) in front of them. And he who says mass is in the middle of the altar, and those who assist him are at the sides. They communicate with salt bread instead of a wafer, and they consecrate of that bread enough for all that are in the church, and they give

[1] These were Nestorians, who call themselves in Mesopotamia Esky Chaldany, old Chaldæans. In 1599 Archbishop Alexander Menezes held a conference at Culam, for the purpose of uniting the Roman Catholics and Nestorians.

it to all of them divided like blessed bread.[1] Each one who communicates goes to receive it at the foot of the altar with his hand.[2] The wine is in this manner, because there is no wine in India; they take raisins which come from Mekkah and Ormuz, and put them for a night in water; and on the next day when they have to say mass they squeeze them and with the juice they say their mass. These priests baptize for money,[3] and go away from this country of Malabar very rich when they return to their own country. And many remain unbaptized for want of money.

TIRINANGOTO.

Further on along the same coast towards the south, is a town of Moors and Gentiles called Tirinamgoto, which also possesses shipping. The town and territory belong to a lord, a relation of the King of Coulam; it is abundantly supplied with provisions, rice and meat.

CAPE OF COMORY.

[Further along the coast is the Cape of Comery where the Malabar country finishes; but the kingdom of Coulam reaches thirty leagues further, as far as a city which is called Cael.][4] [At this Cape Comory there is an ancient church of Christians, which was founded by the Armenians, who still direct it, and perform in it the divine service of Christians and have crosses on the altars. All mariners pay it a tribute, and the Portuguese celebrate mass there when they pass. There are there many tombs, amongst which there is one

[1] Blessed bread, is bread in little pieces distributed in churches on great feast days.

[2] It is hardly necessary to state that this is absolutely opposed to catholic practice.

[3] Selling the sacraments, canonically a great offence: it was condemned by the 48th Canon of the Council of Elvira, A.D. 305.

[4] This passage is translated in the Lisbon edition from Ramusio; the next paragraph is not to be found in either of them.

which has written on it a Latin epitaph: "Hic jacet Cataldus Gulli filius qui obiit anno. . . ."[1]][2]

ARCHIPELAGO OF ISLES.

Opposite this country of Malabar, forty leagues to the west in the sea, there is an archipelago of isles, which the Indians say amount to twelve thousand; and they begin in front of the mountain Dely, and extend southwards. The first are four small flat islands, which are called Malandiva; they are inhabited by Malabar Moors, and they say that they are from the kingdom of Cananor. Nothing grows in them, except palm trees (cocoa-nut), with the fruit of which and rice brought them from Malabar, they maintain themselves. These islands make much cordage of palm trees, which they call cayro (coir).

ISLANDS OF PALANDIVA.

Over against Panam, Cochin, and Coulam, to the west and south-west, at a distance of seventy-five leagues are other islands, of which ten or twelve are inhabited by Moors, brown and small in stature, who have a separate language and a Moorish king who resides in an island called Mahaldiu.[3] And they call all these islands Palandiva. The inhabitants are ill-formed and weak, but are very ingenious and charming. Their king is elected by some Moorish merchants, inhabitants of Cananor, and they change him when they please.

[1] It is vexatious that the date should be wanting; it is probable, however, that this was an Italian and an overland traveller, for if not he could not have been buried more than fifteen years, and a fresh tomb would have hardly called for notice from the writer.

[2] This passage is not in the Italian or Portuguese edition of Barbosa. It is in the MS. No. 571 of the Munich Library, and the date is also wanting; in the Munich MS. No. 570 this paragraph is entirely wanting, as in Ramusio.

[3] This group is called Maldivar in Ortelius, and is there stated to contain seven or eight thousand isles. One of the islands is called Y[a] de Ilheos, or island of small islands, the second word being Portuguese and apparently not understood by the compiler of the atlas.

These persons receive tribute of him every year in cordage and other produce of the country. They go there to load their ships without money, because the people of the country, with or against their will, have to give these said Moors whatever they wish. There is much fish in these islands, of which they prepare much dried,[1] which is a great article of trade. And as ballast for the ships which take on board these things, they carry away sea-snails, which are worth a good deal in many parts, and in some, especially Cambay, they serve as small change. Many fine cotton cloths are manufactured in these islands, and others of silk and gold, which are worth a good deal amongst the Moors. They gather much amber in these islands, of a good quality and in large pieces, white, grey, and brown; and I asked several of these Moors various times how the amber was produced: they hold that it is the droppings of birds, and say that in this archipelago in the uninhabited islands there are some large birds which perch on the rocks near the sea, and there void that amber, which becomes refined by exposure to the air, the sun and the rain, until some storms arise and gales of wind, which drive the sea waves over the rocks, and this bird-dung is torn off the rocks in large and small pieces, and so carried out to sea, where it floats till they meet with it, or it is cast up on some beach, or that some whales swallow it. And they say that what is found of a white colour, and which they call ponabar, has been in the sea only for a short time, and this they value most highly amongst themselves; and that the other which is found of a greyish colour, and which they name puambar, has been, they say, in the sea for a long time, and has taken that colour from floating about in the water; this also is very good, but not equal to the white; and what they find of a brown colour and bruised, has been swallowed, they say, by whales, and turned brown in their bodies, and that it has such a quality

[1] Muxama or mojama, preserved tunny fish.

that the whale cannot digest it, and they eject it whole just as they swallowed it; this they call minabàr, and it is that which among them has least value. In these isles of Maldiva they construct many large ships of palm tree, sewn together with matting, for there is no other wood there. Some of these sail to the mainland, and are ships with keels and of much tonnage; they also construct there other small rowing vessels, like brigantines and *fustas*, very pretty and good for rowing, which they use to go from one island to another; and they likewise cross over to the Malabar country. Many Moorish ships touch at these islands from China, Malacojana, Malaca, Samatra, Bengala, Ceylan, and Peygu, on their passage to the Red Sea: and there they take in water and refreshments for their voyage. Sometimes they arrive so shattered that they unload their cargo there, and they let it be lost. Many of these ships get lost amongst these islands because they do not venture to come to the Malabar coast from fear of the Portuguese.

ISLAND OF CEYLAM.

Leaving these islands of Mahaldiva further on towards the east, where the cape of Comory is doubled, at thirty-eight leagues from the cape itself, there is a very large and beautiful island which the Moors, Arabs, Persians, and our people call Ceylam,[1] and the Indians call it Ylinarim. It is a rich and luxuriant land, inhabited by Gentiles, and ruled by a Gentile king. Many Moors live in the sea-ports of this island in large quarters, and all the inhabitants are great merchants. There are fifty leagues of channel towards the north-east from the said cape until passing the island of Maylepur.[2] Both Moors and Gentiles are well-made men,

[1] "Vês corre a costa celebre Indiana
Para o Sul até o cabo Comori,
Já chamado Cori, que Taprobana
(Que ora he Ceilão) defronte tem de si."
Os Lusiadas, canto x, stanza 107.

[2] There is something wrong here; for, from Cape Comorin to Mayle-

and almost white, and for the most part stout, with large stomachs, and luxurious. They do not understand, nor possess arms, they are all given to trade and to good living. They go bare from the waist upwards, and below that cover themselves with good cloths of silk and cotton, caps on their heads, and the ears pierced with large holes in which they wear many gold rings and jewellery, so much that their very ears reach to their shoulders: and many rings and precious jewels on their fingers; they wear belts of gold richly adorned with precious stones. Their language is partly Malabar and partly of Cholmendel, and many Malabar Moors come to live in this island on account of its being so luxuriant, abundant, and very healthy. Men live longer here than in other parts of India. They have a great deal of very good fruit; and the mountains are full of sweet and sour oranges of three or four kinds, and plenty of lemons and citrons, and many other very good fruits which do not exist in our parts, and they last all the year. And there is plenty of meat and fish, little rice, for most of it comes from Cholmendel, and it is their chief food; much good honey and sugar brought from Bengal, and butter of the country. All the good cinnamon grows in this island upon the mountains, on trees which are like laurels. And the king of the country orders it to be cut in small sticks, and has the bark stripped off in certain months of the year, and sells it himself to the merchants who go there to buy it, because no one can gather it except the king. There are likewise in this island many wild elephants which the king orders to be caught and tamed; and they sell them to merchants of Cholmendel, Narsynga, and Malabar, and those of the kingdoms of Decam and Cambay go to those places to buy them. These elephants are caught in this manner: it must be known that

pur is more than double fifty leagues; the direction of the compass and length of the channel, make it probable that the island of Manar was intended instead of Maylepur.

they have got other elephants with which they manage it, and they fasten them with chains in the mountains and woods where they are bred; and at the foot and all round a tree near the elephant they make three or four very large pits, covered over with slender poles, and they strew earth on the top, so that nothing appears: and the wild elephants seeing the female come to her, and fall into these pits, where they keep them seven or eight days half-dead of hunger, and so many men watch them by day and night, always speaking to them so as not to let them sleep, until they tame and render them domestic, giving them their food with their hands. And after they have got them broken in and tame, they take them with strong chains, and by degrees throw so much earth and branches into the pit that the elephant gradually rises until he comes out of the pit, and then they tie him to some tree and keep him some days watching, with fire, and men who always talk to him, and give him food in moderation until they make him domestic and obedient. And in this way they catch them male and female, great and small, and sometimes two at once in one pit. They make great merchandise of them, and they are worth much, because they are much valued by the kings of India for war and for labour, and they become as domestic and quick at understanding as men. The very good ones are worth in the Malabar country and in Cholmendel from a thousand to one thousand five hundred ducats, and the others from four to six hundred ducats according as they may be, but in the island they are to be had for a small price. And all have to be brought and presented to the king. There are also many jewels in this island, rubies which they call manica, sapphires, jacinths, topazes jagonzas,[1] chrysoliths, and cat's eyes, which are

[1] Jargon or Zircon is a stone having a superficial resemblance to a diamond. Milburn's Oriental Commerce, p. 361. Possibly this stone may be connected with the jarkna stein mentioned in the Edda, and supposed by Grimm to be the opal. In Ramusio the spelling is the

as much esteemed amongst the Indians as rubies. And all these stones are all gathered in by the king, and sold by himself. And he has men who go and dig for them in the mountains and shores of the rivers, who are great lapidaries and who are good judges in those matters: so much so that if they have a few handfuls of earth brought them from the mountain, at once on seeing it they know if it is of rubies or of any other stones, and where it comes from. And the king sends them to look there, and after they have brought them he orders to set aside each kind, and pick out the good ones, and he has them worked to have them sold when cut, which he does himself to foreigners; and the other inferior ones he sells at once to the country merchants. These rubies which grow here, for the most part, are not of so brilliant a colour as those which grow in Ava and Capelam, of which mention will be made further on; and some which come out perfect in colour are much more highly prized by the Indians than those of Paygu, because they say that they are stronger. And in order to make them of a deeper colour they put them into the fire. These lapidaries whom the king has near him, on seeing a stone before it is cut, say: this ruby will endure so many hours of fire, and will remain very good. And the king risks it, and orders it to be put in a very strong charcoal fire for that space of time which the lapidary has mentioned to him: and if it endures it without danger, it comes out more perfect in colour, and is worth very much. And all the other stones are found and worked in the same manner: and some stones are found which are half ruby and half sapphire, and others half topaze and half sapphires, and also cat's eyes. The king has a great treasure of these jewels, for whenever he meets with any very good stone he puts it in his treasury.

Close to this island of Ceylam in the sea there is a sand-

same as in this MS. The whole of this passage is much shortened in the Lisbon edition.

bank covered with ten or fifteen fathoms of water, in which a very great quantity of very fine seed pearls are found, small and great, and a few pearls: and the Moors and Gentiles go there from a city which is called Sael, belonging to the King of Coulam, to fish for this seed pearl, twice a year by custom, and they find them in some small oysters, smoother than those of our parts. And the men plunging under the water, where they remain a considerable time, pick them up: and the seed pearl is for those who gather them, and the large pearls are for the king, who keeps his overseer there, and besides that they give him certain duties upon the seed-pearl.

The King of Ceylan is always in a place called Columbo, which is a river with a very good port, at which every year many ships touch from various parts to take on board cinnamon and elephants. And they bring gold and silver, cotton and silk stuffs from Cambay, and many other goods which are saffron, coral, quicksilver, vermilion which here is worth a great deal; and there is much profit on the gold and silver, because it is worth more than in other parts. And there come likewise many ships from Bengal and Cholmendel, and some from Malaca for elephants, cinnamon and precious stones. In this island of Ceylan there are four or five other harbours and places of trade which are governed by other lords, nephews of the King of Ceylan, to whom they pay obedience, except that sometimes they revolt. In the middle of this island is a very lofty mountain range in which is a very high stone peak, and upon it a pool of spring water, and on this stone there is the form of a man's foot,[1] which the Indians say is the footmark of father Adam, whom they call Adam Baba. And from all those parts and kingdoms the Moors come in pilgrimage, saying that father Adam went

[1] "Olha em Ceylão, que o monte se alevanta
Tanto, que as nuvens passa, ou a vista engana
Os naturaes tem por cousa sancta,
Por a pedra em que està á pegada humana."
Lusiadas, canto x, 136.

up from there to heaven, and they go in the habit of pilgrims, with chains of iron, and clothed with skins of leopards, lions, and other wild animals, and on their arms and legs they inflict wounds continually along the road to keep up open sores, saying that they do that for the service of God, and honour of Mahomed and Adam Baba. And some of them go well provided with money which they carry hidden to spend it on the jewels of Ceylon. Before they arrive at this mountain where Adam's footstep is, they go through swampy land, through valleys full of water, and by the banks of water, and they have five or six leagues to go with water to the waist, and all carry knives in their hands to rid themselves of the leeches which fasten on their legs, and which are innumerable. And on arriving at the mountain they make the ascent of it, and they cannot mount up to the pinnacle except by ladders of iron chains,[1] which it has put round it, of a great thickness. And on the top of it they wash with the water of that pool, and perform their prayer: and they say that with that they remain free and pure of all sin. The said island of Ceylon is very near the mainland, and between it and the continent are some banks which have got a channel in the midst, which the Indians call Chylam,[2] by which all the Malabar sambuks pass to Cholmendel. And every year many are lost upon these banks because the channel is very narrow: and in the year that the Admiral of Portugal went the second time to India, so many ships and sambuks of Malabar were lost in those shallows, that twelve thousand Indians were drowned there, who were coming with provisions, and were determined on driving the Portuguese fleet away from India, without allowing it to take any cargo.

[1] The ascent is still performed in the same manner, and is difficult in windy weather.

[2] Chilao in Ortelius's Map of Asia, the Portuguese way of writing Chilam.

QUILACARE, OF THE KINGDOM OF COLAM.

Leaving the island of Ceylon and returning to the mainland, after doubling Cape Comory at twenty leagues to the north-east, is the country of the King of Colam and of other lords, who live in it subject to him. And the first place is named Quilacare, in which country there are many and great towns of Gentiles and several harbours, where dwell many Moors born in the country. They perform their voyages in small vessels which they call champana.[1] The Malabar Moors come to these towns to trade and to bring Cambay goods, which are worth a good deal there, and a few horses. And they take in rice and cloths for Malabar. And in this province of Quilacare there is a Gentile house of prayer, in which there is an idol which they hold in great account, and every twelve years they celebrate a great feast to it, whither all the Gentiles go as to a jubilee. This temple possesses many lands and much revenue: it is a very great affair. This province has a king over it, who has not more than twelve years to reign from jubilee to jubilee. His manner of living is in this wise, that is to say: when the twelve years are completed, on the day of this feast there assemble together innumerable people, and much money is spent in giving food to Bramans. The king has a wooden scaffolding made, spread over with silken hangings: and on that day he goes to bathe at a tank with great ceremonies and sound of music, after that he comes to the idol and prays to it, and mounts on to the scaffolding, and there before all the people he takes some very sharp knives, and begins to cut off his nose, and then his ears, and his lips, and all his members, and as much flesh off himself as he can; and he throws it away very hurriedly until so much of his blood is spilled that he begins to faint, and then he cuts his throat himself.

[1] Comp. Malay sampan.

And he performs this sacrifice to the idol, and whoever desires to reign other twelve years and undertake this martyrdom for love of the idol, has to be present looking on at this: and from that place they raise him up as king.

SAEL.

Having left Quilacare, further along the coast, at ten leagues to the north-east, is another town called Çael,[1] which belongs to the King of Colam: it is inhabited by Gentiles and great Moorish merchants, and is a seaport where many ships touch every year from Malabar, Cholmendel, and Bengala. They deal in all kinds of goods from all parts at this place. The Chetis of this city are great lapidaries and artists for setting[2] pearls, which fishery belongs to the King of Sahel, who has farmed it for many years forward to a very rich Moorish merchant, who is almost as important in the country as the king. And this person administers justice amongst the Moors, without the king's mixing himself up in it. Those who fish up the pearls, as has been said, fish all the week for themselves, and on the Friday for the owner of the boat; and all of them together fish at the end of the season during which they are there a whole week for this Moor. The king of Colam lives always near this city, and is very rich and powerful on account of his many men at arms, who are very good bowmen. He always has in his guard four or five hundred women, trained from girls to be archers: they are very active. He sometimes is at war with the King of Narsinga, who wishes to take his country, but he defends himself very well.

[1] Cael in Ortelius and Homannus, the cedilla has been omitted in another part of this work.

[2] Maestros: this may also mean dealers.

CHORMENDEL.

Twelve leagues further on the coast turns to the north, the country is called Cholmender,[1] and it extends seventy or eighty leagues along the coast. In it there are many Gentile cities, towns and villages, and it belongs to the King of Narsinga; it is a land abounding in rice, meat and wheat, and all sorts of vegetables, because it is a country which has very beautiful plains. And many ships of Malabar come here to load rice, and they bring goods from Cambay to this country, that is to say, copper, quicksilver, vermilion, pepper and other goods. And throughout all this Cholmender much spice and drugs, and goods of Malaca, China, and Bengal are to be met with, which the Moorish ships bring here from those parts, since they do not venture to pass to Malabar from dread of the Portuguese. And although this country is very abundantly provided, yet if it should happen any year not to rain it falls into such a state of famine that many die of it, and some sell their own children for a few provisions, or for two or three fanoes, each of which will be worth thirty-six maravedis. And in these times the Malabars carry rice and cocoa nuts to them, and return with their ships laden with slaves, and all the chetis, Gentile merchants, who live throughout India, are natives of this country of Cholmender; they are very sharp, great accountants, and dexterous merchants. And many country-born Moors, mercantile and seafaring men, live in the sea-ports.

MAYLEPUR.

Further along this coast, which makes a bend to the north-west and then turns to the north-east, having left the Cholmendel country, at a distance of twelve leagues there is a city almost uninhabited and very ancient, which is called Maylepur; in former times it was a considerable place of the kingdom of Narsinga. In this city is buried the body of the

[1] Cholmandel, Ortelius.

apostle St. Thomas, in a small church near the sea. And the Christians of Cuolam, who are of his doctrine, say that when St. Thomas left Cuolam, on being persecuted by the Gentiles, he went with a few companions to that country, and settled in this city of Maylepur, which at that period was twelve leagues distant from the sea, which later eat away the land, and came in upon it. And there he began to preach the faith of Christ, to which he converted some, whilst others persecuted and wished to kill him, and he separated himself from the people, and went about frequently among the mountains. And one day as he wandered about in that manner, a gentile hunter, with a bow, saw many peacocks together upon the ground in that mountain, and in the midst of them one very large and very handsome standing upon a stone slab; this hunter shot at it, and sent an arrow through its body, and they rose up flying, and in the air it turned into the body of a man. And this hunter stood looking until he saw the body of the said apostle fall. And he went to the city where he related that miracle to the governors, who came to see it, and they found that it was indeed the body of St. Thomas, and then they went to see the place where he had been wounded, and they saw two impressions of human feet marked on the slab, which he left impressed when he rose wounded.[1] And when the governors of the country saw so great a miracle, they said

[1] This story is evidently of Hindu origin, since the peacock is respected by the Hindus. It also in some measure confirms the antiquity of the establishment of Christianity in India, which from this story must have been established before the arrival in India of any of the Nestorian priests: since they came from a country where the peacock is associated with the devil, especially amongst the devil-worshiping Yezidys, who have got a peacock for an idol, which was seen and described by Mr. Layard. Many of their superstitions come down from the Manichees of the second century. Besides this, I have seen an Arabic description of animals written in Syria, in which the peacock is described as the first creature expelled out of Paradise, on account of its pride. This idea and the Yezidy love for it, probably have a common origin.

this man was holy, and we did not believe him; and they took him and buried him in the church where he now is, and they brought the stone upon which he left the said foot-marks, and they placed it close to his grave; and they say that on burying him they could never put his right arm in the tomb, and it always remained outside; and if they buried him entirely, next day they found the arm above the earth, and so they let it be. The Christians, his disciples and companions who built the said church, and the Géntiles already held him for a saint, and honoured him greatly. He remained thus with his arm outside of the grave for a long time, and they say that many people came there from many quarters in pilgrimage,[1] and that some Chinese came also, who wished to cut off his arm and carry it away as a relic, and that when they were about to strike at it with a sword, he withdrew his arm inside, they say, and it was never seen again. So he remains still in that hermitage, very humbly, and lighted up by the grace of God, because the Moors and Gentiles light him up, each one saying that he is something belonging to them. And the house and church are ordered in our fashion, with crosses on the altar, and at the top of the vault a great wooden cross, and peacocks for a device: this church is much deteriorated. All round it there is much brushwood, and a poor Moor takes care of that building and begs alms for it, and for the lamp, which still continues burning. The Christians of India still go there as pilgrims, and carry away thence as relics some little pellets of earth of the tomb of this blessed apostle.

PALECATE.

Further on this coast goes forty-three leagues to the north-east and twelve leagues to the north, there is another city of

[1] Romeria: this word here translated pilgrimage, means a visit to a shrine or holy place, and is inferior to peregrinage: it implies a shorter distance, and is equivalent to ziaret.

the kingdom of Narsinga, inhabited by Moors and Gentiles, great and rich merchants, it is called Palecate,[1] and is a harbour at which many Moorish ships touch, coming from divers parts with all kinds of goods. It also has much trade with the interior of the kingdom, and they sell there many jewels which are brought from Peygu, especially rubies and spinel-rubies of a good quality, and much musk. These jewels may be had for very little there, by whoever knows how to buy well. The King of Narsynga keeps his governors in this city, and collectors of his revenues. In this place they make many good coloured cotton stuffs which are worth much in Malaca, Peigu, and Samatra, also in the kingdom of Guzurate and Malabar they are much valued for the clothing both of Moors and Gentiles. Copper, quick-silver, vermilion, opium, and many Cambay goods fetch a good price, so also scarlet cloth, coral, saffron, velvets from Mekkah, and rose water.

THE MOUNTAIN OF DIGUIRMALE.

Having passed this city of Palecate further along the coast which trends to north-east by north as far as Marepata, a distance of a hundred and forty leagues, in which there are many other places belonging to the kingdom of Narsynga, as far as the kingdom of Horisa.

KINGDOM OF ORISSA.

Further on after passing Marepata, along the coast which trends from hence to north-east by east, the kingdom of Horisa commences. It is of the Gentiles, very good fighting men, and the king is frequently at war with the king of Narsynga, and is powerful in the numbers of his foot soldiers. The greater part of his country is withdrawn from the sea, and has few seaports and little trade. His territory extends seventy leagues along the coast as far as the river Ganges,

[1] Paleacate, Ortelius.

which they call Guenga,[1] and on the other side of this river commences the kingdom of Bengala, with which he is sometimes at war. And all the Indians go in pilgrimage to this river to bathe in it, saying that with this they all become safe, because it issues from a fountain which is in the terrestrial paradise. This river is very great and magnificent, it is studded on both banks with opulent and noble cities of the Gentiles. Between this river and the Eufrates are the first and the second India, a territory very abundant and well provided, very healthy and temperate, and from this river further on to Malaca is the third India, according as the Moors say.

BENGAL.

Having passed the river Ganges, along the coast twenty leagues to north-east by east and twelve leagues to the south-west, and then twelve leagues to the east until reaching the river Paralem,[2] is the kingdom of Bengala, in which there are many towns, both in the interior and on the sea-coast. Those of the interior are inhabited by Gentiles, subject to the King of Bengal, who is a Moor; and the seaports are inhabited by Moors and Gentiles, amongst whom there is much trade in goods and much shipping to many parts, because this sea is a gulf which enters towards the north, and at its inner extremity there is a very great city inhabited by Moors which is called Bengala,[3] with a very

[1] Guenga, Ortelius; it should be Gunga.

"Ganges, no qual os seus habitadores
Morrem banhados, tendo por certeza,
Que inda que sejão grandes peccadores,
Esta agua sancta os lava, e da pureza."—Lusiad. x, 121.

[2] In Ortelius there is a place called Aralem, east of Bengala.

[3] Bengala, Ortelius, and on the same spot in Homannus Chatigan; in our maps Chittagong, which name was changed by the Moghuls in 1666 to Islam Abad.

"Vē Cathigão cidade das melhores
De Bengala provincia; que se preza
De abundante; mas olha, que está posta
Para o Austro de aqui virada a costa."—Lusiad. x, stan. 121.

good harbour. Its inhabitants are white men and well formed. Many foreigners from various parts live in this city, both Arabs and Persians, Abyssinians[1] and Indians, who congregate here on account of the country being very fertile and of a temperate climate. They are all great merchants, and own large ships of the same build as those of Mekkah, and others of the Chinese build which they call jungos, which are very large and carry a very considerable cargo. With these ships they navigate to Cholmender, Malabar, Cambay, Peigu, Tarnasari, Samatra, Ceylon, and Malaca; and they trade in all kinds of goods, from many places to others. There is much cotton in the country, and sugar cane plantations, and very good ginger and much long pepper. They manufacture many kinds of stuffs, extremely fine and delicate, coloured for their own use, and white for trade to all parts; they call them saravetis, and they are excellent for women's head gear, and much valued for that purpose: the Arabs and Persians make caps of this stuff, in such great quantities, that every year they fill several ships with them for different places. And they make others which they call mamuna, and others duguza, and others chautar, and others called topan and sanabafos which are the most valued for their shirts, and which are very durable. They are all of the length of twenty cubits, very little more or less, and in this city they are all at a low price. They are spun by a man with a wheel and woven. White sugar of very good quality is made in this city, but they do not know how to join it to make loaves, and so they pack it up in powder in stuff covered over with raw hide, well sewn up. They load many ships with it and export it for sale to all parts. And when these merchants were accustomed to go freely and without dread to the parts of Malabar and Cambay with their ships, the quintal of this sugar was worth two ducats and a half in Malabar, and a good sinabafo was worth two

[1] Abasis.

ducats, and a piece of muslin for women's caps three hundred maravedis; and a chautar of the best quality six hundred maravedis. And those who brought them gained much money. They likewise make many preserves in this city of Bengal, very good ones of ginger, and of oranges, lemons and other fruits which grow in the country. There are also in this country many horses, cows and sheep, and all other meats in great abundance, and very extremely large hens. The Moorish merchants of this city go into the interior of the country and buy many Gentile children of their fathers and mothers, or of others who steal them, and castrate them, cortandole todo de manera que quedan rasos como la palma de la mano. Some of them die of it, and those who recover they bring them up very well, and sell them as merchandise for twenty or thirty ducats each to the Persians, who value them much as guards to their wives and houses.[1] The respectable Moors of this city go dressed in long morisco shirts reaching to the instep, white and of slight texture, and underneath some cloths wrapped round below the waist, and over the shirt a silken sash round the waist, and a dagger set with silver; they wear many jewelled rings on their fingers, and fine cotton caps on their heads. They are luxurious people, who eat and drink a great deal, and have other bad habits. They bathe frequently in large tanks which they have in their houses: they have many servants, and have each of them three or four wives, and as many more as they can maintain. They keep them very much shut up and very richly dressed and adorned with silks and jewels set in gold; they go out at night to visit one another and to drink wine, and hold festivals and marriage feasts. They make various kinds of wine in this country, chiefly of sugar and palm trees, and

[1] The employment of eunuchs was forbidden by the Prophet, since their employment induced people to supply the demand. Hidayah, vol. iv, p. 121.

also of many other things. The women are very fond of these wines, and are much accustomed to them. They are great musicians both in singing and playing on instruments. The men of the common people wear short white shirts half way down the thigh, and drawers, and very small head wraps of three or four turns; all of them are shod with leather, some with shoes, others with sandals, very well worked, sewn with silk and gold thread. The king is a great lord and very rich, he possesses much country inhabited by Gentiles, of whom every day many turn Moors, to obtain the favour of the king and governors. This king possesses more territory further on the before named gulf, inhabited by Moors and Gentiles, both inland and on the sea coast, which turns to the south.

KINGDOM OF BERMA.

Having passed the kingdom of Bengala, along the coast which turns to the south, there is another kingdom of Gentiles called Berma.[1] In this there are no Moors, nor are there sea ports which can be made use of for trade in merchandise. The people of this kingdom are black men and go naked, for they only cover their middles with cotton cloths. They have their idolatries and houses of prayer. They frequently are at war with the King of Peigu. We have no further information respecting this country because it has no shipping. It is only known that it borders on the kingdom of Bengala on one side, and on the kingdom of Peigu on the other. And it has a gulf in the middle which enters the country in a direction north-east by east forty leagues, and is fourteen leagues wide at the mouth and twenty leagues wide further in, and in the middle of it is a large island which is thirty-six leagues long and from four to ten leagues broad.

[1] Verma, Ortelius and Ramusio.

ERE CAN GUY.[1]

Inland of this kingdom of Berma towards the north is another kingdom of Gentiles, very large and which has no sea ports. It also borders on the kingdom of Bengal and the kingdom of Ava, and it is called Ere can guy. The king and people of this kingdom are Gentiles. It is said that this king possesses many cities and towns, and horses and elephants. These elephants are brought from the kingdom of Peigu. These people are brown men, naked from the waist upwards, and wrapped round below the waist with cotton and silk cloths; they use many ornaments of gold and silver. They venerate idols and have large houses of prayer. This king is very rich in money, and powerful from the number of his men at arms: he is often at war with his neighbours, and some of them obey him against their wills, and render him tribute. He lives in great luxury, and possesses very good houses in all the towns where he resides, which have got many pools of water, green and shady gardens, and good trees. They have also got many women at their caprice, and have no law of marriage. In twelve towns of his kingdom he has twelve first-rate palaces in which he has many women brought up; that is, in each of these cities he has a governor who each year takes twelve girls born in that year, daughters of persons of the highest rank and the prettiest to be found; and he has them carefully brought up at the expense of the king, in these palaces, up to the age of twelve years; they are very well dressed, and taught thoroughly to dance and sing and play on musical instruments; in this way each palace constantly contains many of them of tender age. And at the end of the year the governor conducts to the king at whatever place he may be at, twelve damsels of the age of twelve years. The king orders them to be well dressed and to have the name of each

[1] Aracangil, Lisbon edit.

one written on their clothes, and the next morning he orders them to be sent up to a terrace in the sun, and there remain fasting until midday. And they perspire so much with the heat of the sun that their clothes become damp, and then the king orders them to be taken to a room where they change their clothes. And the damp garments which they have thrown off are all carried to the king, who smells them, and those which do not smell bad he keeps for himself, and those which smell bad from the perspiration he makes a present of to those of his courtiers who are there present, as also the damsels who had worn them, who are known by the names written on the clothes. The other damsels whose clothes did not smell ill from the perspiration the king keeps for himself.[1] And thus he is always accustomed to do, and in this way they bring to him from all these twelve cities a hundred and forty-four girls, whom he distributes in the manner above described. And he has many amusements in the way of hunting, games, music, feasting and other things.

PEYGU.

Returning to the sea coast, after passing the kingdom of Berma, towards the south and south-east, there is another kingdom of Gentiles, very wealthy, well supplied with everything, and of great trade in merchandise by sea. It is called Peygu,[2] and extends seventy-five leagues. This kingdom has three or four sea ports in which are many Moorish and Gentile inhabitants, who are very great merchants. And the actual city of Peigu is seven or eight leagues distant from the sea,[3] on the arm of a very great river which runs through

[1] Here Ramusio adds: "And they say that by this trial they know which of them are healthy and of a good temperament."

[2] Pegu, Ortelius and Ramusio.

[3] The Dicco. Geogo. Universal, Barcelona, states the distance at twelve leagues, as this work is chiefly translated from French authorities, these distances would agree, and the river deposit may have increased the distance.

this kingdom, and comes from some very high mountains. During certain months of the year there is so great an increase of water, that the river leaves its bed and irrigates a large extent of land, from which a great deal of rice is gathered. They ship from these ports a great quantity of provisions in vessels which have three or four high masts, which they call jungos, for Malaca, Samatara, and other parts, and amongst other things much rice is shipped, and cane sugar, brown and loaf. Many Moorish ships from different parts assemble at these ports of Peigu, and bring thither much cloth of Cambay and Palacate, coloured cottons and silks, which the Indians call patola, which are worth a good deal there; they also bring opium, copper, scarlet cloth, coral in strings, in branches, and polished, quicksilver, vermilion, rose water, and a few drugs from Cambay. In this kingdom they ship very fine lac which grows there. There is much trade in cloves and mace and other Chinese goods, and musk and rubies, which come thither from inland from a city called Ava, of which mention will be made hereafter. The people of this kingdom go undressed, they only cover their middles. They are not warlike, and possess few weapons, and those wretched ones. They are very voluptuous, y traen en los capirotes de sus miembros unos cascaveles redondos cosydos soldados entre la carne y el cuero por hazerselos mayores, algunos traen tres, y algunos cinco, y algunos syete, y dellos de oro y de plata, y otros de metal, los quales les van sonando de que andan y an lo por mucha gentileza y las mugeres huelgan mucho con ellos y no quieren hombres que no los tengan, y los que mas honrados son, esos los traen mas y mayores. (*The Lisbon edition continues:* e nom diga mais deste costume pola desonestidade.)[1] The king is called the King of the White Elephant, and in this kingdom there are very high

[1] This is also related by Nicolo Conti, India in the Fifteenth Century, Hakluyt Society.

mountains where many wild elephants are bred; and they have a rule to catch one every day, and the king orders food to be sent them and has them brought up. He has a great quantity of them which he sells to merchants who come there to buy them, to take them to Pelecate, whence they go on to Narsynga, Malabar and Cambaya. There are likewise many small horses which go at an amble, which they make great use of; they also have horses on which they ride à la bastarda,[1] and with these and the elephants, and infantry, they carry on war. There are also many sheep and swine, wild and domestic in this kingdom, and the people are great sportsmen and hunters.

MARTAVAN.

In this same kingdom of Peygu towards Malaca, there are three or four seaports, of which I do not know the name, amongst them is one very good sea port called Martaban,[2] which is seventy-five leagues to the south south-east from the before-mentioned gulf. Many ships touch at it, and trade there and stow provisions and other goods, especially lac of a very good quality, which grows in the country itself; and the Moors of Persia and India call it lucomartaban. And it also grows in the country of Narsinga, but not so good as this: they say of this lac that it is gum of trees, others say that it grows on the slender branches of the trees, just as in our parts the berries grow. And this explanation appears the most natural. And so they bring it in small sticks, which naturally cannot produce so much gum. In this town of Martaban very large and beautiful porcelain vases are made, and some of glazed earthenware, of a black colour, which are highly valued amongst the Moors, and they export them as merchandise, and they also carry away from this country much benjuy in large loaves.

[1] Saddle between *à la gineta*, a high saddle and short stirrups, and *à la brida*, long stirrups and hardly any saddle at all.

[2] Martabam, Ortelius.

AVA.

Inland beyond this kingdom of Peigu between the kingdom of Daran cangui and the kingdom of Dansiam, to the east there is another kingdom of Gentiles which has a king who resides in a very great and opulent city called Ava,[1] eight days' journey from the sea; a place of rich merchants, in which there is a great trade of jewels, rubies, and spinel-rubies, which are gathered in this kingdom. Many foreign merchants flock thither from many parts to buy these jewels, and likewise much musk which is found there. And the king commands all to be gathered for himself, and sells it himself to the merchants of the country who sell it to the foreign merchants. The merchants bring there for sale quicksilver, vermilion, coral, copper, saffron, rose-water, opium, scarlet cloth, coloured velvet from Mekkah, and many other things from the kingdom of Cambay, and the jewels and musk are sold here at a low price in exchange for these goods. These rubies and spinel-rubies are found in the mountains and banks of rivers, by making many holes, and mines where they find these spinel-rubies; and on the surface of the earth and underneath it the rubies are found. The men of the country are very skilful lapidaries who know and cut them well. The musk is found in some small white animals, like gazelles, and they have teeth like elephants, but small.

These animals are born with sorts of tumours under the belly and the breast, and these ripen, and after they are mature and have formed like matter, they have so much itching in them that they go to rub themselves against the trees, and the drops which fall from these tumours are of the best and most excellent musk, and the hunters, who pursue them with dogs and nets and other snares, follow their tracks by the smell, and they find these grains of fine musk, and

[1] Ava, Ortelius.

by following them they catch them alive, and bring them to houses appointed for that purpose, where they entirely cut off these tumours with the skin, and they let them dry. These are the genuine musk pouches, of which very few are exported, because they falsify them, and they do it in this way. It must be known that on taking it from the living animal, they place many leeches on the wounds, and allow them to gorge themselves with blood, and when full they put them in the sun to dry, and of these they put so many that the animal falls dead without any blood, and afterwards they skin it, and with the skin they make several counterfeit pouches, which look like the real ones. Having pounded the leeches and reduced them to powder; with the powder they make grains in their hands, and add one weight of good musk taken from the real pouches, to a hundred of this blood of the leeches, and having mixed up the whole, they fill with it the counterfeit pouches, and they look very good. And they also esteem it in these parts as very fine, because the merchants through whose hands it passes adulterate it still further. The real musk is so strong that on putting it to the nostrils it causes the blood to issue. In this kingdom there are many elephants, horses and men devoted to war: and it is a country well supplied with provisions.

CAPELAN.

Further inland than the said kingdom of Ava, at five days' journey to the south-east is another city of Gentiles which has a ruler who is subject to the said King of Ava. This city is called Capelan,[1] and all round it are likewise found many and excellent rubies, which they bring to sell at the city and fair of Ava, and which are better than those of Ava.

[1] Capelan, Ortelius, near the mouth of the river Menam.

KINGDOM OF ANSIAM.

Having passed the kingdom of Peigu, further along the coast to the south south-east towards Malaca, eighty-seven leagues from Martaban towards Malaca, and further on in the country is the kingdom of Ansiam,[1] which is of the Gentiles. And the king is a Gentile and a great ruler, and inland his borders are from this coast unto the other side, which is the coast of China: and he has seaports on both sides. He is the lord of many people both horse and foot, and of many elephants. And he does not allow any Moor to bear arms in his country. And from the kingdom of Peigu as far as a city which has a seaport, and is named Tanasery,[2] there are a hundred leagues. In this city there are many Moorish and Gentile merchants, who deal in all sorts of goods, and own ships, with which they navigate to Bengal, Malaca, and other parts. In the inland parts of this kingdom there grows much good benjuy, which is a resin of trees which the Moors call luban javi,[3] and it is of two kinds, that is to say, one which does not smell except in the fire, and the other of much scent, of which the good and genuine storax is made in the Levant, before extracting from it the oil, which in the Levant is extracted from it. And many ships of Moors and from other parts congregate at this port of Tanasary, and bring them copper, quicksilver, vermilion, scarlet cloth, silks, coloured velvets from Mekkah, saffron, coral, wrought and in strings, rosewater from Mekkah in little bottles of tinned copper, and it is sold by weight with the bottle; opium, Cambay stuffs, and all these goods fetch a high price at this place.

QUEDA, TOWN OF THE KINGDOM OF ANSYAM.

Having left this town of Tanasery further along the coast towards Malaca there is another seaport of the kingdom of

[1] Sian, Ortelius. [2] Tanazaru, Ortelius. [3] Java frankincense, in Arabic.

Ansiam, which is called Queda,[1] in which also there is much shipping, and great interchange of merchandise. And many ships of the Moors and from other parts come there. Very good pepper grows in the country, which they carry to Malaca, and thence to China. This King of Ansiam has three other sea ports between Malaca and Tenasery, of which I do not know the names, and he possesses many cities, towns, and other villages. Throughout the country in the interior the people are Gentiles, and Moors do not enter there, and if at any time any Moor goes there to trade with them, they do not permit him to carry arms. There is much gold in this kingdom which is collected in the country, particularly in the lordship of Pani, which is beyond Malacca towards China, and has always belonged to the kingdom of Siam, until now that it has risen up against it, and does not obey it, but has rather placed itself in subjection to the King of Malacca. And so likewise in this kingdom of Siam, there is another lordship and country of Gentiles, in subjection to it, which is called Sara hangor,[3] in which there is much tin, which they carry to the city of Malacca as merchandise, and hence they carry it to all parts. The king and people of the kingdom of Ansyam, who are Gentiles, greatly honour their idols, and have many customs different from those of the other nations. They go naked from the waist upwards, and some wear small jackets of silk stuffs. The country is very well supplied with provisions, flesh of domestic and

[1] Queda, Ortelius; Keddah, Malay State tributary to Siam, it derives its name from the Arabic, a cup. Ramusio and Lisbon edit., Quedaa.

> "Olha Tavay cidade, onde começa
> De Syão o largo imperio tão comprido
> Tenessary, Queda, que he so cabeça
> Das que pimienta aly tem produzido;
> Mays avante fareys que se conheça
> Malaca, por Emperio ennobrecido,
> Onde toda a provincia domar grande,
> Suas mercadorias ricas mande."—Lusiadas, x, stanza 123.

[2] Paam, Ortelius; Pahang, now an independent Malay State.

[3] Not in Ortelius; Salangore, an independent Malay State.

wild animals, and rice. They have many horses of a small breed, and much fruit of various qualities. The men are great hunters and sportsmen. In the interior of the country towards China, there is another kingdom of Gentiles which is in obedience to him, (the King of Siam) and there, when a relation or a friend dies, they eat him roasted before a great fire in the middle of a field, where they set up three poles stuck in the earth, and between them a chain with two hooks of iron, and they bring the body of the man who has died of illness or of any other death, and they hang him up there by the hams, roasting him, and his children and relations are there bewailing him, and after he is well roasted they take wine in cups, and they have knives with which they all cut from the body and eat of it, weeping all the while, and they drink their wine; and the nearest relations begin first to eat, and in this manner they finish eating him, and leave only the bones, which they burn afterwards; and they say that they give such a burial to their relations on account of their being of their own flesh, and that they cannot be any where better buried than in their bodies.[1] And in all the kingdom of Ansyam they burn the dead bodies, because that is the custom of all the Gentile countries.

KINGDOM AND CITY OF MALACCA.

The said kingdom of Ansyane throws out a great point of land into the sea,[2] which makes there a cape, where the

[1] "Vé nos remotos montes outras gentes
Que Gueos se chamão de selvages vidas;
Humana carne comem, mas a sua
Pintão com ferro ardente, usança crua."
Lusiade, stanza 126.

[2] "Mas na ponta da tierra Gingapura
Veràs, onde o caminho às naos se estreyta,
De aqui tornando a costa à Cynosura
Se encurva, e para a Aurora se endereyta.
Ves Pam, Patàne reynos, e alongura
De Syão, que estes, e outros mays sogeyta.
Olha o rio Menão, que se derrama
Do grande lago, que Chiamay se chama."
Lusiade, x, stanza 125.

sea returns again towards China to the north; in this promontory is a small kingdom in which there is a large city called Malaca; and in former times it belonged to the kingdom of Ansyam. And the Moors of the town and foreign Moors, established their trade in this city, in which they increased so much in wealth, that they revolted with the country and caused the neighbouring inhabitants to turn Moors, and they set up a Moorish king over them, without paying further obedience to the said King of Ansyam. Many Moorish merchants reside in it, and also Gentiles, particularly Chetis, who are natives of Cholmendel: and they are all very rich and have many large ships, which they call jungos. They deal in all sorts of goods in different parts, and many other Moorish and Gentile merchants flock thither from other countries to trade; some in ships of two masts from China and other places, and they bring thither much silk in skeins,[1] many porcelain vases, damasks, brocades, satins of many colours, they deal in musk, rhubarb, coloured silks, much iron, saltpetre, fine silver, many pearls and seed pearl, chests, painted fans, and other toys, pepper, wormwood,[2] Cambay stuffs, scarlet cloths, saffron, coral polished and rough, many stuffs of Palecate, of coloured cotton, others white from Bengal, vermilion, quicksilver, opium and other merchandise, and drugs from Cambay; amongst which there is a drug which we do not possess and which they call puchô, and another called cachô, and another called magican, which are gall nuts, which they bring from the Levant to Cambay, by way of Mekkah, and they are worth a great deal in China and Java. There also come thither many ships from Java, which have four masts, very different from ours, and of very thick wood. When these

[1] The Lisbon edition has *sulia*, and explains the word in a note as translated above.

[2] Encienço is the old word for ajenco, absinthe, or it may be the old form of incenso, incense.

become old they fish[1] them with other new planks, and in this manner they carry three or four coverings of planking one above the other; and the sails are of woven osiers,[2] and the cordage of the same. These bring much rice, meat of cows, sheep, pigs and deer, dried and salted, many chickens, garlic and onions. They also bring thither many weapons for sale, that is to say, lances, daggers and swords, worked with inlaid metal and of very good steel, they bring likewise cubebs and a yellow die which they call cazunba, and gold which is produced in Java. They bring their wives and children in these ships, and there are some mariners whose wives and children never leave the ship to go on shore, nor have any other dwelling, but there are born and die. From this place many ships sail to the Molucca Islands, which will be mentioned further on, to ship cloves, and they carry there as merchandise Cambay cloths, and all sorts of cottons, silks, and other stuffs of Palacate and Bangala, quicksilver, tin, copper unwrought and wrought into bells, and in a coin which they bring from China, like ceutis[3] of Portugal, pierced in the middle, pepper, porcelain, garlic and onions, with other things and drugs from Cambay; and they traffic much in them. So they navigate in these ships to other islands which are scattered over all the sea, that is to say, to Timor, whence they bring white sandal, which the Indians make great use of; and they carry to them iron, hatchets, knives, swords, cloths of Palacate and Cambay, copper, quicksilver, vermilion, tin and lead, little beads from Cambay of all sorts. And in exchange for these things they carry away the before named sandal, honey, wax, slaves; and at the Isles of Bandam they ship nutmeg and mace.

[1] The English word to *fish* a mast or fishing rod, comes from the Spanish word used here, fajar; anciently pronounced as the Catalan faixar, to wrap or wind a sash, to swathe.

[2] Rattan.

[3] Small coins, three ceutis make one blanca, an ancient coin. Escuela de leer letras Antiguas, p. 207: not in the dictionaries.

These islands supply themselves with goods from Cambay. These ships also fetch pepper from Samatra, silk in skeins, benjuy, and fine gold; and from other islands they fetch camphor and aloes wood; and they also navigate to Tanasery, Peygu, Bengala, Palecate, Cholmender, Malabar, Cambay, and Aden, with all kinds of goods, so that this city of Malaca is the richest trading port and possesses the most valuable merchandise, and most numerous shipping and extensive traffic, that is known in all the world. And it has got such a quantity of gold that the great merchants do not estimate their property, nor reckon otherwise than by bahars of gold, which are four quintals each bahar. There are merchants among them who will take up singly three or four ships laden with very valuable goods, and will supply them with cargo from their own property. They are very well made men, and likewise the women, they are of a brown colour, and go bare from the waist upwards, and from that downwards cover themselves with silk and cotton cloths, and they wear short jackets half way down the thigh of scarlet cloth, and silk, cotton or brocade stuffs; and they are girt with belts, and carry daggers in their waists wrought with rich inlaid work, these they call querix.[1] And the women dress in wraps of silk stuffs, and short shirts much adorned with gold and jewellery, and have long beautiful hair. These people have many mosques, and when they die they bury their bodies. Their children inherit from them. They live in large houses, and have their gardens and orchards, and pools of water outside the city for their recreation. They have got many slaves who are married with wives and children. These slaves live separately and serve them when they have need of them. These Moors who are named Malayos are very polished people, and gentlemen, musical, gallant, and well proportioned. The Chety merchants from Cholmendel are for the most part stout and corpulent. They

[1] Kris.

also go bare from the waist upwards. In this city there are also many people from Java dwelling in it; they are small stout men, whose breasts and faces are long and ill formed. They are Moors and go bare from the waist upwards, and wear cloths ill put on from the waist downwards. They wear nothing on their heads, and their hair is curled with art, and some of them are shaved. They are ingenious and subtle in all their work, and very cunning and treacherous, and of little truth, daring in all mischief, and unto death. They have very good arms and fight valiantly. There are some of them who if they fall ill of any severe illness, vow to God that if they remain in health they will of their own accord seek another more honourable death for his service,[1] and as soon as they get well they take a dagger in their hands and go out into the streets and kill as many persons as they meet, both men, women and children, in such wise that they go like mad dogs, killing until they are killed. These are called amuco. And as soon as they see them begin this work, they cry out saying, amuco, amuco,[2] in order that people may take care of themselves, and they kill them with dagger and spear thrusts. Many of these Javans live in this city with wives and children and property. This city possesses very good water and fruit, and is very healthy. Other provisions are brought from outside. The King of Malaca has got much treasure, and a large revenue from the duties which he collects. To him the lord of Pam made himself tributary, who was a ruler in the kingdom of Ansyam, and he raised himself up against it. In this country of Pam much gold of inferior quality is found. This country of Malaca was discovered by Diego Lopez de

[1] This passage fixes the Hindu origin of running amok, which from this seems to have been connected with the worship of Shiva or Bhowani. Now it would be difficult to get any other explanation than that of *adet*, custom.

[2] The Barcelona MS. has plainly Amuco, which is correct. Ramusio has Amulos, and the Lisbon edition Guanicio.

Sequeyra, a Portuguese gentleman, and after it was discovered the Moors of the country took certain Portuguese and merchandise by stratagem,[1] and killed some, on account of which Alfonso de Alborquerque, Captain General of the King of Portugal in the Indies, moved his fleet, and went against Malaca to avenge this event, and he attacked and took it by assault, and drove out the King of Malaca, notwithstanding that the Moors made a vigorous defence with artillery, spears, arms, guns, and arrows, and with elephants armed with wooden castles, in which were good soldiers with their weapons. So that the merchants and traders of this city surrendered into subjection to the King of Portugal, without any vexations being done to them. And the Portuguese immediately built a handsome fortress in this city, which entirely commands the town and all its trade, as it was before. Much spoil was taken in this city, and great wealth from those who had fled. The ruler of Pam, the lord of a gold mine, on knowing that Malaca was in subjection to the King of Portugal, at once sent an ambassador to this Captain Major General, offering obedience to the King of Portugal.

ARCHIPELAGO OF MALACA.

In front of the before named island of Samatra across the Gulf of the Ganges, are five or six small islands, which have very good water and ports for ships, they are inhabited by Gentiles, poor people, they are called Niconbar,[2] and they find in them very good amber, which they carry thence to Malaca and other parts.

ISLAND OF SAMATRA.

Having passed these islands near the Cape of Malaca,

[1] Thirty men according to other accounts.

[2] Nicobar, Ortelius' map of Asia, and Nicovan in map of India; Ramusio, Navacar.

about twenty leagues to the south[1] there is a large and very beautiful island which is called Samatara,[2] which has in circumference seven hundred leagues reckoned by the Moors, who have sailed all round it: and it has many seaports and kingdoms of Moors and Gentiles. The Moors live in the seaports, and the Gentiles in the interior of the country. The principal kingdom of the Moors is called Pedir.[3] Much very good pepper grows in it, which is not so strong or so fine as that of Malabar. Much silk is also grown there, but not so good as the silk of China. Another kingdom is called Birahem,[4] and another Paser,[5] and another Campar,[6] another Andraguide,[7] another Manancabo,[8] where much fine gold is collected, which is taken thence to Malaca, most of it in dust; and another kingdom called Haru, of Gentiles, who eat human flesh, and any person whom they can catch, they eat him without any mercy. And it also contains many other kingdoms of Gentiles in the interior of the country. In some parts of this island there grows much benjuy, pepper, and long pepper, camphor, and some ginger, and wax. Many ships sail to this island for these goods. Cloths and goods from Cambay are worth a good deal in it, and so also coral, quicksilver, rose-water, dried fish from Maldiu. These Moors are very disloyal, and often kill their kings and set up others who are more powerful. The King of Portugal has a fortress in this island, and trade. And having passed Samatara towards Java there is the island of Sunda,[9] in which there is much good pepper, and it has a king over it, who, they say, desires to serve the King of Portugal. They ship thence many slaves for China.

[1] Medio *giorno*, Italian. [2] Samotra and Sumatra, Ortelius.
[3] Pedir, Ortelius. [4] Biraen, Ortelius, on the north-west coast.
[5] Pasem and Pazer, Ortelius; Passam, Homannus.
[6] Camper, Ortelius and Homannus, between Siuk and Jambi.
[7] Amdaragui, Ortelius; Andragari, Homannus; east coast.
[8] Menancabo, Ortelius, south-west coast.
[9] Sunda, Ortelius.

JAVA MAJOR.

Further on than this said island towards the western quarter and the south[1] there are many islands small and great, amongst which there is one very large which they call Java the Great;[2] it is one hundred and twenty leagues distant from the Cape of Malaca to the south south east, and it is inhabited by many Gentiles and Moors. And in its seaports there are many towns and villages and large settlements of Moors, with Moorish kings. But they are all obedient to the king of the island, who is a Gentile, and lives in the interior of the country, and is a great lord called Patevdara,[3] and sometimes some rebel against him, and afterwards he again subjugates them. Some of these Moorish rulers and inhabitants of Java desire to serve the King of Portugal, and others are ill affected towards him. They say that this island is the most abundant country in the world. There is in it much good rice, and various meats of all kinds, domestic and wild, they make in this place much dried and salted flesh for many parts. There grows in this island pepper, cinnamon, ginger, bamboos, cubebs, and gold. Its inhabitants are short and stout in stature with broad faces.[4] Most of them go bare from the waist upwards, others wear silk clothes down to the middle of the thigh, and their beards thin;[5] the hair shaven on the top and curled upwards, they wear nothing on their heads, and say that nothing must be on their heads, nor anything whatever, and if any person were to put his hand upon their head they would kill him: and they do not build houses with stories, in order that they may not walk over each other's heads. They are very proud

1 Ramusio has here translated south-east, the Lisbon edition has south-west.

2 Java Maior, Ortelius. It is still called Java Major by the Arabs.

3 Ramusio, Palevdora; Lisbon, Pateudru.

4 They look very like Crim Tatars.

5 Raydas.

men, liars and treacherous; very ingenious as carpenters and masons, and very good artillerymen. They make in this country many guns and long muskets, and many other fireworks. And in all other parts they are much esteemed for this and as artillerymen. They have got many ships and great navigation, and many rowing galleys. They are great corsairs and mariners, and they make many kinds of arms of good temper and of good steel, wrought with very pretty inlaid work of gold and ivory: they are great sorcerers and necromancers, and they make arms in certain places and hours, and they say that those cannot die by steel who wear them, and that they kill by drawing blood: and others of which they say that those who bear them cannot be conquered. And they say that there are arms which they employ eight or ten years to complete, watching for places, hours and minutes, disposed for these effects: and the kings prize and take great care of these. They are great sportsmen and hunters, they have plenty of horses and many good hunting dogs, and birds of prey for the chase. When they go to hunt they take their wives with them in handsome carts with canopies and curtains; and the kings and great lords also go in those carts, which are drawn by horses when they go hunting. The ladies are white and very pretty in figure and of pleasing countenances though rather long; they sing well, are polished in manner, and are very industrious workwomen.

JAVA MINOR.

Further out to sea five leagues to the east of the said island of Java Major is another island also very well supplied with provisions of all kinds, inhabited by Gentiles, with a Gentile king, and a language of its own. A few Moors subjects of the Gentile king live in the seaports. This island is called amongst them Sumbava, and the Moors, Arabs, and Persians call it Java Minor.[1] And after passing the said island there

[1] Java Minor, Ortelius, now Bali, the inhabitants are still pagans;

is another small island called Oçare, and a fire always burns in the centre of it. They go much on horseback and are hunters, and the women take much care of the flocks.

TIMOR.

Having passed these islands of Java Major and Minor, forty-two leagues distant from Java Minor to the east south-east there are many other islands great and small, inhabited by Gentiles and by a few Moors, amongst which there is an island called Timor,[1] which has a Gentile king, and a language of its own. Much white sandal grows there, and those who go for it carry as goods to this island iron hatchets, large and small, knives and swords, stuffs from Cambay and Palecate, porcelain, small beads of all kinds, tin, quicksilver and lead. They also ship in this island honey, wax, slaves, and some silver which is found in these islands.

ISLANDS OF BANDAN.

Fifteen leagues more to the north-north-west there are five other islands almost close together, which make a pool between them into which ships enter. And they enter there on two sides, and these are called the Bandan Islands,[2] they

the island Sumbawa also in Ortelius is not the same as Java Minor, but apparently the one here called Oçare, as it contains a great volcano. Here Ramusio says some lines are wanting; he calls the island Oçare, Nucopora.

[1] Timor, Ortelius :—

"Aly tambien Timor, que o lenho manda
Sandalo salutifero, e cheyroso.
Olha a Sunda tão larga, que humabanda
Esconde para o Sul difficultuoso.
A gente do sertão, que as torras anda,
Hum rio diz que tem miraculoso,
Que por onde elle so sem outro vae
Converte em pedra o pao que nelle cae."

Lusiad. x, stanza 134.

[2] Bandan, Ortelius :—

"Olha do Bandá asilhas que se esmaltão
Da varia cor, que pinta o rosco fruto,
As aves, variadas, que aly saltão,

are inhabited by Moors and Gentiles, and in three of them there grows much nutmeg and mace upon trees like laurels, whose fruit is the nutmeg, and upon the nutmeg is the mace like a flower, and above this there is another thick rind: and in these islands one quintal of mace is worth as much as seven of nutmeg, for there is such a quantity of the nutmeg that they burn, so that it is almost worth nothing. And to purchase this mace and nutmeg the merchants carry the following goods: cotton and silk stuffs of all kinds from Cambay, drugs from Guzerat, copper, quicksilver, lead and tin; and some coloured caps[1] with long pile, which they bring from the Levant, and bells from Java which are worth each one of the large ones twenty bahars of mace, and each bahar is four quintals. From this island of Bandam to Maluco, which is towards the north, there are many islands inhabited and uninhabited, in these they keep as treasure very large metal bells; ivory, Cambay silk stuffs which they call patolas, and very fine porcelain. There is no king in these islands, nor do they obey any one: on some occasions they obey the King of Maluco.

DANDON.[2]

A hundred leagues further on to the north-east towards Maluco, there are many other islands peopled by Gentiles, they are called the Dandon islands, each one has a king and a language of its own. In these islands there are many rowing boats which go out to rob one another, and make prisoners, whom they kill, or ransom for Cambay stuffs, which are highly valued amongst them; and each man labours to obtain such a quantity of these cloths that when

Da verde Noz tomando seu tributo.
Olha tambem Borneo, onde não faltaõ
Lagrimas, no licor qualhado, e enxuto,
Das arvores, que camphora he chamado
Com que da ilha o nome he celebrado." Lusiad., 133.

[1] Chapel is also the same as chapin, a slipper or sandal.

[2] Ramusio, Ambon; Lisbon, Andam.

placed upon the ground the bundle would rise to the height of a man's stature; and those who have as much as that consider themselves as free, since the ransom of those who are captured is not greater than this quantity.

ISLANDS OF MALUCO, WHICH ARE FIVE.

Beyond these islands twenty-five leagues towards the north-east there are five islands one before the other, which are called the islands of Maluco,[1] in which all the cloves grow, and they are of Gentiles and Moors. Their kings are Moors, and the first of them is called Bachan, the second Maquian, which contains a very good harbour, the third is called Motil, the fourth Tidory, and the fifth Ternaty,[2] in which there is a Moorish king who is called Sultan Benarra Sorala. He was king of all these islands of cloves, and now all the four have revolted, and have each got a king of their own. The hills in these five islands are all of cloves, which grow on trees like laurel, which has its leaf like that of the arbutus, and it grows like the orange flower, which in the beginning is green and then turns white, and when it is ripe it turns coloured, and then they gather it by hand, the people going amongst the trees, and they put it to dry in the sun, where it turns brown, and if there is no sun they dry it with the smoke, and after it is very dry they sprinkle it with salt water for it not to crumble, and that it may preserve its virtue. And there are such quantities of these cloves that they never can finish gathering them, so that they let much of it be lost. And the trees from which they do not gather it for three years, after that become wild, so that their cloves are worth nothing. Every year the people of

[1] Molucos, Ortelius.

[2] Bachian, Machian, Motir, Tidore, Tarenate, Ortelius; Bluteau's dictionary names them Bachan, Maquien, Moutel, Tidor, Ternate, and says they were anciently named Seque, Mara, Moutil, Duco, Gape. The only remaining possession of the Portuguese in the Malay Archipelago is Dili in the island of Timor.

Malaca and Java come to these islands to ship cloves, and they bring as merchandise, quicksilver, vermilion, stuffs from Cambay, Bengal and Palecate, drugs from Cambay, some pepper, porcelain, large metal bells which are made in Java, dishes of copper and tin. The cloves are worth very little in these islands, so as to be almost for nothing. This King of Maluco is a Moor, and almost a Gentile; he has a Moorish wife, and three or four hundred Gentile damsels whom he keeps in his house, and he has of many of them Gentile sons and daughters, and only the children of the Moorish women become Moors. He is served by hump-backed women, whom he orders to have their spines bent from childhood, for state and show; and he may have eighty or a hundred of these, who always go with him and serve him as pages; some give him betel, others carry his sword, and they render all other services. In these islands there are many coloured parrots, of very splendid colours; they are tame, and the Moors call them nure,[1] and they are much valued amongst them.

ISLAND OF CELEBE.[2]

Having passed these islands of Maluco to the west of Motil and Machian, at a distance of a hundred and thirty leagues, there are other islands to the west, from which sometimes there come white people, naked from the waist upwards, and they wear cloths round them made of straw, and have a language of their own. They bring some ill made boats to ship cloves in the before mentioned islands, and copper, tin and Cambay stuffs. They bring for sale very long and broad swords of one edge and other manufactures of iron,[3] and much gold. These people eat human

[1] Nury is the real name of Molucca parrots, which has been changed to loro and lori. Ramusio calls them mire, and the Lisbon ed. noire.

[2] This section is not in the Lisbon MS.

[3] The Bugis of Celebes still make the best krises.

flesh, and if the King of Maluco has any person to execute they beg for him to eat him, just as one would ask for a pig, and the islands from whence they come are called Celebe.[1]

BANGAYA.[2]

At no great distance from this island to the west-south-west, at thirty-six leagues off, is another island of Gentiles which has a Gentile king over it. The inhabitants of it are accustomed to saw off their teeth at the roots of the gums. It is called Bangaya,[3] there is much iron in it, which they carry to all parts.

SOLOR.

Seventy-five leagues further on to the north-east in the direction of China is a very large island and well supplied with various provisions, which is called Solor,[4] it is inhabited by Gentiles, almost white men, and well made; they have a Gentile king and a language of their own. In this island there is much gold, which is found in the earth; and all round this island the Moors gather much seed pearl and fine pearls of perfect colour and not round.

BORNEY.

Beyond this island to the north more towards China is another island also very well supplied with provisions, inhabited by Gentiles, who have a Gentile king and a language of their own. In this island much camphor for eating is gathered, and the Indians value it highly. It is worth its

[1] Celebes, Ortelius.

[2] This section is not in the Lisbon MS.

[3] Ramusio and the Lisbon ed., Tendaya. Banguey island, north of Borneo, 7 deg. 13 min. N. lat. and 120 deg. 12 min. E. long.; $6\frac{3}{4}$ leagues long and $3\frac{1}{2}$ broad: it is desert. Geographical Dict., Barcelona, 1831.

[4] The island now called Solor is in another direction E. of the island Flores, 8 deg. 30 min. S. lat. and 126 deg. 52 min. E. long.

weight in silver, and some of it even more. They bring it made into powder in tubes of cane; and it is worth a great deal in Narsinga, Malabar, and Decan.[1] This island is called Borney.[2]

CHAMPA.

Having passed this island thirty leagues to the west towards the country of Ansiam and China, there is another great island of Gentiles, which is called Champa,[3] which has a king and a language of its own; and many elephants which are bred there, and they carry them to many places. There also grows in it aloes wood which the Indians call eagle, and calambuco; it must be said that the very fine calambuco and the other eagle wood is worth at Calicut a thousand maravedis the pound.[4] Between these islands there are many other islands inhabited by gentiles, and others uninhabited amongst which there is one in which there are many diamonds which the people of the country collect and export for sale to many parts but they are not such nor so fine as those of Narsynga.

CHINA.

Leaving these islands which are many, almost unnumbered, of all of which the names are not known; and they are towards the north and in the direction of China, and there is not much information about them; it is only known that after passing the kingdom of Ansyam and other kingdoms, there is the kingdom of China, which they say is a very extensive dominion, both along the coast of the sea and in the interior of the country; it is a country of Gentiles, and

[1] Ramusio stops here and says several lines are wanting.

[2] Borneo, Ortelius.

[3] Champa, Ortelius and Homannus, the southern portion of Cochin China next to Cambodia; it is not an island as here stated.

[4] Ramusio says three hundred maravedis, the Lisbon MS. says thirty or forty pardoes.

it possesses many islands in the sea also inhabited by Gentiles, subject to it, in which the King of China keeps his governors and officers of his appointment. This king always resides in the interior of the country in very large and good cities. No foreigner enters within the kingdom, they can only trade in the sea ports, and in the islands; and if any ambassador from another kingdom comes to it by sea, he first gives information of it in order that he may enter, and afterwards the king bids him be conducted to where he is staying. The inhabitants of the country are white men, tall, well-made and gentlemen; and so likewise the women. They have got only one defect, that their eyes are very small, and on their chins they have three or four hairs and no more; the smaller their eyes are, so much the prettier they think them; and the same as regards the women. They are very smartly dressed, clothed in silk and cotton and woollen stuffs, and their costumes are like those of Germans; they are shod with soft leather boots[1] and shoes, like the people of a cold country. They have a language of their own, and the tone of it is like that of Germans. They eat on high tables like ourselves, with their napkins, and for as many as may be there to eat, they set before each one a plate, a small roll, and a knife, and a silver cup; they do not touch the food which they are going to eat with their hands, but eat it with little pinchers of silver or wood, and they hold in their left hand the dish or porcelain in which they eat, brought very close to the mouth, and with those pinchers they eat very quickly. They prepare various kinds of viands, and eat all meats, and wheaten bread. They drink several kinds of wine, and many times during their meals. They also eat the flesh of dogs which they hold to be good meat. They are men of truth and[2] good gentlemen: they are great mer-

[1] Borceguies—the Turkish mest.

[2] There is a *no*, not, here in the manuscript, which seems to be put in by mistake; the Spanish idiom does not allow of adding another nega-

chants of all sorts of goods. They make much porcelain in the country, and very good, which is a great article of commerce for all parts. They make them of sea snail shells well ground and with the whites and shells of eggs, and of other materials, of which they make a dough, which they put under the earth to ripen and mature itself, for a space of eighty or a hundred years, and they leave this mass as a treasure and inheritance, because as the time approaches for working it so it becomes more valuable, and in this way they leave it to their sons and grandsons;[1] and after the time has arrived they work it into vases of all patterns, and after they are made they enamel and paint them. There also grows and is produced in this country of China much very good silk, of which they make a great quantity of stuffs; that is to say, damasks of all colours, satins of several kinds, and brocade. There is much rhubarb in this country, and much musk, very fine silver, seed pearl, and pearls that are not very round. They also make many other very pretty gilded things in this country; that is to say, very rich chests and trays of gilt wood, salt dishes, fans, and other delicate works of ingenious men. They are also great navigators in very large ships which they call jungos, of two masts, of a different make from ours, the sails are of matting, and so also the cordage. There are great corsairs and robbers amongst those islands and ports of China. They go with all these goods to Malaca, where they also carry much iron, saltpetre and many other things, and for the return voyage they ship there Samatra and Malabar pepper, of which they use a great deal in China, and drugs of Cambay, much anfiam, which we call opium, wormwood, Levant gall nuts, saffron, coral wrought and un-

tive at the beginning of the sentence; the one negative alone makes nonsense, and is contrary to what has been said above.

[1] A French missionary, quoted in the "Dictionnaire de la Conversation," does not believe this story, which he assumes to be invented for the sake of increasing the value of the porcelain.

wrought, stuffs from Cambay, Palecate and Bengal, vermilion, quicksilver, scarlet cloth, and many other things. In this country of China the pepper is worth fifteen ducats the quintal, and more according to the quantity they carry there, which pepper they buy in Malaca at four ducats the quintal. Many of these Chinese take their wives and children continually in the ships in which they live without possessing any other dwelling. This China borders on Tartary towards the north, and it is a thousand leagues distant to the north-north-west from the Malucos.

LEQUEOS.

Opposite this country of China there are many islands in the sea, and beyond them at a hundred and seventy-five leagues to the east there is one very large which they say is the mainland, from whence there come each year to Malaca three or four ships like those of the Chinese, of white people whom they describe as great and wealthy merchants. They bring much gold in bars, silver, silk and many very rich silk stuffs, much very good wheat, beautiful porcelain and other merchandise. And they ship pepper and other things which they carry away. These islands are called Lequeos,[1] the people of Malaca say that they are better men, and greater and wealthier merchants, and better dressed and adorned, and more honourable than the Chinese. There is not much information about these people up to the present time, because they have not come to India since the King of Portugal possesses it.[2]

FINIS.

[1] The Liu Kiu Islands. Lequio major and minor, Ya. Fermosa, and Reix magas, form a group in Ortelius: in Homannus Formosa is in its proper place, and the group is called Lequeyo or Riukiu Islands.

[2] Here the Lisbon edition says that the manuscript of Duarte Barbosa ends, and that what follows about the precious stones has been translated from the Italian of Ramusio: this appendix about precious stones is wanting in the Munich MS. No. 570.

An end was made of transferring this book from its original in the Portuguese language, translated into Castilian language, in Vitoria, the Emperor and King of Spain residing there, on the first day of March, of the year one thousand five hundred and twenty-four years, by Min. Cinturion,[1] Ambassador of the Community of Genoa, with the interpretation of Diego Ribero, Portuguese, Cosmographer of His Majesty, and Master of the Sailing charts.

ACCOUNT OF THE RUBIES, WHERE THEY GROW, OF THEIR VARIETY, AND OF HOW THEY ARE SOLD IN THE MALABAR COUNTRY.

Firstly, the rubies grow in the third India, and are for the most part gathered in a river which is called Peygu, and these are the best and the finest, which the Malabars call nir puco. Those which are sold for the prices written below must be very good, without any blemish: and in order to know their fineness the Indians put the point of their tongue upon them, and that which is the coldest and hardest is best: and in order to see its purity they take it up with wax by the finest point, and so look at it by the light, by which they see any blemish which it may have got. They are found in very deep caves which there are amongst the mountains. And in this river and country of Peygu they clean them, but do not work them, for they take them to other parts to be worked, principally in Palecate and the country of Narsynga.

[1] Martin Centurion according to the Munich MS. No. 571, where the name is given in full.

In Calicut and the whole Malabar country, eight fine rubies of the weight of one fanam are worth ten fanaes[1] - - x fs. 10

[1] Fano, fanam, fanão—a weight for weighing rubies, according to Bluteau=1 quilat or carat; according to the Dicco. Enciclopedico, Madrid, 1853, and the Encyclopedie of Diderot and D'Alembert=to 2 carats of Venice. Also a coin equal to two Spanish reals or twenty Portuguese reis, or ten of which made a cruzado. The author has said in another place that it is equal to thirty-six maravedis. The following table of coins will be useful with reference to the prices named in this work.

Ducado =	375 maravedis.
Dobla =	365 „
Florin =	265 „
Real =	34 „

These maravedis were worth double those of the present time, in which a real contains 34 maravedis, so that a fanam would be worth 2 reals or half a peseta=6d. The author of the Escuela de leer Letras Antiguas, from which these figures are taken, has added lists of prices at different times as guides to the value of coins.

In 1348, law of Don John I.

Fanega of wheat	15 maravedis.
Ditto barley	10 „
Ditto oats	8 „
Cubit of French cloth	60 „
Ditto Flanders or English cloth	50 „
Day's wages from November to March	3 „
Ditto ditto March to November	4 „
Each yoke for ploughing all day	10 „
A servant by the year	100 „
A maid ditto	50 „
For grinding a fanega of wheat	2 „
A thousand tiles	60 „
Ditto bricks	55 „
A fanega of mortar	6 „
Ditto lime	5 „
An ox	200 „
A calf	180 „
A pound of mutton	2 „
A hare	3 „
A rabbit	2 „
A fowl	4 „
A goose	6 „

Four rubies of the said weight in perfection xx fanaes - - -	xx fs.	20
Two weighing one fanam - -	xl fs.	40
One weighing one fanam - -	l fs.	50
One weighing three quarters of a fanam -	xxx fs.	30
One weighing a fanam and a quarter -	lxxv fs.	75
One weighing a fanam and a half is worth -	c fs.	100
One which should weigh a fanam and three quarters - - -	cl fs.	150
A ruby which weighs two fanaes is worth	cc fs.	200
One which should weigh two fanoes and a quarter - - - -	ccl fs.	250
One of two and a half - -	ccc fs.	300
One of two and three quarters and a half -	cccc fs.	400
One of three fanoes - - -	ccccl fs.	450
One of three fanoes and a quarter -	d fs.	500
One of three and a half - -	dl fs.	550
One of three and three quarters -	dc fs.	600
One of three fanoes three quarters and a half - - - -	dcxxx fs.	630
One of four fanoes - - -	dclx fs.	660
One of four fanoes and a quarter -	dcc fs.	700
One of four fanoes and a half - -	dcccc fs.	900
One of five fanoes - - -	ɪↄ fs.	1,000
One of five fanoes and a half - -	ɪↄcc fs.	1,200
One of six fanoes - - -	ɪↄd fs.	1,500

They are usually worth these prices if they are perfect, and those which should not be perfect, or may have any spots,

A pigeon . . . . . . 3 maravedis.
A partridge . . . . . . 5 "

These maravedis were worth 22½ actual maravedis, or about 2d. each.

In 1524 the fanega of wheat was fixed at 70 maravedis.
Ditto ditto of barley " 40 "

These maravedis were worth two of the actual ones.

1865, a fanega of wheat = . 50 reals.

or have not got a good colour are worth much less, according to the choice of the buyer. A fanam weighs something more than two carats of our parts, and eleven fanoes and a quarter are a mitigal,[1] and six mitigals and a half make an ounce, and each fanan is worth here a real of silver.[2]

ACCOUNT OF THE SPINEL RUBIES.

There is another kind of rubies which we call spinel rubies, and the Indians call them carapuch, which are produced in the same country of Peygu, where the fine rubies grow, and they find them in the mountains near the surface of the ground. These are not so fine nor of so bright a colour as the rubies, but they have rather the colour of scarlet: and those which are perfect in colour and pure, are worth half less than the rubies.

ACCOUNT OF OTHER RUBIES OF CEYLON.

In the second India there is an island called Ceylan, where many rubies are found, which the Indians call manica, most of these do not reach the perfection of the others in colour, because they are red, and pale, and ruddy.[3] They are very hard and very cold, and those which are found in all their perfection of colour are very highly valued amongst them. And the king of that island has them found, and keeps the perfect ones for himself, which he sells with his own hand: and when the lapidaries clean them if they find one very white they put it by his orders into the fire for a certain number of hours, and if it endures the fire and comes out sound it remains of a brighter colour. Such a stone is of great value, and those of this kind which the King of Narsynga can get into his hands, he orders them to be bored

[1] A miskal.

[2] A real de plata means two reals vellon, or actual reals of the present time.

[3] Son bermejos y deslavados, y encarnados.

with a very fine hole on the underneath side so that the hole reaches to the centre, and they do not pass it, because the stone can no longer leave the kingdom, and that it may be known that it has been tried in the fire. And so also these are worth more than those of Peygu. Their prices are the following if they are perfect in colour and purity:—

One which weighs a carat, which is half a fanam, is worth in Calicut thirty fanoes	xxx fs.	30
One of two carats - - -	lxxv fs.	75[1]
One of three carats - - -	cl fs.	150
One of three carats and a half - -	cc fs.	200
One of four carats - - -	ccc fs.	300
One of four carats and a half - -	cccl fs.	350
One of five carats - - -	cccc fs.	400
One of five carats and a half - -	ccccl fs.	450
One of six carats - - -	dxxx fs.	530
One of six carats and a half - -	dlx fs.	560
One of seven carats - - -	dcxxx fs.	630
One of seven carats and a half - -	dcclx fs.	760
One of eight carats very good and tried in the fire is worth - - -	dccc fs.	800
Such a one of eight carats and a half -	dcccc fs.	900
Such a one of nine carats - -	IUC fs.	1,100
Such a one of ten carats - -	IUCCC fs.	1,300
One of eleven carats of this kind -	IUdc fs.	1,600
One of twelve carats - - -	nU fs.	2,000
One of fourteen carats - -	mU fs.	3,000
One of sixteen carats - -	VIU fs.	6,000

ACCOUNT OF THE BALASSES, WHERE THEY GROW AND WHAT THEY ARE WORTH IN CALICUT.

These balasses are of the class of rubies but not so strong as them, their colour is rosy and some are almost white, they

[1] 65 in Ramusio.

are found in Balaxayo[1] which is a kingdom of the mainland near Peygu and Bengal. The Moors bring them out of that country to all parts; that is to say, the good and picked ones, cut or uncut, they clean and work them in Calicut, and they are sold for the prices of spinel rubies. Those which are not good, and are bored, are bought by the Moors of Mekkah and Aden for the whole of Arabia, where they are accustomed to take them.

ACCOUNT OF THE DIAMONDS OF THE OLD MINE.

These diamonds are gathered in the first India in a kingdom of Moors called Decan, and they carry them thence to all parts. There are other diamonds which are not so good; some are white and are said to be of the new mine which is in the kingdom of Narsynga; these are worth less by a third in Calicut and the country of Malabar, than those of the old mine; and they are worked in the kingdom of Narsynga itself. And those of the old mine are not worked in India. They likewise make false diamonds in India with white rubies, topazes and sapphires, which look like fine gems and these are found in Ceylon, and they only differ from diamonds in the colour which they have by nature. And some of these stones are found half of which have the colour of the ruby and the other of the colour of the sapphire, and others of the colour of the topaze, and some of them have got all these colours mixed. They bore these stones with two or three very fine threads through them, and they remain as cats' eyes. And with the stones which turn out white they make a great quantity of small diamonds which cannot be distinguished from the other genuine ones, except by the touch[2] and by those who have much acquaintance with them.

[1] Balassia in Ramusio. [2] Toque or proof.

Eight fine diamonds which weigh a manjar[1] are worth xxv or - - -	xxx fs.	30
Six weighing one manjar - -	xl fs.	40
Four weighing one manjar - -	lx fs.	60
Two weighing one manjar - -	lxxx fs.	80
One weighing one manjar - -	c fs.	100
One weighing a manjar and a quarter -	clxv fr.	165
One of one and a half - -	clxxx fs.	180
One of one and three quarters - -	ccxx fs.	220
One of one and three quarters and a half	cclx fs.	260
One of two manjars - - -	cccxx fs.	320
One of two and a quarter - -	ccclx fs.	340
One of two and a half - -	ccclxxx fs.	380
One of two and three quarters if in full perfection - - -	ccccxx fs.	420
One of this said perfection of three manjars	ccccl fs.	450
One of three manjars and a half -	cccclxxx fs.	480
One of four manjars - - -	dl fs.	550
One of five manjars - - -	dccl fs.	750
One of six manjars - - -	dcccc fs.	900
One of seven manjars - -	IUCC fs.	1,200
One of eight manjars - -	IUCCCC fs.	1,400

These go on increasing in price in proportion, and each manjar weighs two taras and two-thirds, and two taras make a carat even weight, and four taras weigh a fanam.

ACCOUNT OF THE SAPPHIRES.

The best and most genuine sapphires are found in Ceylon, they are very strong and fine, and those which are in all perfection, and purity, and of a fine blue colour, are worth the following prices.

One which weighs a carat two fanaes -	ii fs.	2
One weighing two - - -	vi fs.	6

[1] Equal to a carat and a third.

One weighing three carats - -	x fs.	10
One weighing four carats - -	xv fs.	15
One weighing five carats - -	xviii fs.	18
A weight of six - - -	xxv fs.	25
One of seven - - -	xxxv fs.	35
One of eight carats - - -	l fs.	50
One of nine - -	lxv fs.	65
One of ten carats - - -	lxxv fs.	75
A sapphire weighing eleven carats is worth	xc. fs.	90
One of twelve - - -	cxx fs.	120
One perfect in purity and colour weighing thirteen carats - - -	cxxxv fs.	135
One of fourteen carats - -	clx fs.	160
One of sixteen two hundred fanoes -	cc fs.	200
One of eighteen - - -	ccl fs.	250
One of twenty - - -	ccc fs.	300
One weighing a mitical which is xi fanams and a quarter - - -	cccl fs.	350

There is also in Ceylam another kind of sapphires, which are not so strong, which they call quirin genilam,[1] and they are of a darker colour. These are worth much less, however good they may be, for one of the above-mentioned is worth as much as thirteen of these.

In the kingdom of Narsynga in a mountain above Bancanor and Mangalor there is another kind of sapphires softer and inferior in colour, which they call cringanilan;[1] they are somewhat whitish; these are worth very little, so much so that the most perfect of them which weighs twenty carats will not be worth a ducat. Their colour is also somewhat yellow.

There is another sort of sapphires which are found on the sea beach of the kingdom of Calicut in a place called

[1] These two names must be the same word Kringa-nila; blue stone, perhaps. In Ramusio, Quiniganilam.

Capucad,[1] the Indians call these carahatonilam, they are very blue and cloudy and do not glitter, except setting them in the light.[2] They are soft and break like glass. An opinion is held by some who say that in former times there was by the sea of this Capurad the house of a king and that its windows were of blue glass, and that the sea having covered it over the pieces of glass are thrown up ashore; but they are very large, and on the other hand they seem to be glass. These are worth very little among them.

ACCOUNT OF THE TOPAZES AND OF THEIR PRICES IN CALICUT.

The natural topazes are found in Ceylon which the Indians call pur ceraga, it is very hard stone and very cold and heavy like the ruby and sapphire, because all three are of one kind. Its perfect colour is yellow like beaten gold, and when their colour is perfect and pure, whether they be great or small, in Calicut they are worth their weight in fine gold, and this is their price usually; and if the colour is not so perfect they are worth their weight in gold of fanams which is less by half, and if it is almost white they are worth much less, and they make small diamonds of them.

ACCOUNT OF THE TURQUOISES, AND OF THEIR PRICES IN MALABAR.

The true turquoises are found in Niexer[3] and Quirimane,[4] country of Sheikh Ismail, in mines and dry ground,[5] and they are found upon black stones, and the Moors detach them there in small pieces, and bring them thence to Ormuz, whence they are sent out to many countries by sea. The Indians call them peyrosa. It is a soft stone and of little weight, and not very cold; and in order to know that it is

[1] Capucar in Ramusio. [2] A jour.
[3] Excr in Ramusio. [4] Kerman. Chiraman, Ortelius.
[5] In the MS. the passage reads *as mina y tierra seca.*

good and true, by day it will seem to you of a blue colour, and at night by candle light it turns green ; and those which are not so perfect, do not change from one appearance. If this stone is pure and of a fine colour, underneath at its base it will have brown stone upon which it grew, and if any little vein or point were to come out above the black stone itself, then it is known as very genuine indeed, and of greater value, because it is a sign of being a true turquoise, and for greater certainty putting upon it a little virgin lime, white and moistened like ointment, the lime will appear coloured. And when they have this perfection they are worth the following prices :—

If the turquoise is of the said perfection and weighs a carat, it will be worth in the Malabar country - -	xv fs.	15
One of two carats - - -	xl fs.	40
One of four carats - - -	xc fs.	90
One of six carats - - -	cl fs.	150
One of eight carats - - -	cc fs.	200
One of ten carats - - -	ccc fs.	300
One of twelve carats - - -	ccccl fs.	450
One of xiiij carats - - -	dl fs.	550

They take no account of the larger ones, from their being light pieces of much bulk. The Moors and Guzuratys wear the large ones.

ACCOUNT OF THE HYACINTHS.

The hyacinths are produced in Ceylan, and are soft yellow stones, and those which are of a stronger colour are the best; most of them have within some grains which impair their beauty, and those which have not got them, and are pure, in perfection of this colour, are worth little in Calicut where they arrange them ; one which weighs a fanam is not worth more than three fanams, and one of xviij fanams is not worth more than xvi fanams.

There are also other gems, cat's eyes, chrysoliths, and amethists, of which no other distinction is made on account of their being of little value, and so also with regard to the jagonzas.[1]

ACCOUNT OF THE EMERALDS.

The emeralds are produced in the country of Babilonia, which the Indians call Maredeygua;[2] and they likewise grow in many other parts; they are green stones of a good colour and pretty; they are light and soft, and many counterfeits are made of them which resemble them, but looking at them in the light they show the counterfeit and some little globules such as all glass makes; and if they were genuine they would not show any. But the sight of them would give great satisfaction and the good ones shew rays inside them like of the sun, and being touched by a touchstone leaves on it a copper colour. And the real emerald is such that they are worth the same as diamonds in Calicut, and something more, not according to the weight but the size, because the diamond is much heavier than it.

There are likewise other emeralds which are green stones, and these are not so much valued, but the Indians make use of them in jewellery. These do not leave a copper colour on the touchstone.[3]

[1] The *Times* reviewer of Mr. Emmanuel's book *On Precious Stones*, April 5, 1866, is in error in saying that "the zircon is known in trade as the jacinth or hyacinth".

The jargon, corindon or circon, which was much used in the xvi^th^ century, is not held in any estimation at the present time; it has the merit of possessing the hardness of the sapphire.

[2] Mar Deignan in Ramusio.

[3] I have been informed by Mr. Capt, jeweller, of Geneva, that the proportions of the prices of precious stones, according to their weight, are still very exact for uncut stones in the Indian market, and that the general accuracy of the details given in this MS. is very great. With respect to the doubts which had been expressed as to the stones of combined colours, they do exist, but are held in no estimation in Europe. Experiments have been made in Europe, and especially in Germany, for

SUMMARY ACCOUNT OF THE SPICES, WHERE THEY GROW, AND WHAT THEY ARE WORTH IN CALICUT, AND WHERE THEY ARE EXPORTED TO.

Pepper grows in all Malabar, firstly in the kingdom of Calicut, and there it is worth from two hundred to two hundred and thirty fanoes the bahal, which weighs four quintals of the old weight of Portugal at which all spice is sold in Lisbon: and they pay twelve fanoes per bahar duty for taking it out of the country to the King of Calicut; and those who buy it are used to take it to Cambay, Persia, Aden, Mekkah, from whence they also transport it to Cayro, and thence to Alexandria. And now they give it to the King of Portugal at the rate of iiijulx (4,060)[1] the bahar, with the duties, which are cxciij fanoes (193) and ¼, on account of so great a variety of merchants no longer resorting there to buy it, and on account of the agreement which the King of Portugal made with the kings and Moors and merchants of the country of Malabar. Much pepper also grows in Sumatra which is an island near Malaca, and it is larger and better looking than that of the Malabar country: but this pepper is not so fine nor so strong as that. This pepper is carried to Bengal and China and Java, and some of it is carried to Mekkah without the knowledge of the Portuguese, who do not allow it to be taken. It is worth 400 to 600 maravedis the quintal of Portugal, in this case of the new weight. And between the new and the old one in Portugal there is a difference of two ounces per pound.

ACCOUNT OF THE CLOVES.

The cloves grow in an island beyond Java called Maluco, and from thence they bring it to Malacca, and from there to Calicut and all the Malabar country. Each bahar is worth

the purpose of deepening the colour of precious stones, particularly rubies, by the process here mentioned; but success was so hazardous, and so costly, that speculators would no longer incur the risks of it.

[1] 6562 in Ramusio.

in Calicut 500 and 600 fanoes, and if it is clean of husks and sticks, at seven hundred fanoes, and xviiij fanoes per bahar are paid as export duty. At Maluco where it grows it is worth from one to two ducats the bahar; according to the multitude of buyers who go for it. In Malacca the bahar of these cloves is worth as much as fourteen ducats the bahar according to the demand of the merchants.

CINNAMON.

Good cinnamon grows in the island of Ceylam, and in the county of Malabar there grows a very inferior quality; the good sort is worth little in Ceylam, and in Calicut it is worth three hundred fanoes the bahar, new and very choice.

BELEDYN GINGER.

Beledyn[1] ginger grows at a distance of two or three leagues all round the city of Calicut, and the bahar is worth lx[2] fanoes, and sometimes fifty, they bring it to the city for sale, from the mountains and estates. The Indian merchants buy it in detail and collect it together, and then in the season for loading ships they sell it to the Moors at prices from ninety to a hundred and ten fanoes; its weight is the greater weight.[3]

ELY GINGER.

The Ely ginger grows in the mountain Dely as far as Cananor, and is smaller and not so white, nor so good. The bahar in Cananor is worth forty fanoes, and six fanoes duty is paid per bahar, and it is sold without being packed.[4]

[1] Beledin, of the country, local; Arabic. Ramusio has not translated it.

[2] xl in Ramusio.

[3] El peso del es el mayor. This may refer to the old and new weights, or it may mean that this ginger is heavier than the other ginger.

[4] Syn enbarar.

GREEN GINGER FOR CONSERVES.

In Bengal there is also much ginger of the country and there they make with it a large quantity of preserves with sugar, very well made; and they bring it in Martaban jars to sell at Malabar, and the farazola, which is twenty-two pounds, is worth xiiij and xv or xvj fanoes. And that which is now preserved with sugar in Calicut is worth xxv fanoes the farazola on account of sugar being dear there.

Green ginger for making preserves is worth three quarters of a fanam the farazola[1] in Calicut.

ACCOUNT OF THE DRUGS AND SPICES IN CALICUT AND ALL THE MALABAR COUNTRY.

Lac of Martaban, very good, is worth the farazola, which is twenty-two pounds and six ounces and a half of Portugal, of xvj ounces to the pound - -	xviij fanoes	18
Lac of the country, the farazola -	xij fs.	12
Coarse camphor in loaves of lxx to eighty fanoes the farazola - - -	lxxx fs.	80
Very good borax[2] in large pieces at xxx, xl, or l fs. the farazola - -	xl fs.	40
Camphor for anointing the idols at the rate of one fanam and a half the mitical, six and a half of which make an ounce -	i fm. & a half	$1\frac{1}{2}$
Camphor for eating and for the eyes at iij fs. the mitical - - -	iij fs.	3
Eagle wood at cccl and cccc fs. the farazola	ccclxxv fs.	375
Genuine aloe-wood, and very choice black and heavy is worth i fs. the farazola -	iu fs.	1,000

[1] Faratela, Indian weight equal to seven and a quarter pounds. Enciclopèd. Dict., Madrid, 1853.

[2] Atincar, Anglicè tincal, when refined, borax.

Musk in powder of good quality, the ounce xxxvi fs. - - -	xxxvi fs.	36
Benjuy each farazola lx and the very good lxx fs. - - -	lxv fs.	65
Fresh tamarinds at iij fs. the farazola -	iij fs.	3
Sweet flag[1] the farazola - -	xij fs.	12
Indigo, coarse and heavy, which contains sand, seventeen to twenty-two fs. the farazola - - - -	xx fs.	20
Encienzo the best when in grain is worth	v fs.	5
Encienzo[2] in paste and inferior is worth -	iij fs.	3
Very good amber is worth ij to iij fs. the mitical - - - -	iij fs.	3
Mirobolans in sugar conserve are worth from sixteen to xxv fs. the farazola -	xx fs.	20
Coloured sandal v and vi fs. the farazola -	vi fs.	6
Spikenard, fresh and good, from xxx to xl fs. the fa. - - -	xl fs.	40
White sandal, and of a lemon colour xl to lx fs. the farazola, it grows in an island called Timor - - -	l fs.	50
Nutmeg x and xi fs. the farazola, it comes from Bandam, where the bahar is worth viij or x fs. - - -	xi fs.	11
Mace from xxv to xxx fs. the farazola, this also comes from Bandan, where it is worth l fs. the bahar.	xxx fs.	30
Good herb lonbreguera[3] at xv fs. the farazola	xv fs.	15
Turbiti,[4] at xiij fs. the farazola - -	xiij fanoes	13

[1] Calamo aromatico, also called acoro, a kind of aquatic plant used in medicine.

[2] This may be either incense or wormwood. Incenso in Ramusio.

[3] Lombriguera, southernwood, wormwood : Artemisia abrotanum.

[4] Turbith, Convolvulus turpethum ; its root is used as a purgative, and it comes from India and Ceylon.

Zerumba is worth the farazola - -	ij fs.	2
Zedoary is worth the farazola - -	i fm.	1
Serapine gum[1] is worth the farazola -	xx fs.	20
Socotra aloes are worth the farazola -	viij fs.	8
Cardamums in grain at xx fs. - -	xx fs.	20
Rhubarb, there is much of it in the Malabar country, and what comes from China by Malaca is worth cccc to d fs. the farazola - - - -	ccccl	450
Mirobolans, ynblicos, are worth, the farazola - - - -	ij fs.	2
Mirobolans, belericos, are worth, the farazola - - - -	i fm.	1
Mirobolans of a citron colour and quebulos which are one kind - -	ij fs.	2
Mirobolans yndos, which are from the same trees as the citron coloured, are worth - - - -	iij fs.	3
Tutty,[2] the farazola - - -	xxx fs.	30
China cubela,[3] which grows in Java, is given there at a low price without weight or measure, by eye.		
Opium is worth the farazola in Calicut, and comes from Aden, where they make it, it is worth from cclxxx to cccxx fs. - - -	ccc fs.	300
Another opium which is prepared in Cambay is worth from cc to ccl fs. the farazola - - - -	ccxxv fs.	225

[1] Gum from the giant fennel: also called sagapeno, is known in commerce as yellowish white drops of a strong aromatic smell something like garlic; is used for diachylum.

[2] Atulia, a sublimate of calamine.

[3] Probably cubebs.

ACCOUNT OF THE WEIGHTS OF PORTUGAL AND OF THE INDIES.

IN PORTUGAL.

A pound of the old weight contains xiiij oz. A pound of the new weight contains xvi oz., eight quintals of the old weight make seven quintals of the new, and each quintal of the new weight is of cxxviij pounds of xv oz., each old quintal is three quarters and a half of a new quintal, and is of cxxviij pounds of xiiij oz. each.

INDIES.

A farazola is xxij pounds of xvi oz. and vi oz. $\frac{2}{7}$ more. Twenty farazolas are one bahar. One bahar is four old quintals of Portugal.[1] All spices and drugs and anything which comes from India is sold in Portugal by old weight, at present all the rest[2] is sold by new weight.

[1] Or four hundredweight English.

[2] Lo al, old Spanish.

VOYAGE WHICH JUAN SERANO MADE WHEN HE FLED FROM MALACA, WITH THREE PORTUGUESE AND CRISTOVAL DE MORALES OF SEVILLE, IN A CARAVEL WHICH HE STOLE IN MALACA, IN WHICH HE PUT CERTAIN MALAY MARINERS, NATIVES OF MALACA, ABOUT THE YEAR OF OUR LORD JESUS CHRIST ONE THOUSAND FIVE HUNDRED AND TWELVE YEARS.[1]

In the name of God: we left the city of Malaca in a caravel with five Malay mariners and pilots; the captain was Fran^co^ Serano, with three other Christians, who in all were nine; the mariners, natives of Malaca; the Christians, three Portuguese and a Castilian. In the year one thousand five hundred and twelve we sailed to the city of Pegu, and this city is on the mainland, and not very far from the sea, more on this side of Malaca, east (and) west[2] of the island Care ca Faya, north (and) south, with the Malacca channel and island Quendan, it must be said, the river higher up towards the east passes close by it: this river is very large and clear, by it enters and goes forth the merchandise, which many Christians traffic with; these are clothed in camlets and bocasi.[3] They believe in one only true God. They are natives of these parts these married Christians. They trade with Upper and Lower India. The king of this country is an idolator; he uses another dress, which reaches from his head to his feet, full of gold rings and jewellery and seed pearl. These stones are brought from the kingdom of Pegu itself, about three days' journey inland.

In this country, when the husbands die, their wives burn themselves and throw themselves into the fire.

[1] This voyage is not in Ramusio nor in the Lisbon edition, and apparently has been hitherto unpublished. The Munich MS., No. 570, gives the date 1522, but 1512 is the correct reading.

[2] Leste o este.

[3] Surat glaized cotton stuff.

This King of Pegu is continually at war with some other powerful king, who may be the King of Camboja, Siam, or Conchin Chinan.

Leaving Pegu and the bar of the river and continuing to the south-west, inclining to the south south-west,[1] we arrive at the island Samatra, for so is named a city of this northern part, as I will relate further on, at a port which is very large and called Pedir. It is near the extremity of the island, placed more to the north, which looks to the north west.[2] The harbour of Pedir is very large and the city very populous, the best of the island, which the Malay pilots said had a circuit of two hundred and fifty leagues, according as we can collect from their day's journey and our day's run.[3] We gathered from the position of the country and sayings of the pilots and ancient geographers that this island is Traprobana, in which there are four idolatrous kings. The wives of the natives of the country burn themselves when their husbands are dead, as in Pegu and in Malabaria.

The people are white; they have wide foreheads, the eyes greyish and round, the hair long, the nose flat; they are small in stature. Much silk is produced in this island, and grows of itself on the mountains, in which there are many trees of storax and benjuy some way inland; and if it is not brought so much hither, the reason is that they use it there, for they all anoint themselves: many various kinds of lignum aloes grow in the mountains.

Having left Pedir and gone down the northern[4] coast, I drew towards the south and south-east[5] direction, and reached to another country and city which is called Samatra, in which we saw many merchants; and in a single quarter

[1] Sudueste and su sudueste, these terms have not been ever used in the body of the book.

[2] Norueste.

[3] Singaduras for Singladuras, Portuguese Singradura, derived by Bluteau from French Cingler, and that from the German Segelen.

[4] Setentrional.

[5] Del sur al sueste.

we counted five hundred changers, besides other quarters where there were many others. There are innumerable silk workshops. The people are all dressed in cotton. They navigate with vessels made of a certain wood which looks like canes: they call them juncos in Malay language: they carry three masts and two helms: when they pass any stiff gulf, the wind being contrary they hoist other sails, and they are raised on the second mast, and so they make their voyage.

The houses of this city of Samatra and its island, which are all named from it, as I said speaking of Pedir, are of stone and lime, low and covered with shells of tortoises or turtles. Each one of these shells covers as much as two or three bucklers; they are painted of their natural colour like ours. From here we stood to the east until the Bandan Islands, and we found near this, which gives name to the others, twenty islands. It is a dry country which bears fruit; some of these islands are inhabited, the people are like the peasants of Malabaria and Calicut, who are called poliares and gicanales,[1] they are of a low way of living, and coarse intelligence. A profitable commodity is found in Bandan, namely nutmeg, which grows here in great quantity and kinds. Thence we departed to other islands standing to the north-east and east-north-east[2] through many channels as far as the islands of Malut. In them grows much cloves, they are five in all, the largest of them is smaller than Bandan. The Maluquese people are very wretched, and worth little, they are very beastly, and of a brutal mode of living, they do not differ from animals in their customs but only in possessing the human face. They are whiter than other races of these islands. The cloves grow in another island which is smaller, and is called Tidory, the tree on which it grows is like the box or buxo. When the cloves are ripe on the trees they stretch cloaks or sheets on the ground and sweep the tree, and the inhabitants

[1] Or Colayres and giravales according to another reading.

[2] Les nordeste.

gather the most they can. The country is of earth clay and sand; it is so near the line that the north star cannot be seen, and then they sail by certain stars which the orientals are accustomed to. And having departed from here to another second isle, there we the four Christians and some Malays remained; and there the King of Maluco shewed great honour to Fran^{co} Serano, the beforenamed captain, and married him with honour to his daughter, and to the others who wished to go he gave permission to go and see the city and island of Java. On the road we found an island which is called Borney, which is fifty leagues from Maluco, and it is somewhat larger than Maluco, and much lower. Its people adore idols, they are rather white, and go dressed with shirts like those of sailors, and in face they are like the people of the city of Cayro: they dress in camlets.

From this island we went to another and took other mariners. In this country there grows much camphor, because there are many trees in which it grows, and from there we set out to the island of Zaylon, at which we arrived in three days; and so the mariners whom we took in Borney carried a map for navigating, and they had a needle and loadstone, and a chart in which they had many lines and strokes at which we were greatly amazed, and spoke to them of it in the Malay language: and the north star having disappeared from us in those countries the mariners told us that they guided themselves throughout all that region by five stars, principally by one star opposite to the north to which they continue to navigate, and for this they always carry a needle and loadstone because that stone always follows the north, towards which they continue to sail, and it never turns away from the north, and they look on it on that account;

[1] This passage is important. Los marineros q. tomamos en borney llevaban carta de marear e trayan una aguja y piedra yman e una carta en q. trayan muchas rayas e lineas de lo qual nos espantamos mucho. See the Pillars of Hercules, by D. Urquhart with respect to the Phenician compass.

and the mariners of Borneo told us that in that part of that island there was a people which used the contrary stars opposite to the north, for their navigation; and which seemed to be almost the antipodes of Tropia and Sarmatia, and that this people inhabited in the frigid zone near the antarctic pole, which appeared in that country not to have more than four hours of daylight; for the country is very cold to a wonderful degree, on account of the climate being like that which exists near the Arctic Pole.

Having left this island, we went to the island of Java, in which we found four kinds of kings, who follow different rites, all idolators, who worship idols, others the sun, others the moon, and others worship the cows, and things to eat, and others worship the devil. There are other races which go dressed with cloaks and bornusses of silk and camlet.

There are in this Java some who sell their parents when they see that they are old and decrepit, to another nation, who are called canibals or anthropophagi, who are pagans, and likewise brothers sell their brothers when they are sick: when their recovery is despaired of they bring them out into the market-place and sell them to those Caribs, saying that man's flesh is brought up with so much care and luxury, that it would not be in reason that the earth should consume it.

NOTE TO DESCRIPTION OF PRECIOUS STONES.

I have read with great interest the passages of the manuscript relating to precious stones, and I have admired their conscientious appreciation and exactness in details.

A doubt was raised with respect to stones of combined colours; they do exist, but are by no means valued in Europe.

The proportions of the prices in regard to weights, are still very exact as to the Indian market, and uncut stones.

Experiments similar to those here described have been made in Europe, and chiefly in Germany, to heighten the colour of gems, rubies especially, by exposing them to fire, but their success has been so hazardous, nay costly, that speculation has been unwilling to expose itself to so much risk.

Jargon-corindon or circon was much used in the sixteenth century, and is now without value: it has the merit of possessing the hardness of the sapphire.

HENRY CAPT,
Jeweller.

17, Rue du Rhône, Geneva.

NOTE TO PAGE 30.

The Munich MS. No. 571, like the Barcelona MS., has: "y las naos de alli se enpeguen el dicho yncenso el qual le vale alli de ciento cinquenta mrs el quintal." But the Munich MS. No. 570 has: "e las naos desta costa son *embreadas* en el e vale el quintal de ciento o ciento y cinquenta reaes en la tierra en donde nace."

So that the meaning of the passage is that the ships are caulked or pitched with this herb or gum.

NOTE TO PAGE 35.

The Munich MS. No. 571 is like the Barcelona MS., but the MS. No. 570 gives this list of places:—"Lefete, quesebey, tabla, beroho, cal, cor, juza, mohymacim, lima, horbaz, alguefa, carmoni, cohmobarque, conch, conga, ebrahemi, xenaa, menacio, xamyle, leytan, bamtani, doam, loram," and leaves out the words which in the other two MSS. follow after the names of *Quesebi*, *Carmoni*, and Ebrahemi. From this MS. No. 570 it is clear how *tabla* got into the maps.

NOTE TO PAGE 93.

Devadachi, femmes des Pagodes, servantes des dieux. Chap. 17.

Ce sont ordinairement les tisserants qui vouent leurs filles aux pagodes, les parents ne leur demandent pas pour cela leur consentement, ils n'attendent pas même qu'elles soient en age de le donner, puisqu' ils les destinent au service des dieux dès qu'elles commencent de naître : ils ont grand soin de les préparer à cet état par un continuel exercice de la danse, du chant, et des jeux ; il y a un maître exprès de ces exercises, qui enseigne les jeunes filles que l'on a destinées et devouées aux pagodes, et qui les dirigent dans les cérémonies : lorsqu' elles sont devenues devadashi, c'est à dire servantes des dieux, lorsqu' elles ont atteint l'âge de 9 ou 10 ans, leurs pères vont convier toutes les castes de venir assister à la consécration de leurs filles. On les conduit solemnellement à la pagode, devant d'y entrer elles donnent à tout le monde des marques de leur habileté dans la danse, dans le chant, et dans le jeu, et selon qu'on est content d'elles on leur fait des présents, ensuite elles entrent dans la pagode, elles se prosternent devant les dieux. Les Brahames qui sont là présens, les font relever, allors le prêtre offre la fille aux dieux, en leur disant, Seigneurs voilà une fille que je vous offre, daignez la prendre pour votre servante. Le Brahame officiant met dans la main de la fille un peu de Tirouniron, et un peu de l'eau qui a servi à laver l'idole : elle delaye tout cela ensemble, et elle s'en met au front pour marquer qu'elle se devoue d'elle-même avec joye pour être toute sa vie la servante des dieux. Cette cérémonie suppose que c'est à la pagode de Siva qu'elle se devoue particulièrement, car si c'est à la pagode de Vishnou elle se met le tirounamam[1] et on lui fait boire un peu de l'eau dans laquelle il y a quelques feuilles de Toulachi qui est une espèce de basilic. Ensuite soit que ce soit dans l'une ou dans l'autre pagode, le Brahamme officiant delaye dans un bassin de cuivre un peu de sandale avec de l'eau qui a servi à l'idole, et il en jette avec les doigts sur la fille. Cela marque la consécration parfaite. Il met au col une guirlande qui a servi à l'idole pour luy témoigner qu'elle est agréable aux dieux et qu'ils l'ont prise sous leur protection : le Brahamme luy dit qu'elle est présentement Devadashi, et qu'il l'exhorte à se comporter en digne servante des dieux, après cela elle se prosterne devant l'idole : le Brahamme la fait relever et ordonne à ses parents de l'aller conduire dans une maison particulière qui est proche la pagode, les parents y donnent du Bethel aux conviez et regalent toutes les devadachis. Toutes celles qui sont ainsi consacrées aux pagodes ne peuvent jamais se marier, ny elles ne peuvent plus retourner à leurs

[1] Line across the forehead.

familles, ny en hériter. Elles font profession d'etre publiques à tout le monde, et les malabares croyent qu'il y a du mérite d'habiter avec les servantes des dieux. Elles n'ont point parmy elles de supérieures; chacune fait son menage separément si elles veulent on tire leur subsistance des revenus de la pagode, mais ce n'est pas ce qui les enrichit beaucoup; le commerce charnel qu'elles entretiennent avec tout le monde leur est bien plus lucratif, et celles qui font ainsi fortune ont grand soin de se bien habiller et de s'orner de pendants d'oreilles, de colliers et d'anneaux d'or, et de cercles d'argent aux bras et aux pieds l'employ des Devadashis et d'aller trois fois le jour à la pagode, c'est à dire le matin vers le midi et le soir, qui sont les temps que ce font les sacrifices et les cérémonies de la pagode, elles y dansent et chantent, et font des jeux pour le divertissement des dieux; elles font la même chose aux processions, et aux mariages.

"Tout est odieux et criminel dans la condition de ces Devadashis, la cruauté des pères qui forcent la liberté de leurs enfants, l'impiété des pères qui prostituent leurs filles."

The above extract is taken from a manuscript in the Royal Library, Munich, No. 1165 (Gall. 666), called La Religion des Malabares; it is supposed to have been written between 1705 and 1720, and to have belonged to the Missions Etrangères; later it was presented by the Abbé Clément to the library of the Oratoire St. Honoré. The MS. contains 546 pages and three parts. The first is an exposition of Christian doctrine; the second of the Malabar religion; the third sets forth the doctrinal differences between the Christians and Hindus, and shows how to proceed in arguing with the latter. The whole tenour of the book is, however, chiefly an attack on the Jesuits, whom it accuses of laxity, and of having sought to multiply the number of Christians rather than to secure the truth. It reproaches them with allowing Christian Malabars to play musical instruments in the pagodas, and pagan Malabars to play their instruments in Christian churches, and with having allowed various idolatrous ceremonies to have become perpetuated under a fresh dedication. This tenour of the MS. is the cause stated in a manuscript note by Abbé Clément, for the book having been removed from the missions étrangères when the credit of the Jesuits prevailed, and caused the departure from that establishment of the missionaries who were hostile to that body. From this work marriage seems to have been more general amongst the Malabars than would be supposed from the account of the early Portuguese voyagers in which much stress is laid upon the absence of marriage amongst the nairs. This missionary in treating of divorce amongst the Malabars says the husband retains the children, if there are any, and the wife returns to the husband the *taly* which she had round her neck (probably the jewel which has been mentioned in the text;) and she resumes her dower if she brought any at her marriage. Amongst other objectionable practices of the Jesuits, blamed in this work, is the having adopted the Malabar name of Sarounasouren (signifying Lord of all) for the True God, since Sarunasuren is properly applied to Siva because he is the first human form which Carsa (or the most subtle of the five elements) took on forming the world ; whilst the True God is neither Carsa nor Siva, and Sarunasuren is the name of an idol.

Carsa is further described as supreme intelligence, the soul of the universe, and the most subtle of the five elements, water, fire, earth, air, and wind, and is said to have taken a human form which he called Shiva ; and as Shiva was to disappear into Sattyaloguen or the most perfect heaven, he transformed himself into another human figure which he named Roudra, and also in others called Vishnou and Broumha. Carsa filled these three persons with intelligence, in order that they might remain in the world with men. *Section de la divinité des Malabars et de leur fausse Trinité.* Maycereni, the name of the third person of the Indian trinity given in the text, does not appear in this work, and may be an epithet of Rudra. The following is one of the most remarkable passages in this manuscript, and is much in accordance with M. E. Burnouf's recent publications in the Revue des deux Mondes. " Et comme ils ne rendent en particulier aucun culte extérieur à Carsa, ils croyent le dédommager suffisament par celui qu'ils rendent à tous les dieux ; on voit par là combien l'erreur aveugle l'esprit des hommes qui s'éloignent du vray Dieu. Il n'est personne qui ne convienne que la cause est plus noble que son effet. Si donc ils supposent que ces dieux sont les effets de la puissance de Carsa, pourquoi leurs rendent-ils plus de culte qu'à ce Dieu, qu'ils disent être le principe de toute chose. N'est-ce pas faire de Carsa un dieu chimérique ?" p. 539.

The reader may see in Mr. Frank's book on the Kabbala, with respect to the Adam Kadmon, how much Hindu ideas, and especially the Hindu theory of the formation of the world, had penetrated into Syria, and corrupted the Jews, before the Christian era.

INDEX.

LONDON: T. RICHARDS, 37, GREAT QUEEN STREET.